THE ONLY
CLEANSE

ALSO BY SAMANTHA HELLER, M.S., R.D.N., C.D.N.

Get Smart: Samantha Heller's Nutrition Prescription for Boosting Brain Power and Optimizing Total Body Health

THE ONLY CLEANSE

A 14-Day Natural Detox Plan to Jump-Start a Lifetime of Health

Samantha Heller, M.S., R.D.N., C.D.N.

The Countryman Press
Woodstock, Vermont
www.countrymanpress.com

A division of W. W. Norton & Company, Inc.,
500 Fifth Avenue, New York, NY 10110
www.wwnorton.com

For information about special discounts for bulk purchases, please contact W.W. Norton Special Sales at specialsales@wwnorton.com or 800-233-4830.

Design by LeAnna Weller Smith
Printed in the United States of America

The Only Cleanse
978-1-58157-303-9

10 9 8 7 6 5 4 3 2 1

THIS BOOK IS DEDICATED TO:

My sister Susi who lights up the world with
her intelligence, beauty, creativity, insight, compassion,
sass, and zany sense of humor.

ACKNOWLEDGMENTS

The Only Cleanse would never have happened without the guidance, insistence, and literary help of my talented agent Sharon Bowers. She was the one who brought me to Ann Treistman, my editor at Countryman Press. Ann is a veteran writer and editor and her keen eye has helped this book take shape.

The designers at Countryman Press have helped visualize and format *The Only Cleanse* into a reader-friendly, engaging book. I thank you. Thanks too, to the copy editor.

Many thanks to my 14-Day Plan testers, whose feedback helped iron out the kinks.

Check out registered dietitian Dana Angelo White's delicious recipes in the book. She was kind enough to share them with me. Thanks, Dana!

Thank you to Cynthia and James Love Lee whose delicious humor, warmth of spirit, and abiding friendship have helped make this book possible and made life a lot more fun

A big thank you to the folks at NYU Langone Medical Center's SiriusXM Doctor Radio. What a pot of jam I landed in getting the gig hosting *Samantha Heller's Health & Nutrition Show* every week for so many years. I am fortunate to work with a terrific staff at both SiriusXM and NYU Langone Medical Center, including Maurice Tunick, Emily Anton, and Dr. Marc Siegel. I have had the good fortune to interview top health, nutrition, and medical experts from all over the world. A thank you to my guests from whom I have learned so much.

I am blessed to have the support of so many friends and colleagues throughout the writing process of this book. Love to you all. You know who you are.

Thank you to Mollie Katzen, whose cookbooks literally taught me how to cook, for sharing her recipe with me.

The "Fusion of Science and Song" keynote and book presentations I give on *The Only Cleanse* (and many other topics) all over the country are made possible by the extraordinary talent of jazz musician and guitarist Michael Coppola. He is the innovator of the nine-string guitar. You should hear him play! When I approached Michael about the possibility of working together, he said yes even before he had ever heard me sing or seen me perform. It is such a joy to work and create with Michael. For more on the Fusion of Science and Song presentations, go to www.hellerhealth.com. For more on Michael Coppola go to www.9string.com

My appreciation to those who were kind enough to let me interview them for this book.

To my dear, sweet friend Michael Kevin Walsh, a talented performer and musician. Thank you for the laughter, the hugs, and the music.

Thanks to my BFF, Pam Drummond for her support and insight. We have been hanging out since seventh grade, and she has contributed to this book in many ways.

And thanks to my brother Chris because he has great hair and can always make me laugh.

CONTENTS

INTRODUCTION

- Boost Energy
- Ignite Your Inner Cleansing Systems
- Ramp Up Your Health
- Dodge Disease

YOU DESERVE TO FEEL FANTASTIC and healthy. You want to be energized and vibrant. That's why you picked up *The Only Cleanse*. *The Only Cleanse* is the only evidence-based, common-sense approach you need to fire up your body's purification systems, boost energy, and dodge disease. This is not your typical, run-of-the-mill "cleanse" or "detox" program. Those fads and trends, while popular, do nothing to keep your body running at its peak. Your body already knows how to cleanse itself. It is cleansing and detoxing 24/7. The best way to "cleanse" your system is by supporting your body's innate, amazing, complex, integrated detoxification systems. These systems, including the skin, liver, gastrointestinal tract, and kidneys, are detoxifying toxins, fighting off microbial invaders, cleaning up metabolic debris, and seeking inner balance every second of every day. What you eat, how you think, and the quality of your sleep all affect your health and well-being. *The Only Cleanse* offers an easy-to-follow, fourteen-day, multi-phased plan designed to nourish, energize, and revitalize your body and your mind.

Through the years everyone from St. Augustine to King Louis XIV to Beyoncé has partaken in cleanses, fasts, detoxes, and purification rituals. Detoxing is wildly popular, and devotees are fierce in their beliefs that all manner of cleanses, from water fasts to yogurt enemas, are going to purify and purge their bodies. As a bonus, they will lose weight and look decades younger. The allure of detoxing and purification has been around for centuries, but the notion itself is flawed. The fact is, the human body would cease to exist if it were sterilized from the inside out.

The Only Cleanse is designed to fully integrate the body's biochemical balance. And since your mind is inextricably connected to your body, a mental and personal-space cleanse is an essential part of the process. Concrete changes such as altering your external environment are combined with a flexible-yet-structured physical, dietary, and psychological guide that will help you optimize your total body health. This is a refreshingly truthful, clean approach that will help you understand what your body needs and why.

There is enough physiological evidence that making lifestyle changes like those outlined in *The Only Cleanse* can have a significant impact on your health in two weeks or less.

The Only Cleanse reveals the bizarre past and current use of enemas, fasts, juicing, pills, teas, and products that claim to cleanse and detoxify the body, cure lethal diseases, and rid the body of deadly poisons. There are hundreds of thousands of detox products on the market. *The Only Cleanse* dives into the vat of controversy to untangle the twisted mass of confusions and claims, myths and medicine.

The Only Cleanse is not some faddy detox. It's a lifestyle, a change that you can keep forever. It's not deprivation-based, complicated, impractical, or unrealistic. Simply put, it will get you and your loved ones on a healthy track so you can focus on enjoying the rest of your life. Please join me on this journey. You'll be so glad you did.

NOTE: *All the stories in this book are true. I have changed the names of friends, colleagues, and patients to protect their privacy.*

The Only Cleanse

1. *Your Colon*

Bottom's Up: *The Colon*

➤ **A Brief Yet Fascinating Tour of the Anatomy and Physiology of the Colon**
➤ **Fiber Fest**
➤ **Short-Chain Fatty Acids—A New Miracle Food?**
➤ **Classical Gas**

Colon or bowel cleanses, enemas, and high colonics have been around for eons. The idea that you can scour stinky, noxious goo from your colon to prevent or cure disease or obliterate harmful toxins seems like a good one. After all, poop is made up of the body's waste materials. But there is a whole lot more to your colon than being a holding tank for body waste. Trying to render this complex organ all shiny and clean can lead to serious, even life-threatening problems. However, there are times when a foray into the body's exit portal may be necessary. Here we will separate fact from fiction.

Your Colon

Your colon may not be a hot topic of conversation on Jimmy Fallon, but in some circles it's all they talk about. While younger people rarely give their colons a second thought, older people obsess about theirs. It makes sense because as we age we become more prone to gastrointestinal (GI) problems like constipation, diverticulosis, or diarrhea. Unfortunately, this paradigm is shifting, and globally more people of all ages are being diagnosed with inflammatory and irritable bowel diseases and other gastrointestinal malfunctions. If you or someone you know is suffering from a GI disease or disturbance, you know how it can take over your life. With the surge in bowel diseases, and with colon cancer being the third most-diagnosed cancer in the United States, colon health may just become the newest Twitter trend.

How It Works

We should all have a love affair with our colons and treat them with great respect. The colon plays multiple roles in maintaining the body's immune system, ridding the body of toxins and keeping it well nourished. In fact, 70 to 80 percent of your immune cells reside in your GI tract. The GI tract houses trillions of bacteria (yes, *trillions*). The colon plays host to over four hundred species of bacteria. These microcreatures have far-reaching effects on total body health (see Chapter 2, "The Microbiome," for more). Our lifestyle and what we eat affects their ability to keep us healthy.

The colon, also called the large intestine or bowel, makes up about five feet of your gastrointestinal tract and is the major site for the absorption of water, salt, and certain vitamins. The colon is the lower part of your digestive tract that begins where the small intestine ends and ends at the anus. This wrinkled tube has several distinct sections:

- The cecum
- The ascending colon
- The transverse colon
- The descending colon
- The sigmoid colon
- The rectum

A lot goes on in the colon before fecal matter is formed and makes its exit from the body. This doesn't make great dinner conversation for sure, but it's a good idea to have a basic understanding of how your body works. You may be surprised to learn that the primary function of the colon is to absorb water and salt. A slushy mix of partially digested food from the stomach, called chyme, wends its way through the small intestine and eventually arrives at the colon. By this point most of the vitamins, minerals, fats, carbohydrates, and proteins have been broken down and absorbed in the small intestine and are on their way to being metabolized. However, vital nutrients remain in the chyme that can only be broken down and utilized by the colon. The chyme moves through the colon at about two inches (five centimeters) per hour. The slow pace ensures that almost all of the remaining nutritional value is absorbed.

The colon wall, if ironed out, has a big surface area of approximately sixty-six feet (two-thousand centimeters), the size of an eleven-by-six foot rug. This is designed to maximize water and electrolyte absorption, every bit of which is soaked up by the colon walls except that which passes out through the colon as stool. The functions of the electrolytes, which include sodium, potassium and chloride, are to regulate hydration, nerve and muscle function, blood pH and more. As the colon absorbs water via a complex process involving sodium, potassium, and—believe it or not—electricity, chyme solidifies into feces. Diarrhea is the result of a portion of water not being absorbed: thus the loose, watery stools

The Colon

- *Is the primary site of water and salt absorption*
- *Plays host to over four hundred species of bacteria*

Fiber Fest

The large population of bacteria that live in the colon digests and ferments small amounts of dietary fiber and proteins that are not broken down and digested in the small intestine. This bacterial activity forms vitamin K, vitamin B12, thiamin, riboflavin, biotin, short-chain fatty acids (SCFA), and gases. The colonic vitamin B12 is excreted in the feces. Vitamin K and SCFA are absorbed in the colon. Vitamin K is essential for blood clotting and healthy bones. SCFAs are emerging as new stars in the keeping-our-bodies-healthy pantheon. Scientists are still investigating how much of the other vitamins the colonic cells can absorb.

SCFAs: *Why They Are Important*

- ⇒ **Help keep the colon walls healthy**
- ⇒ **Reduce inflammation**
- ⇒ **Enhance salt and water absorption**
- ⇒ **Keep out the bad bacteria**
- ⇒ **Are involved in the production of healthy probiotic bacteria such as lactobacilli and bifidobacteria**
- ⇒ **Maintain the physiology and metabolism of the colon**
- ⇒ **Play a role in the prevention and treatment of diseases of the colonic mucosa, such as distal ulcerative colitis and cancer**
- ⇒ **May help keep cholesterol levels in check**
- ⇒ **May improve glucose tolerance**
- ⇒ **Detoxify potentially harmful substances**

SCFA: *The New Miracle Detoxification Food?*

Short-chain fatty acids (SCFAs) are pretty much what the name implies: rather short molecules of fat. They are a food but not one you find on the grocery store shelf. SCFAs are produced from the digestion of fiber and resistant starch by the bacteria in the colon. Resistant starch comes from foods such as legumes, bananas, and temperature-cooled starchy foods like pasta salad. Since fiber and starch comes from plants, not animals, carbohydrates like whole grains, vegetables, fruits, legumes, nuts, and seeds provide the banquet for colonic bacteria to feast on and produce SCFAs. SCFAs in turn are the food the cells in the colon (colonic cells) use for fuel. Because SCFAs reduce inflammation, scientists are examining ways that SCFAs may help prevent or treat inflammatory bowel diseases and reduce the risk of colorectal cancer.

A Potent Detoxifier

SCFAs are one of the colon's natural detoxifiers. The three major SCFAs are:

- Acetate
- Propionate
- Butyrate

Butyrate, for example, helps prevent the accumulation of potentially toxic by-products, such as D-lactate. D-lactate is a normal part of metabolism in the colon. But if for some reason—like a malabsorption problem—D-lactate levels rise, they can cause a rise in acid production. Excess acid can lead to all sorts of other problems. SCFAs help keep colonic D-lactate in balance.

Colonic bacteria eat the fiber from plants such as vegetables, fruits, and beans to produce a powerful detoxifier called short-chain fatty acids. Another good reason to eat healthy, high-fiber carbohydrates daily.

Classical Gas

The Roman emperor Claudius apparently suffered from chronic, smelly flatulence to the extent that he passed a law legalizing public farting: "No Roman need feel reticent about passing flatus in public," it declared. Alas, while farting in public remains legal in today's society, it's embarrassing (for most of us) and can cause those in the vicinity to roll their eyes and cover their noses.

Passing gas is a normal part of gastrointestinal biology. Intestinal gas is the result of several factors, including swallowing air, colonic bacterial activity, back passage of gas from the bloodstream into the intestines, and other biochemical processes. Some foods like broccoli, cabbage, and beans may cause undue flatulence. The foods themselves don't produce gas; it's the healthy gut bacteria chowing down and fermenting the undigested food and fiber particles in the colon that emit the gas that eventually passes out the rectum (think, if you will, tooting bacteria).

You may have noticed that not all toots are smelly. The smell-o-meter depends on the type of gas that is produced. Gases produced and expelled from the colon include hydrogen (H_2), methane (CH_4), and carbon dioxide (CO_2). H_2 and CH_4 are flammable gases. You will be relieved to know that despite the flammable nature of the H_2 and CH_4 in flatulence, working near open flames is not hazardous. Some bacteria consume large amounts of hydrogen gas in the colon, which in turn gives them gas. So these little critters release small amounts of methane or sulfur-containing gases. These are the stinky gases. If you are talented enough to avoid expelling loud, stuttering farts and instead emit the SBD (silent-but-deadly) ones, you can always blame the dog or, in lieu of a handy dog, a barking spider.

NOTE: *People experiencing excessive gas emissions, bloating, abdominal discomfort, or other GI symptoms should see their physician as these may be symptoms of an underlying disorder that requires medical attention.*

Facts about Flatulence

- *Passing gas around 13 to 21 times a day is normal*
- *Daily gas expulsion averages 600 to 700 mL (depending on what you are eating)*
- *Gases produced and expelled include hydrogen (H_2), methane (CH_4), and carbon dioxide (CO_2)*
- *H_2 and CH_4 are flammable gases, hence the great hilarity when kids hold a lighted match near their rectum, fart, and a plume of flame erupts.*

2. *The Microbiome*

It's Complicated: *The Microbiome Relationship*
⟫ **What Is the Microbiome?**
⟫ **Where Did It Come From?**
⟫ **Gut Instinct**
⟫ **Two Heads Are Better Than One.**
⟫ **Community Revitalization**
⟫ **What to Eat**
⟫ **The Pres and the Pros**
⟫ **The Best and Worst Foods for your Microbiome**
⟫ **Fun and Interesting Bits and Pieces**

How do you dodge heart disease, obesity, rheumatoid arthritis, diabetes, liver disease, ulcerative colitis, cancer, and a host of other maladies? The answer may well be hidden in the trillions of microbes that are hitching a ride on and inside your body. Contrary to the notion that you need to eradicate bacteria and fungi from your body with cleanses and detoxes, human life is in fact dependent upon them.

Imagine an island city with neighborhoods populated by people from various cultures, backgrounds, talents, and skills—like Manhattan. Imagine now that your body is that island and the inhabitants are the microbes that live on and in it. Basically that is the microbiome. The human body contains trillions of microbial creatures that are not human, but are microbial, and these diverse, interdependent communities of microbes live on our skin, feet, lungs, ears, scalp, gastrointestinal tract, and mouth. We are the landlords and these creatures are our tenants. They pay rent by helping metabolize foods we eat, manufacturing chemicals that reduce inflammation, detoxifying toxins, promoting healing, and fighting off pathogens. Pathogens are biological agents like bacteria or viruses that can make us sick.

Cutting-edge research on the microbiome is exploding.

The term "microbiome" includes not only microbes, but the entire collection of genes found within microbes. Scientists believe that our microbiomes, which include different kinds of microbes including bacteria, protists, and fungi, may be the backbone of our very existence. Indeed, it is reasonable to characterize the microbiome as a newly recognized organ that affects the very survival of the human species. Yes, we are discovering that our microbiomes are *that* important. Of the hundreds of thousands of kinds of microbes on Earth, about one thousand have been found associated with humans. So the microbes on and in the human body are there specifically to support human life. Experts believe that the answers to many medical mysteries may be found in the human microbiome.

The Only Cleanse teaches you how to befriend bacteria, favor fungi, promote protists, and value viruses, all of which live in your body and dwell in the land of the Microbiome. By learning the care and feeding of these internal guests you will be firing up your body's natural ability to cleansify, detoxify, and healthify itself.

How did all these microbes get inside your body? They came from other humans.

Newborn babies encounter microbes for the first time during birth. As the baby is being born, it is coated with microbes from the mother's birth canal. Babies that are born by Caesarean section first encounter microbes from the mother's skin. Babies come in contact with more microbes from other people who touch, carry, and cuddle them. Another early source of microbes is breast milk. As babies grow more mobile and begin to explore the world, they encounter both environmental microbes (like those that live in soil and water), and microbes that have been shed by other people, pets, and plants. They also ingest microbes from food. As we grow up our microbiomes adjust to what we eat and even where we live.

A Cleaner You Begins with a Dirtier You

The premise of *The Only Cleanse* is to support the body's innate ability to cleanse and detoxify itself. That does not mean you shouldn't get dirty. Experts recommend taking your kids and plopping them in a pile of dirt to play. You might want to join them. Research shows that people who grow up on farms, live in or near green spaces, whether it's a park, forest, seaside, mountains, or jungles, have fewer diseases including heart disease, allergies, asthma, and mental illnesses like depression. The reason is that they are exposed to a greater variety of microbes, plants, and animals (called biodiversity), nurturing a more diverse microbiome. A diverse microbiome is a healthy microbiome. As in any balanced society, the more varied the population, the healthier the communities. Scientists

POINT OF INTEREST

FOR *LAW AND ORDER* VIEWERS

In the future, detectives may use microbiome maps instead of fingerprints to identify criminals because, like fingerprints, apparently no two human microbiomes are exactly alike.

believe that one reason there is a rise in immune dysfunction, inflammatory diseases, and autoimmune diseases is the urban environments in which kids and adults live; they have higher exposures to chemicals and limited exposure to nature's microbes. The theory is that the shift to living in a less biodiverse world is reflected in the world of the human microbiome, making it less diverse and thus vulnerable to infection and disease.

If you live in a city, seek out green spaces and bring your family. Leave the city as often as possible and go hiking, walking, swimming, camping, or visit farms. Get involved with local conservation groups, where you can be in the woods or on the beach, joining their efforts to improve the environment and protect wildlife and natural resources.

Gut Instinct

In this chapter we are focusing on the microbiome that lives in your gut. The gut microbiome reflects your overall state of wellness. You will learn what you need to do to maintain thriving bacterial communities that support total body health. The role of the microbiome is multifaceted. The healthy microbes help digest and retrieve energy from foods and create anti-inflammatory and anti-cancer compounds, all while fighting off invading pathogens like viruses.

Simply Put

A healthy gut keeps unwanted microbes from entering into the rest of the body and boosts total body immunity. Emerging research suggests that the gut microbiome may affect sleep patterns, mood and mental health, and the genesis of diseases such as cancer, heart disease, diabetes, and inflammatory bowel diseases.

The relationship between humans and their microbiota has evolved over millennia. Each has learned to support and protect each other for their mutual survival. That relationship is now threatened by the changes in the environment, diet, and lifestyle that have occurred over the past fifty to a hundred years. Our air, soil, and water is polluted. We eat more animals and processed foods than ever before. And we have become a primarily sedentary society. Perhaps, scientists hypothesize, this is another reason why diseases such as celiac disease, auto-immune diseases, certain cancers, asthma, and allergies are on the upswing.

Microbes, a.k.a. the microbiota, include an assortment of one thousand or so species of bacteria that inhabit our digestive tract.

Two Heads Are Better Than One

Have you ever had "butterflies in your stomach" when you are excited or nervous? Our minds and emotions are intimately linked with our GI tract, and vice versa. The gastrointestinal tract is called the second brain for good reason. The GI tract is lined with some one hundred million neurons that act as radar centers to register what is going on inside and outside the body. These radar centers are nerve, immune, and endocrine (hormonal) cells. They send informational and chemical signals to organs and glands all over the body. These signals influence hunger, satiety, digestion, muscle function, immune system, and emotions. It is important to note that the microbiota in the gut influence how well the radar centers work.

The microbes and the brain communicate by sending text messages to each other. But instead of using their smartphones they use chemicals to send the messages. This is called the gut-brain axis. The microbes produce hundreds of neurochemicals that get sent to the brain in order to regulate mental and physiological processes such as learning, memory, and mood. For example, gut bacteria manufacture about 95 percent of the body's supply of serotonin, which influences both mood and GI activity. Disruptions in the ability of the brain and gut to communicate have been associated with psychiatric symptoms such as anxiety and GI disorders like irritable bowel syndrome. Because the gut-brain axis is like an intimate, on-going discussion, many believe that certain mental illnesses may be treated by manipulating that gut-brain conversation—by altering the gut microbiome. The way to a healthier mind and brain may just be through the "stomach."

The surface area of the GI tract ranges from about 322 to 430 square feet, about the size of a studio apartment. That makes sense since we are housing trillions of microbiomic tenants.

Community Revitalization Project

We all know of communities that are crime ridden, in ruins, and poverty stricken. In order to revitalize these communities, a multi-system cleanup project must be undertaken. The bad guys need to be controlled; the streets, parks, homes and buildings need to be cleaned up and renovated; and healthy families and businesses need to move in and settle down. For many of us, our gut microbiomic communities need to be revitalized in a similar fashion. We've taken too many antibiotics and eaten too much meat and processed foods; we are sedentary and overweight. All of these factors have a huge, defining influence on the balance of good-guys-versus-bad-guys in our gut. Overgrowth of bad microbes, weak or damaged structures like the intestinal wall, and chronic inflammation need to be replaced with healthy microbes that can help protect and rebuild the gut wall and provide nutrients that strengthen and heal the body. A full body intervention that supports the body's natural ability to revitalize and detoxify itself is in order for all of us. *The Only Cleanse* plan is designed to launch a community effort to revitalize your gut microbiomic communities.

The population in various intestinal neighborhoods varies among individuals and is affected by your genes, age, antibiotic use, diet, and lifestyle. Microbes, a.k.a. the microbiota, include an assortment of one thousand or so species of bacteria that inhabit our digestive tract. There are a mind boggling one hundred trillion of these microbes housed in the human body. How much of which kind of microbes set up house in various neighborhoods in your gut will affect your overall health and risk of disease.

There are two main families that inhabit the gut microbiome neighborhood, called the Firmicutes and the Bacteroidetes. In a healthy gut there is a balance of the two families.

The Microbiome, in a Nutshell:

- *Consists of over a thousand species of microbes that live in your gastrointestinal tract*
- *Human life may be more reliant on these microbes than anyone ever knew*
- *Diet, exercise, and lifestyle have a huge impact on the health of the gut microbiome*
- *Antibiotics, infections, stress, obesity, and poor diet negatively affect the microbiome*
- *The good microbes regulate immunity, total body health, brain and hormonal functions, digestion, mood, and cognition*

A HEALTHY MICROBIOME:

- *Resists autoimmune diseases such as rheumatoid arthritis, ulcerative colitis, and multiple sclerosis*
- *Fights infections*
- *Reduces inflammation*
- *Detoxifies and cleanses the system*
- *Staves off diseases such as cancer, cardiovascular disease and diabetes*
- *Communicates effectively with the brain*
- *A diverse biocommunity is a healthy one*
- *Antibiotic overuse, red and processed meat, and highly processed foods have a negative effect on the microbiome.*
- *There are over one hundred trillion microbes in the human gastrointestinal tract.*
- *A balance of the different kinds of microbes is important for a balanced body.*

DO THESE BACTERIA MAKE ME LOOK FAT?
Want to lose weight? Change your gut microbes. Preliminary-but-intriguing research has found that altering the types of microbes in their gut may help people to lose weight.

Bacteroidetes and Firmicutes compose the largest population of microbiota in the gut, and a healthy gut has a nice balance of the two. What scientists have found is that obese people's balance of these microbes is thrown off. They have fewer Bacteroidetes and more Firmicutes than lean people. Moreover, the proportion of Bacteroidetes increases with weight loss. Bacteroidetes and Firmicutes help digest plant fiber and produce important compounds such as butyrate, which has anti-cancer properties. They regulate bile acid metabolism and detoxify mutagenic (cancer-causing) compounds. A sure way to knock off the balance in the gut community is with what scientists refer to as the "Western diet." The Western Diet refers to the typical American diet, which is high in red and processed meat, fat, refined sugar, and junk and processed foods. The Western diet creates an environment that pushes out the good guys and brings in the bad guys. It also shifts the equilibrium of the microbial population, and in the process the biochemical checks-and-balances system among the microbiota is thrown off. This can create an overflow of toxic substances such as endotoxins, which can cause insulin resistance, lower immunity, and increase the risk of diseases such as diabetes and cardiovascular disease.

The ratio of Firmicutes/Bacteroidetes appears to be strongly influenced by obesity and may have an influence on who is more likely to become obese. Research is ongoing, and new discoveries are happening all the time. The take-home message is that diet and weight have a profound effect on the health and well-being of the gut microbiota. Studies looking at the microbiomes of various cultures have found that those who eat a more plant-based, high-fiber diet and eat few (if any) processed foods have a healthier balance of gut microbes than those that eat the high-fat, low-fiber Western diet. A healthy weight plus a healthy diet supports a healthy microbiome.

Translocation: *A Little is Good, More is Not*

The gut wall is a multilayered organ. It's not only a tunnel through which food and fluids pass, are digested, and absorbed, but it also keeps tight control over what gets in and out of the wall itself. The gut wall profiles bacteria, viruses, toxins, and other substances and carefully decides which ones can and cannot cross the border into the body. When tiny amounts of bacteria, toxins, or other substances cross through the wall of the intestine and travel throughout the body, it is called bacterial translocation. You might think that letting these un-wanted visitors into your body would be a disaster. Yet it isn't. These interlopers trigger the body's defense system, and by doing so they help to strengthen it. Problems arise when the gut wall, known as the epithelial mucosa, is weakened and becomes flimsy, holey, or easily penetrated. This can be the result of poor diet, overuse of antibiotics, infection, or a dramatic shift in microbial composi-tion. If this happens, a flood of unwanted endotoxins, bacteria, and viruses can escape the gut by breaching the wall and invading the body. The unwelcome pathogens can overwhelm the system, resulting in metabolic chaos, disease, and even organ failure.

**The Only Cleanse kicks off with a 14-Day plan
because your gut microbiota can be shifted to a
more favorable balance in a short period of time.**

What to Eat

What we eat and our daily lifestyle can help keep the gut microbiome healthy and happy, which in turn helps fight infection and disease. A happy microbi-ome means an ongoing detoxification and cleansing system is operating in your body 24/7. We want to help colonize our GI tract with healthy microbes, and then we have to feed them. Fortunately our bodies are pretty good land-lords and provide other amenities, such as a warm environment and cushy, comfy intestinal walls for our tenants to occupy.

One of the reasons *The Only Cleanse* kicks off with a 14-Day plan is that studies are suggesting that your gut microbiota can be shifted to a more favorable balance in a short period of time with diet and exercise. The studies tend to be small because it is difficult to wrangle enough people who are willing to have their lives, diet, and bowel habits literally put under the microscope and have them follow carefully orchestrated protocols, day after day. This is the bane of human research in general. That said, there is enough physiological evidence to show that making lifestyle changes like those outlined in *The Only Cleanse* can have a significant impact on your health in two weeks or less. What we eat changes the concentrations of certain types of gut bacteria and their genetic behavior. We know fast food is not good for us, but who stops to think that the junky foods we covet can provoke a genetic response in gut bacteria that can affect our total body health? No one, except a few scientific outliers. That is, until now.

A GUT REASON TO BREASTFEED IF YOU CAN
According to a 2013 article in the *Journal of Food Science*, the type of feeding is one of the most essential factors that affect the infant's gut microbiotic composition. In studies, breast-fed infants were mainly colonized with healthy bacteria called bifidobacteria (up to 90 percent of flora). Breast milk components function as growth factors for beneficial gut bacteria, help bind invading pathogens, and may promote development of the early immune system.

The Pres and the Pros

The Pres

Grandma was right when she told you to eat fiber. Fiber is famous for reducing constipation, but it does a whole lot more than just move things along in your GI tract. The 2011 the NIH-AARP Diet and Health Study found that people who ate more fiber lived longer than those who ate less, and they lowered their risk of death from cardiovascular, infectious, and respiratory diseases. One reason that fiber offers a feast of benefits is that it is the ambrosia that feeds microbiota in our GI tract, especially bifidobacteria and lactobacilli, two species of gut-friendly bacteria. The kinds of fiber that feed our friendly microbes are called "prebiotics."

Plant fibers are forms of carbohydrates, but because of their structure they resist digestion in the human GI tract. When fiber gets to the colon the bacteria happily nosh on it. This is known as fermentation. The process of fermentation is what produces compounds that bolster immunity and reduce inflammation. Eating more prebiotics by eating more plants helps support a vigorous and diverse gut community.

Another terrific benefit of dietary fiber is that it binds bile acids and removes them from the body (see pg. 39 for more on bile acids), lowering cholesterol and the production of cancer-causing substances. Fiber is filling, too. So you eat less, and thus it helps with weight management. A plethora of studies show that people who eat a high-fiber diet (e.g., more plant based) have a smaller waist, lower body mass index (BMI), better weight management, lower risks of type 2 diabetes, and fewer GI maladies such as diverticulitis and Crohn's disease.

Health Benefits of Prebiotics

➠ Reduce the prevalence and duration of infectious and antibiotic-associated diarrhea

➠ Reduce the inflammation and symptoms associated with inflammatory bowel disease

➠ Exert protective effects to prevent colon cancer

➠ Enhance the bioavailability and uptake of minerals, including calcium, magnesium, and possibly iron

➠ Lower risk factors for cardiovascular disease

➠ Promote satiety and weight loss and prevent obesity

➠ Foster growth of good gut bacteria

In the Grocery Aisle

Inulin is a type of plant fiber that is a favorite meal for your gut bacteria. When used as a supplement or added to foods, inulin comes primarily from chicory root. Asparagus, Jerusalem artichokes, bananas, leeks, onions, and garlic are good sources of inulin. Food companies are fortifying all kinds of foods like candy, juices, sugary cereals, and even waters, with inulin and other prebiotic fibers such as beta-glucan and resistant starches. Just because your favorite ice cream has been fortified with fiber doesn't mean it magically becomes a healthy food. You know that, right? Food companies are hoping you don't. They want you to think that processed foods loaded up with fiber and pre- and probiotics, are good choices. If you really want to support your inner cleansing systems, stick with less processed, real foods. It is best to eat as many foods in their whole form as you can because they are loaded with a synergistic blend of a multitude of

POINT OF INTEREST

FOR ANTHROPOLOGY AFICIONADOS

Foods high in prebiotic fiber have been consumed since prehistoric times. As far back as ten thousand years ago, people were eating desert plants high in inulin fiber. Archeologists found evidence of this in caves in the northern Chihuahuan Desert, near the modern town of Del Rio, Texas. Analysis of well-preserved coprolites (also known as fossilized poop) showed that the typical male hunter-forager, following a plant-based diet, consumed about 135 grams a day of inulin. In today's world the current daily intake of prebiotic fiber is a lot less; one to four grams a day, and three to eleven grams a day in Western Europe.

FOR BIO-CHEM PROFESSORS AND REGISTERED DIETITIAN-NUTRITIONISTS

Prebiotics are short-chain carbohydrates that alter the composition or metabolism of the gut microbiota in a beneficial manner. Good examples of prebiotics are fructooligosaccharides (FOS), inulin, galacto-oligosaccharides (GOS), soybean oligosaccharides, and complex polysaccharides that constitute dietary fiber.

compounds like fiber, vitamins, and minerals, to provide your body and gut with optimal nutrition. That is not to say that foods like bread, pasta, yogurt, or dark chocolate, none of which grow on trees, should be avoided. They all fit into *The Only Cleanse* plan's realistic and practical approach to a healthy body.

Beta-glucan

Remember several years ago when the news broke that oats could lower cholesterol, and every box of oatmeal flew off store shelves? Beta-glucan, a kind of fiber found in plant foods like oats, instigated that frenzy. Beta-glucan helps lower cholesterol and blood pressure and helps limit the rise in blood sugar that occurs after a meal. The fiber is found in whole grains (especially oats, wheat, and barley) and fungi such as baker's yeast and the medicinal mushrooms maitake and reishi. Beta-glucan is currently being investigated by researchers for its beneficial effects on the immune system.

The Pros

Probiotics are very different from prebiotics. While prebiotics refers to the fiber in foods that we eat and that subsequently feed our microbial companions, probiotics are actually bacteria or yeasts that we ingest. Probiotics mingle with gut microbes, boosting health in many ways such as acting as powerful anti-inflammatory agents and pumping up immunity. The Food and Agriculture Organization of the United Nations and the World Health Organization define probiotics as "live microorganisms which, when administered in adequate amounts, confer a health benefit on the host." These live bacteria and yeasts are found in fermented foods like yogurt and tempeh, sold as supplements, and added to foods including chocolate, juices and granola bars. The three most extensively studied probiotics are Lactobacillus and Bifidobacterium, which are live bacteria, and Saccharomyces, which is derived from yeast. Each of these probiotics has family members, called strains. Different strains or combinations of strains have different effects on different illnesses.

FOR EXAMPLE:

In the Lactobacillus family:
- *Lactobacillus casei* Shirota supports the immune system.
- *Lactobacillus bulgaricus* may help relieve symptoms of lactose intolerance.

- In the Saccharomyces family, *Saccharomyces boulardii* has been shown to help reduce antibiotic-associated diarrhea. One reason is that *Saccharomyces boulardii* is a yeast and not a bacterium, so it is naturally resistant to antibiotics.

Health Benefits of Probiotics:
➠ **Boost bacterial performance**
➠ **Detoxify toxins**
➠ **Produce B vitamins necessary for metabolizing food**
➠ **Ward off anemia caused by deficiencies in B6 and B12**
➠ **Help maintain healthy skin and a healthy nervous system**
➠ **Fortify the gut wall**
➠ **Reduce antibiotic-associated diarrhea**
➠ **Reduce severity and duration of all cause and infectious diarrhea**
➠ **Reduce the severity of pain and bloating in patients with irritable bowel syndrome**
➠ **Immunostimulating activities**
➠ **Anti-inflammatory properties**

Check the label of the products to be sure there are live, active cultures. The amount of cultures should be listed on the label. In general the dosage recommendations are five to ten billion CFUs (colony-forming units) per day for children; ten to twenty billion CFUs per day for adults.

Should Everyone Be Taking Probiotics?
I have asked several gastroenterologists this question and gotten both yes and no answers and an "eat yogurt everyday instead" response. To get a better perspective I went to my go-to gastroenterologist, Dr. Ira Breite, Clinical Assistant Professor of Medicine/Gastroenterology at the NYU School of Medicine in New York City and asked him if we should all be taking a probiotic. "I do not recommend that everyone takes a probiotic every day," he replied. "Although we know the benefits of probiotics in a 'researchy' sort of way, we still have very little evidence as to which specific probiotics works in each specific population."

Good point. But what about all the products and websites that make us feel like if we don't take probiotics we will be at the mercy of plague and pestilence? Ira smiled. "If you are happy with your digestion, I wouldn't mess with mother nature."

Who Should Take a Probiotic?

Again, I sought Dr. Breite's expertise: "I recommend probiotics for irritable bowel syndrome (IBS) and inflammatory bowel disease (IBD) at this time. The question of how long is very interesting as there is some evidence that the positive effect of the probiotic fades over time. For IBS I usually start with three months and reevaluate. Many times, I keep the person on the probiotic as long as it is effective. For IBD I use them indefinitely."

There may be other instances when taking a probiotic is advantageous as well, such as when someone is taking antibiotics or recovering from certain illnesses. Speak with your physician to find out if and when you need to take a probiotic.

A Lot of Choices

Because probiotics are considered dietary supplements, they are not regulated by the FDA the way prescription drugs are. Probiotics are not standardized, meaning they are made in different ways by different companies, have different additives, and there will be varying kinds of strains in various products. Adding to the confusion, many products make baseless health claims. Stick with name-brand products with a good track record such as those by Attune Foods, Bicodex, Culturelle, Dannon, General Mills, Kraft, Nestlé, Procter & Gamble, VSL Pharmaceuticals, and Yakult.

NOTE: *People with impaired immune systems and those who are debilitated should not take a probiotic supplement without first speaking with their physician. Because probiotics help strengthen the immune system, it may seem logical to take a probiotic if you are immunocompromised, for example HIV/AIDS patients, stem cell transplant patients, or those undergoing treatment for cancer. There are reports, though rare, of immunocompromised patients suffering from sepsis due to probiotic supplementation. Probiotic sepsis occurs when the probiotic leaches into the bloodstream, triggering a systemic, inflammatory, and potentially lethal response.*

A Warning from The American Gastroenterological Association:
Beware of the Internet.

If you order products from the Internet, make sure you know the company from which you are ordering. There are scammers out there who are willing to send you fake products labeled as probiotics. At best, the ingredients could be harmless, like garlic powder. At worst, they could be laced with powerful herbs, prescription medications, or illegal drugs. Some companies may simply take your money and disappear.

In Agreement

Every scientific article I have read and every expert with whom I have spoken about the gut microbiome all agree on one thing: A plant-based diet is the cornerstone of a healthy gut microbiome. That's not to say you can't enjoy some BBQ on a holiday weekend. Just not every day. Or every week. One small study of humans in the journal *Nature* compared the effects on the gut microbiome of an animal-based diet to those of a plant-based diet. They found that guts of the people who ate the animal food diet (e.g., meat, ice cream) had an increased concentration of a secondary bile acid called deoxycholic acid (DCA). High levels of DCA promote liver, colon, esophageal, and other cancers. The animal based diet also increased levels of a bacterium called *B. wadsworthia*, whose production of hydrogen sulfide is thought to inflame intestinal tissue and trigger inflammatory bowel diseases. Only good can come from increasing your intake of plant foods such as broccoli, artichokes, lentils, and apples and limiting animal foods such as beef, cheese, and pork.

The Best Foods for Your Gut Microbiota
- Lentils, split peas
- Kidney, black, cannellini, red and pinto beans
- Chickpeas, black eyed peas, and other legumes
- Garlic
- Radishes
- Prunes
- Jicama
- Asparagus
- Leeks
- Onions
- Bananas
- Jerusalem artichokes
- Apples
- Oats
- Barley
- Quinoa
- Wild rice

POINT OF INTEREST

BECAUSE IT IS A COOL THING

The microbiome provides a rapid means for humans to adapt and thrive when environmental conditions change. One example of such an adaptation is the discovery of a gene for digesting seaweed in the microbiome of some Japanese people. The gene is rarely found in human microbiomes outside of Japan.

FOR SCIENCE NERDS

The wall of the gut is called the epithelial mucosa.

Fermented Foods to Feed the Pros

(*high sodium)
- Sauerkraut* (unpasteurized and fermented without vinegar)
- Pickles* (fermented without vinegar)
- Miso*
- Kimchi*
- Yogurt (with live, active cultures)
- Kefir (with live, active cultures)
- Tempeh

The Worst Foods for Gut Health

- Hot dogs
- Deep fried anything, including chicken, french fries, tempura, onion rings, calamari, and Twinkies

- Cheeseburgers
- Sausage
- Sweets, e.g., cookies and cakes (especially commercially baked goods)
- Cheese
- Pork
- Lamb
- Beef
- Luncheon meats and cold cuts
- Non-nutritive sweeteners
- Partially hydrogenated oils (a.k.a. trans fats)

A Note of Caution

You will be hearing a lot about the microbiome, microbiota, probiotics, prebiotics, synbiotics, gut flora, and healthy bacteria in the coming years. Enterprising businesspeople will try to leverage current media headlines by selling all kinds of microbiome-related products. The science and commercial buzz is advancing quickly, as evidenced by the emergence of companies offering to sequence samples of your personal bacterial DNA. For a mere $89-$399 the folks at UBiome (http://ubiome.com) will send you a kit to swab your microbes and mail them back to them for analysis. It's worth noting that knowledge of which species are sharing real estate in your body is of little value, especially to the lay person, until we have more data on what the one-thousand or so species, their genomes, and their concentrations mean to our health. There are hundreds, maybe thousands of pro-, pre- and synbiotic supplements on the market already. The products are "miraculous," "astounding," and mostly ridiculous. Bloggers, websites, and "authorities" are having a field day shelling out advice and shilling products they say will boost your microbiome. Please have a very critical eye when reviewing all of the above. For good information and data refer to the NIH Human Microbiome Project: http://hmpdacc.org

Like the gluten-free craze, coconut oil hype, and paleo promotion, microbiomic mania is bound to ensue and may be hazardous to your health. In the scientific journal *Nature* in 2014, Dr. William P. Hanage, Associate Professor of Epidemiology at the Harvard School of Public Health, writes "The hype surrounding microbiome research is dangerous for individuals who might make ill-informed decisions, and for the scientific enterprise, which needs to develop better experimental methods to generate hypotheses and evaluate conclusions."

If you have a medical problem for which knowledge of certain bacterial species is necessary, you should work with a health professional well versed in this field to determine what, if anything, needs to be done. In the meantime adopt lifestyle changes, such as those I recommend in *The Only Cleanse*, that will help establish a more balanced microbiome. *The Only Cleanse* is all about balance.

Main Functions of Gut Flora:

METABOLIC
- *Fermentation of nondigestible dietary residue and endogenous mucus:*
  - *salvage energy as short-chain fatty acids*
  - *production of vitamin K*
  - *absorption of ions*

TROPHIC
- *Control of epithelial cell proliferation and differentiation*
  - *development and homoeostasis of the immune system*

PROTECTIVE
- *Protection against pathogens (the barrier effect)*

The Gluten Phenomenon Deconstructed

When I had Dr. Alessio Fasano, founder and director for the Center for Celiac Research at Massachusetts General Hospital, on my SiriusXM radio show, I asked him what he thought about the gluten-free craze that is sweeping the world of fad diets, throwing in my two cents that I thought it was out of control. His answer, live on air, was stunning. "I am probably to blame for this trend."

"Wow," I said. "Why is that?"

Dr. Fasano explained that it is his seminal research on celiac disease that has prompted the deluge of fad diet books, blogs, websites, and products denouncing gluten and suggesting that every human on the planet needs to avoid this deadly toxin. Dr. Fasano went on to say that the authors of these books, even though some are written by MDs, are misinterpreting his research. I would add that they are *badly* misinterpreting the research, scar-

POINT OF INTEREST

FOR IT START-UPS:
THERE'S AN APP FOR THAT!

The microbiome is becoming so popular that in July of 2014 researchers began using apps to track how certain daily health events affect gut microbiota. In a teeny, tiny one-year study using only two people, re-searchers had the participants track things like bowel movements, food intake, exercise, fitness, location change, medication, mood, oral hygiene, sleep, urina-tion, and vitamin intake on a smart phone app. Inter-estingly, researchers found that the balance of the gut microbiome was fairly stable, though it was affected daily by diet. For example, a high-fiber diet boosted good gut bacteria. However, big events such as mov-ing overseas or a bout of food poisoning caused big changes in gut microbiota.

ing people with sensational headlines such as "Gluten Is a Universal Human Poison," and causing a lot of confusion and consternation among consumers.

Here is the simple truth about gluten and whether you should be eating it or not: Gluten is a protein found in grains such as wheat—any kind, includ-ing semolina, durum, whole, and refined—its relatives such as spelt, faro, barley, and rye. Gluten is what gives bread its elastic texture and structure. Dr. Fasano's research has found that gluten, which is a combination of two proteins called gliadins and glutenins, is indigestible in humans. The body

POINT OF INTEREST

A MINI-RANT

Researchers are discovering that diets high in red and processed meat alter the gut microbiome and increase the risk of serious diseases like heart disease and cancer. Their solution is to find "therapeutic ways" to manipulate the microbiome, such as inventing pharmaceutical products that will undo the ill effects of a poor diet. Instead, why not spend all those research dollars on educating, motivating, and empowering people to eat a more plant-based diet? Our sociopolitical focus is slanted toward putting pharmaceutical Band-Aids on problems that can be resolved with lifestyle and behavior changes.

sees these undigested particles as an enemy that needs to be destroyed, and this stimulates an immune response. In some *genetically susceptible* people, like those who develop celiac disease, gluten can trigger an aggressive immune response in the gut, resulting in inflammation, dysfunction, and gut microbiomic imbalance. For the rest of us, while we still cannot fully digest gluten, the immune response is not nearly as intense or damaging. Our bodies engage daily in a war with all kinds of substances, such as bacteria and viruses, but rarely do we lose this battle. Many of us eat gluten daily and our bodies manage this intestinal conflict quite well with no repercussions. We drink alcohol, which is technically poisonous to the body. We encounter all kinds of germs and toxins every day, which is why our bodies have highly complex,

The B&B: Bile Acids and Bacteria

Bile acids are substances made in our liver to help the digestion of the fats that we eat. Bile acids are made from cholesterol (which is also made in the liver) and transported to your nearby gallbladder. The gall bladder's job is to serve as a holding tank for bile. When you eat food that has fat in it, whether it's a peanut butter sandwich or potato chips, the gall bladder contracts and releases bile acids into the intestine to break down globules of fat into smaller globs for easier absorption. Being a very green organism, your body reabsorbs and recycles what is left of the bile back to the liver. One reason eating lots of fiber helps lower cholesterol is simply that the fiber binds the bile in the intestine and carries it out of the body. The liver then has to make new bile using the available pool of cholesterol, thus lowering the cholesterol content in the body.

High levels of bile aids caused by diet, genetics, or illness can lead to cancer, diabetes, and other diseases. The body keeps very tight control over the amount of bile acids produced in order to prevent the buildup of toxic substances. It's only when these fine levels of control are breached that bile acids become associated with disease. This violation of the control mechanisms can occur through dietary means—e.g., high fat diets—where excessive levels of bile acids are produced and converted (via the bacterial flora) to damaging deoxycholic acid (DCA), which at high levels can cause cancer. A plant-based diet can make a big difference in reducing the production and amount of DCA and other secondary bile acids. The fiber alone helps manage the amount of bile acids in the body. The Physician's Committee for Responsible Medicine reports that because plant fiber changes the type of bacteria that is present in the intestine, there is reduced production of carcinogenic secondary bile acids. Plant foods are also naturally low in fat and rich in antioxidants and other anti-cancer compounds. Not surprisingly, vegetarians are at the lowest risk for many cancers and have a significantly reduced risk compared to meat eaters.

multi-leveled defense systems. Thus, saying gluten is a universal poison is like saying we should all stop breathing because there are airborne pathogens that can make us sick: a bit of truth mixed with a lot of sensationalism.

In Dr. Fasano's book *Gluten Freedom* he writes: "I do not share the position of the proponents of a 'gluten-free' world, who cite my work to support their position." He cannot be any clearer on the subject. There is no reason to avoid eating gluten-containing foods unless you have a medical reason to do so. People with celiac disease cannot have any gluten, ever. People who have a wheat allergy or feel that they may be intolerant to gluten should avoid it. Otherwise, go for whole grains and enjoy your bread and pasta.

Animals and Antibiotics

Stay away from eating animals fed antibiotics. This is one urban legend that is actually true. When animals are fed antibiotics, their bacteria become resistant to those antibiotics. When you eat that meat, that resistance is transferred to you. The complex relationship of gut bacteria and pathogens, and the introduction of antibiotic resistant bacteria into your gut, can lead to pathogenic influx and unwanted bacterial overgrowth. There is strong evidence that human consumption of animal foods like beef, chicken, and pork that carry antibiotic-resistant bacteria has resulted in human acquisition of antibiotic-resistant infections including E. coli, campylobacter, and salmonella. Infections with these bacteria can decimate the healthy gut microbiota and cause diarrhea, vomiting, neurological disorders, renal failure, and in some cases death. If you choose to eat animals, it is worth spending the extra money on those that are organically and sustainably raised. The law prohibits the use of antibiotics in organic foods.

MICROBES IN MOTION
Exercise increases the diversity of gut microbiota.
A study out of Ireland compared rugby players with sedentary subjects. The rugby players had healthier balances of gut microbes than the sedentary people. The athletes also ate more grains, fiber, fruits, vegetables, unsaturated fats, and protein (in the form of whey protein) than the nonathletes. The researchers believe that both exercise and diet have big impacts on gut microbial diversity.

POINT OF INTEREST

FOR ALL OF US

The Natural Resources Defense Council reports that antibiotic use on farms threatens public health. Feeding low levels of antibiotics to healthy farm animals simply to prevent illness or to fatten them up breeds "superbugs," dangerous germs that are able to fight off antibiotics and that spread to our communities and families.

SWEET

"What's in a name? That which we call a rose by any other name would smell as sweet."

–WILLIAM SHAKESPEARE

...Unless it was a fake rose.

I have never been a fan of artificial or non-nutritive sweeteners for most people. Products including saccharin, sucralose, aspartame, neotame, Acesulfame-K, and stevia can run between two-hundred and thirteen-thousand times sweeter than real sugar. Do we really need to eat something thirteen-thousand times sweeter than sugar? In a sense these non-nutritive artificial sweeteners (NAS) are tricking the body into thinking sugar is being consumed. The body revs up to metabolize it, releasing hormones like insulin and glucagon-like peptide-1 into the blood stream. Having no sugar or glucose on which to act confuses the brain and the body and leaves

41

these hormones in circulation, where they can do damage. Over time this can result in a metabolic mess. Scientists believe that NAS contribute to weight gain, alterations in the gut-brain axis, glucose intolerance, and an unhealthy shift in the gut microbiome. Several studies have shown that both children and adults who consume NAS are at risk for weight gain. Emerging research has found that consuming NAS can alter the brain's response to foods and that this may increase the risk for obesity, insulin resistance and other metabolic dysregulation.

In September 2014 a study in the journal *Nature* found that in both mice and humans, consuming the artificial sweeteners saccharin, aspartame, and sucralose altered the gut microbiota, which may increase the risk for glucose intolerance, type 2 diabetes, insulin resistance, and obesity. Granted, the study was done primarily on mice, the results of which cannot be generalized to humans. However, in the very small part of the study that involved humans, researchers looked at seven healthy adults and had them consume NAS for only one week. Four of the seven subjects developed significantly poorer blood sugar responses five to seven days after NAS consumption, and a pronounced change in their gut microbiota was observed. The other three subjects had little gut or blood sugar response. What this means, in terms of this very small group, is that while people's guts may react differently to NAS, NAS affects multiple physiological parameters, including the messages sent between the gut and the brain. Overall, my recommendation is to avoid them.

Labelese:
Avoid products containing these faux sweeteners:
- Sucralose
- Saccharin
- Aspartame
- Neotame
- Stevia
- Acesulfame potassium (Acesulfame K)
- Monk fruit [also called Swingle fruit extracts (SGFE)]
- Luo Han Guo, Lo Han Kuo
- Tagatose
- Isomalt
- Sugar alcohols
- Monatin

POINT OF INTEREST

FOR DNA ENTHUSIASTS FROM THE FOLKS AT THE U.S. NATIONAL LIBRARY OF MEDICINE:

A genome is an organism's complete set of DNA, including all of its genes. Each genome contains all of the information needed to build and maintain that organism. In humans, a copy of the entire genome— more than three billion DNA base pairs—is contained in all cells that have a nucleus.

Emerging Research on the Microbiome

Here is a smattering of what research is exploring in the relationships between our gut microbiomes and their effects on diseases. Of note is what we can do to keep certain genes in our bodies, and those of the microbiota inhabiting our bodies, from being turned on or off. Genetics is incredibly complicated, but the brainy folks who study genomes are investigating just how much control over our genetics we have. It seems our lifestyles can be deciding factors in flipping on or off certain genes. Smoking and eating a lousy diet can flip the switch on genes that open the door to cancer, diabetes, obesity, and heart disease. Conversely, a healthy lifestyle can help flip on good genes and keep the bad ones off. In the case of the gut microbiome, evidence is mounting that the foods we consume not only affect our personal genomes but the genomes of the trillions of bacteria we house. You'll see a solid through-line here: The typical American or Western diet is the springboard to an adulterated microbiome and the onset of chronic and serious diseases; a more plant-based diet and a physically active lifestyle support a healthy microbiome and will result in fewer chronic diseases.

Diabetes

Studies are looking at how the microbial composition in our guts influences whole-body metabolism and contributes to insulin resistance and diabetes. Differences in the gut microbiome have been noted between people with type 2 diabetes and healthy individuals. Scientists are hoping to discover a way to shift gut microbes to a favorable balance in the hopes of reducing the onset or severity of type 2 diabetes. Whatever the balance of microbes you have in your gut is, being overweight or obese and remaining sedentary remain the biggest risk factors for developing type 2 diabetes.

The microbiome throws its hat into the ring with type 1 diabetes, too. We now know that alterations in the gut microbiota contribute to the development of autoimmune disorders such as type 1 diabetes. New data suggests that gut microbiota play a critical role in the prevention or the triggering of type 1 diabetes.

Inflammatory Bowel Disease (IBD)

A variety of factors, which may be environmental, genetic, immunological, and microbial in nature, contribute to the development of inflammatory bowel disease (IBD).

IBD has been repeatedly linked to the overall ecology of the human gut microbial ecosystem, including the community and the range of microbial over- and under-abundances. Intestinal microbiota play an important role in the pathogenesis of inflammatory bowel disease. There is good evidence supporting the use of certain probiotics and prebiotics in the therapy of ulcerative colitis and pouchitis, whereas their beneficial role in Crohn's disease has not yet been proven. Do not start taking probiotics or other supplements without first speaking with your gastroenterologist. She/he will be on top of the current research and can guide you to the best choices to meet your particular medical needs.

Liver Disease

When your gut microbes are out of balance because of diet and lifestyle, your liver can become inflamed and suffer from tissue injuries. You do not want to mess with the health of your liver, since it is a major detoxification organ. It filters metabolic byproducts, keeps substances from accumulating and reaching toxic levels in the body, and filters and removes toxins such as alcohol and drugs. Researchers are looking at how alcohol, drugs, and the typical Western diet can disrupt the gut microbiome and lead to liver diseases such as cirrhosis, nonalcoholic fatty liver disease, and nonalcoholic steatohepatitis.

Colon Cancer

Scientists are wondering how what we eat affects the production of toxic byproducts in the gut microbiome that could damage cells and cellular DNA and lead to cancer. For example, Mayo Clinic researchers are looking at two metabolic pathways with toxic potential, including sulfate-reducing bacteria and methanogens in the archaea family (these microorganisms produce the byproduct methane). In one small but interesting study, scientists from America and Africa collaborated on a study that compared the gut microbiota of native Africans with those of African Americans. Can you guess what they found? The native Africans consumed more fiber and vegetables and less animal and processed foods than African Americans. The native Africans' guts had a healthier balance and more diverse population of microbes than the African Americans, who were eating the typical "Western" diet—high in fat and red and processed meat. The African American microbiota had more methanogens and secondary bile acids than the native Africans and thus were at greater risk of getting colon cancer.

H. pylori

Conventional thinking was that the hydrochloric acid in our stomachs was so powerful it kept the stomach sterilized. When the bacteria *Helicobacter pylori* (H. pylori) was discovered in the stomach it turned GI science on its ear. Scientists found that the stomach supports over one hundred types of bacteria and is a key player in the world of the gut microbiome. *H. pylori* infects approximately fifty percent of the world's population. *H. pylori* infection occurs when *H. pylori* infects your stomach, which usually happens during childhood. Complications from *H. pylori* infection include peptic ulcers and gastric cancers. When *H. pylori* settles into the nooks and crannies of the stomach it can increase inflammation. Excessive salt and nitrate intake (found in foods like bacon, hot dogs, and cold cuts, pickled or smoked foods), a high meat intake, and a diet low in fruits and vegetables may impair the stomach's ability to handle the inflammation, which in turn can lead to bacterial imbalance and disease. There is a lot of ongoing research, but until scientists figure out how to keep H. pylori in check, skipping processed, smoked, and cured meats, and eating more fruits and vegetables is a good idea.

POINT OF INTEREST

FOR A FRAME OF REFERENCE

It is estimated that there are more than five hundred thousand cases of CDI in the United States, and fourteen thousand associated deaths each year.

Neurological Disorders

It's weird to think that the bacteria in your gut can affect the onset of neurological diseases like multiple sclerosis, amyotrophic lateral sclerosis (ALS) and Alzheimer's disease, but that is what scientists believe may be happening. And they say that our diets are game changers. A 2014 study in the journal *Frontiers in Neurology* found that typical Western diets with their high-fat, cholesterol, sugar, and sodium and low fiber intakes caused unwanted bacterial translocation. These escapees from the GI tract can migrate to the extensive neurovasculature of the central nervous system, which may trigger neurological diseases.

Clostridium difficile Infection (CDI or *C. diff.*)

CDI is one of the most common hospital-acquired infections and the leading cause of healthcare-associated diarrhea in the US. *Clostridium difficile* is a bacteria that is passed in feces and can live on surfaces like toilets, sinks or doorknobs for weeks or even months. You can become infected by touching a contaminated surface (including someone's hand) and then your mouth. *C. diff* can invade the large intestine and overwhelm the good bacteria in the colon. Once established, *C. diff* starts to produce virulent toxins. These toxins are called Toxin A and Toxin B. Toxins A and B poison the gut, causing severe inflammation (colitis), diarrhea, dehydration, and in some cases, death. I'll tell you a story I have not gone public with before now. I got CDI in 2010, following a bout with the stomach flu. Since my GI tract was already inflamed and fighting a viral infection, the microbiota was stressed and depleted and thus more susceptible to infection and invasion by CDI. I was probably directly exposed to CDI at the nursing home I was visiting daily to see my mother. It used to be that mostly older people who were in hospitals got CDI, but that profile has been changing in recent years. Because of the overuse of antibiotics, some *Clostridium difficile* strains have become resistant to treatment. This means that the *C. diff* bacteria has morphed itself into a superbug that deflects antibiotic treatment. Recurrence rates are up in 40 percent of patients of all ages and are climbing. I was one of the unlucky forty percent.

The CDI made me very sick, and the oral Vancomycin antibiotic treatment I was being given could not stem the toxic invasion. I was scared and felt miserable. The doctors did not know why the CDI was so persistent in a relatively young and healthy person. At the time there was no readily available treatments for antibiotic-resistant CDI. After ten months, thousands of dollars spent on medications, and dangerous weight loss, I finally got better. Healthy eating, regular exercise, oral probiotics, and the Vancomycin all finally kicked in and slammed down the CDI for good. Fast forward just a few years, and by 2014 a new approach to treating intractable CDI has emerged; it has everything to do with the gut microbiota. It's called fecal microbiota transplantation (FMT). FMT transplants another person's fecal matter into the patient's gut to help recolonize the gut with the donor's healthy microbes. Sounds revolting, I know. However, the use of FMT has a reported 90 percent success rate for recurrent CDI, which is great news. **NOTE:** *Washing hands regularly helps reduce CDI. Also, keeping a healthy gut will help your body fight these kinds of infections.*

Cardiovascular Disease

The old saying "The way to someone's heart is through their stomach" is a lot truer than ever before. Investigators believe that there is a connection between the way food is digested by a person's gut bacteria and the development of atherosclerosis (hardening of the arteries) and cardiovascular disease. To test this hypothesis, researchers are looking at inflammatory markers in the blood and at the genome of the bacteria in the gut to determine how they affect a person's risk of heart disease. What this means to you right now is that the healthier you eat, the happier your gut microbes will be and the less likely it is that a heart disease gene will be flicked on.

3. Enemas and Clysters

Enemas and Clysters: *High Fashion, Sexual Perversions, Murder, and Fetishes*

Enemas, formerly known as clysters, have been used for centuries to cure everything from headaches to cancer, purify the system, alleviate constipation, rid the body of gas, toxins, and germs, deliver medications, and help the patient lose weight. They have also been used to assassinate, baptize, and exorcise. Throughout history enemas have been depicted in art and theater, in medical and religious texts. Yes, it is true: There are actual paintings of people getting enemas. For those of you who have not had the pleasure of having one, an enema is a procedure where fluids are introduced into the lower part of the colon via a syringe or tubing inserted into the rectum.

As far back as ancient Egypt enemas, or clysters, were believed to be an essential part of good health. Pharaohs each had their own personal "Guardian of the Anus" (I'm curious as to what would lead one to make this career choice).

In 431 BC the Greek historian Herodotus mentioned clysters, saying that Egyptians performed enemas to be healthy, believing that disease came from the foods they ate. He also said Egyptians vomited several days a month to promote healing and ate raw birds and fish.

Apparently the Egyptians got the idea of the clyster from watching the ibis, a bird that was sacred in Egypt. Ancient manuscripts attribute this notion to a Roman scholar named Pliny the Elder (23-79 CE): "The ibis... having a crooked and hooked bill, useth it in steed of a syringe or pipe, to squirt water into that part, whereby it is most kind and holsome to void the doung and excrements of meat, and so purgeth and cleaneth her bodie." In other words, the Egyptians believed the ibis was giving himself an enema as part of his daily bathing routine and decided it would be a good idea for humans to do so, too.

Centuries later, physicians in the fifteenth and sixteenth centuries were still going at it, administering enemas to help relieve stomach pain, constipation, fevers, and headaches. The seventeenth century is known as the "golden age of the clyster." Parisians in high society, mimicking the fashion of King Louis XIV's court, are reported to have had three or four "lavements" or "remedies" a day to purify their complexions. Enema fluids may have included colored water or perfumes—another curiosity. Why colored water? Who would see it?

There are numerous references in historical articles about King Louis XIV and his obsession with enemas. It is a widely reported that Louis XIV had over two thousand enemas during his reign. The king was so enamored with the experience that he would have his physicians administer them even while he was holding court.

The popularity of clysters in France inspired the playwright Molière to spoof them in his plays. In *The Imaginary Invalid*, Molière made great fun of Argan, the hypochondriacal main character and his doltish physicians who recommended clysters as a cure for all the world's ills. Molière himself played the lead role on opening night in 1673.

Getting Away with Murder

The toxic cluster had the advantage of being the instrument of the perfect crime. An article in the 1901 medical journal *The Cincinnati Lancet* reported that in the 1700s "rump and syringe went much together so there was a fine opportunity for clyster poisoning." Patients and police would have no suspicion because the poisonous fluids administered via enema were in small doses. The results were intestinal ulcerations, perforation, peritonitis, and ultimately death. Poet and essayist Sir Thomas Overbury was famously murdered with a poisoned clyster in 1613. He was outwardly against the marriage of his longtime friend Sir Robert Carr and the recently divorced Countess of Essex, Frances Howard. The Countess, furious that Overbury was standing in her way, contrived with Carr to have Overbury imprisoned on trumped-up charges. But prison was not enough for the vindictive Countess; she wanted Overbury dead. Through a series of machinations and court intrigues Carr and the Countess gathered a team of co-conspirators and managed to have Overbury's prison food poisoned. To their disappointment, instead of killing him, the tainted vittles just made him ill. Eventually, the Countess and her murderous team opted for the poisoned clyster, which did in fact kill Overbury. Several accomplices were convicted and hanged for the murder. Years later Carr and the Countess, now married, were tried and convicted of the murder of Sir Thomas. Eventually, however, they were let off the hook.

Fast forward to the nineteenth century: Enemas remain quite popular in Europe, and their popularity had crossed the Atlantic to the United

States. Dr. John Harvey Kellogg of Battle Creek, Michigan—the inventor of Kellogg's Cornflakes—was arguably America's first holistic health guru. He ran a health sanatorium that promoted a vegetarian diet, exercise, healthy eating, and enemas. Kellogg was obsessed with bodily cleanliness, both external and internal. Patients at the sanatorium received daily yogurt enemas to "clean" their intestines. In 1888 Kellogg claimed to have invented the first oxygen enema. His premise was that oxygen could be absorbed via the lining of the colon in cases of hypoxia (lack of oxygen). This was never proven medically.

Enemas can be an effective delivery system for medications. For example, in some patients with distal colitis, butyrate, cyclosporine, or nicotine enemas may be helpful in reducing symptoms. Use only under the guidance of a qualified medical expert.

Enemas in the Twenty-First Century

Today, when you stroll down the aisle in your local pharmacy, the green and white Fleet sodium-phosphate enema box is as familiar as aspirin and cough drops. These over-the-counter home enema kits seem to have been around forever. Unfortunately enemas as constipation relievers have been killing people, says a 2012 report in the *Archives of Internal Medicine*. Physicians are so concerned about the use of Fleet enemas that they recommend making sodium-phosphate enemas available by prescription only. People receiving sodium-phosphate enemas, whether self-administered or performed in the hospital, can end up with renal failure, hypernatremia, hypokalemia, hyperphosphatemia. In normal language this means failing kidneys, too much sodium or phosphate, and too little potassium in the blood—any of which can kill you. Your colon can suck up these minerals and fluids, rapidly flooding the circulatory system and wreaking havoc. If you are suffering from chronic constipation, you need to see your physician to determine the cause. Speak with your healthcare practitioner if you are thinking about using an over-the-counter enema product.

Who killed Marilyn Monroe?

John W. Miner, a former Los Angeles County prosecutor who attended Marilyn Monroe's autopsy in 1962, is convinced Monroe died as the result of a poisoned enema. The Los Angeles times reported that Miner believed someone dissolved Nembutal in water by breaking open thirty or more capsules and then administered the lethal solution to Monroe by enema.

Hydrogen Peroxide

Don't try this at home folks: A report in the *Journal of Clinical Gastroenterology* is just one of multiple accounts in medical journals of people ending up in the ER because of hydrogen peroxide enemas. This report details an account of a fifty-nine-year-old man who gave himself a hydrogen peroxide enema because he was constipated. He ended up in the emergency room with abdominal pain, bloody diarrhea, rectal bleeding, necrosis (cell or tissue death), swelling, and a raw, inflamed, and ulcerated colon wall.

Doctors warn that hydrogen peroxide enemas are dangerous and potentially lethal. There are numerous websites and blogs advocating hydrogen peroxide enemas. The people writing them are irresponsible—and just plain stupid.

Coffee Enemas

Coffee is one of the world's favorite elixirs. People are passionate about their coffee: the roast, beans, temperature, aroma, and taste. Coffee baristas rank right up there with wine sommeliers. There is a Starbuck's on every corner, international coffee tastings and seminars, coffee bloggers, baristas and aficionados. Imagine my amusement when, while researching this book, I came across this ad for coffee:

"We offer ground and whole bean enema coffee. The made-for-enemas blend of coffee beans are chosen for their high caffeine and palmitic acid content, which are the elements in coffee that have the greatest benefits for liver detoxification, pain reduction, and the complete colon cleanse enema."

A Seriously Bad Idea

**FROM THE JOURNAL OF CLINICAL GASTROENTEROLOGY,
A MEDICAL DESCRIPTION OF WHAT HAPPENS WHEN A HYDROGEN
PEROXIDE ENEMA IS ADMINISTERED:**

*The pathogenesis of hydrogen peroxide colitis is thought to
be secondary to the chemical reaction (2HO-2HO+O) resulting
in penetration of highly reactive oxygen species, resulting in
damage to colonic mucosa. Within moments after exposure the
colon becomes distended with reduced blood flow. Blanching
occurs as peroxide contacts catalase within capillaries, forming
microbubbles of oxygen, which forces blood from the vasculature.
If the quantity of oxygen produced exceeds maximum blood
solubility, venous gas formation within the mesenteric and portal
venous system can occur, resulting in systemic embolization.*

There are special coffee-enema blends? Based on what? Taste? Of course the health claims are bogus, but people are laying out good money for these products. What is scary is that there are those who forego medical treatment for serious diseases such as cancer with the belief that coffee enemas can cure their disease. According to the American Cancer Society, coffee enemas have been associated with serious infections, dehydration, constipation, colitis (inflammation of the colon), electrolyte imbalances, and even death. A quick search of the medical literature finds reports of rectal burns, intestinal perforations, acute colitis, and proctocolitis (inflammation of the rectum and colon) from coffee enemas. Coffee enemas made national headlines in 2013 when a couple in Florida went public on a cable TV show in the US with their "coffee enema addiction." Apparently, their obsession with coffee enemas has taken over their lives, and takes up five hours of every day; the couple does not travel or leave the house for long periods of time.

One of the biggest proponents of coffee enemas is the Gerson Institute. Developed by Dr. Max Gerson in the 1920s, the Gerson approach to healing and curing diseases was transformed into an institute by Gerson's daughter in 1977. The Gerson Institute's website claims that their approach

POINT OF INTEREST

FOR IDIOMATIC PHRASE HISTORIANS

You are familiar with the saying "He's just blowing smoke up her . . .," meaning that the person being discussed is conning or lying to someone.

You guessed it. The origin of that colorful phrase comes from "vapor" clysters, in which tobacco smoke was quite literally blown into the colon via the rectum. Vapor clysters were used to revive those who had fainted or succumbed to asphyxiation.

to therapy, which includes vegetarian diet, raw juices, and multiple coffee enemas daily, "boosts the body's own immune system to heal cancer, arthritis, heart disease, allergies, and many other degenerative diseases. Coffee enemas are the primary method of detoxification of the tissues and blood on the Gerson Therapy." In 2014 the Gerson Clinic in Tijuana, Mexico, cost $5,500 a week. The clinic requires a two-week minimum stay. While there are ardent believers in Gerson's therapy, there is currently no scientific evidence or proof showing any benefit or a cure for any disease with these treatments.

Most of us have been touched by cancer in one way or another. I have worked with cancer patients daily. They and their families would go to the ends of the earth to find a cure. So too would they do just about anything to avoid surgery, radiation, or chemotherapy. I don't blame them. Unfortunately, there is no scientific proof that Gerson Therapy or any other nontoxic, alternative approaches cure cancer. There is no proof that coffee enemas detoxify anything. Folks, if a program like Gerson's really cured disease, there'd be clinics and programs all over the world advocating this kind of therapy. But there aren't.

Sure, vegetarian diets and raw juices are healthy. Up to 90 percent of cancers are lifestyle related. Smoking tobacco, drinking alcohol, the Western diet and being sedentary, all contribute to cancer risk. Sellers of cancer cures, whether it be a therapy, enema, pill, or tea, are taking these basic truths and twisting them into money-making opportunities by preying on people's desperation. Your money is better spent on proven medical treatments, buying healthy foods, joining a fitness center, and keeping up with health screenings such as mammograms, colonoscopies, and prostate exams.

Stupid Enema Tricks

The alcohol enema, a.k.a. "butt chugging" (even the name has an ew factor) is where alcoholic beverages are delivered via enema so the recipient can get drunk quickly. This is extremely dangerous because the alcohol is absorbed directly into the blood stream through the colon walls, spiking blood alcohol levels and rapidly leading to alcohol poisoning. In 2004 a Texas woman was charged with negligent homicide after she gave her husband a sherry enema and he died. It was reported in September 2012 that a twenty-year-old University of Tennessee student almost died as a result of an alcohol enema delivered at a fraternity party. Seriously dudes, there are other ways to have a good time.

The Bottom Line

Today, enemas are used regularly to relieve constipation. Over-the-counter products are readily available. The barium enema, where an x-ray-sensitive solution is delivered into the colon, is sometimes used as diagnostic procedure (though colonoscopies are done more frequently now). A warm mineral-oil enema may be used to help soften hardened stools. In certain circumstances, enemas may be used to deliver medications, since they can be absorbed through the sensitive colon wall. While alleviating constipation is important, there is no research to suggest that enemas detoxify or cleanse the body. In fact, enemas have been linked with eating disorders, toxicities, cramping, pain, and even death. The attraction to enemas as cleanses is being fueled by well-oiled marketing and advertising campaigns, showing green meadows, snow-capped mountains, and waterfalls. These ads are designed to present the enema as a safe and effective tool for body detoxification, spiritual well-being, and curing disease.

Many products advertise herbal or "all natural" enema preparations. There are several reports of serious side effects from people using these products. An article in the *Journal of Family Practice* in 2011 reported on a forty-nine-year-old man who after taking an herbal colon-cleansing product he bought on-line became very sick. The man told the doctors that he had read "testimonials" on the product's website by people who had supposedly done the "cleanse". They claimed renewed energy, better skin, and weight loss. The man was intrigued and bought a one-month supply. He, like many people, was attracted to the idea of cleansing his colon— and maybe he could lose a few pounds in the process. Not long after he ingested the product he experienced vomiting, diarrhea, and "twisting" abdominal pain. Days later he ended up in the emergency room after having rapidly lost twenty-four pounds. He was dehydrated, his pancreas and colon were inflamed, and his potassium levels were dangerously low. Low potassium levels in the bloodstream can lead to cardiac arrhythmia (irregular heartbeats) and death. His gastroenterologist diagnosed him with "herbal intoxication." Unfortunately, this man's story is not unusual. Since the FDA regulates dietary supplements under a different set of regulations than those covering drug products, you have no idea what substances are actually in these "cleansing" products and they have not been tested for safety. The man in this case study was lucky. He was admitted to the hospital, where he was rehydrated and his potassium levels were restored. After five days he was deemed well enough to go home.

The truth is enemas may be medically necessary at times, but there is no evidence to suggest that they cure or alleviate disease or decontaminate the human body.

High Colonics
Let's get high

Higher into the colon that is. Enemas only flush out the lower, sigmoid part of the colon. With high colonics, also known as colonic irrigation or hydrotherapy, a flexible tube is inserted into the anus all the way up to the beginning of the

POINT OF INTEREST

FOR ELVIS FANS

Did constipation kill Elvis Presley? Urban myths suggest that Elvis died with forty or more pounds of impacted fecal matter in his colon. This is definitely not true (see below). Other reports point out that Presley was a regular prescription drug user. Many believe he died from a drug overdose. There is also the fact that prescription pain medications tend to cause chronic constipation. To alleviate the constipation, Presley was apparently tossing back laxatives like they were jelly beans. Laxative overuse can reduce the colon's ability to function properly and can make constipation worse. Presley's personal doctor, Dr. George Nichopoulous (who some saw as a nefarious character), says the cause of death was straining at the stool, which caused a heart attack. The real cause of Presley's death remains a mystery.

colon, called the cecum. Colonic cleansing is usually performed by hygienists or colon therapists, who may or may not have any training to do so (a problem in and of itself). Unlike the enema, colonics sluice a larger volume of water into the colon—up to sixty liters. The fluid and fecal matter it washes out is expelled through a second tube.

Colonics were initially based on the theory of autointoxication. It was believed that over time toxic sludge collected in the colon, became putrefied, and was absorbed into the body through the colon wall, causing no end of illnesses, ailments, and disease. Washing out the colon seemed like a reasonable solution to rid the body of these poisons. In the late 1800s Charles A. Tyrell, a not-quite medical professional, marketed his version of an enema device he called Cascade and made a fortune doing so. Tyrell aggressively promoted the use of colonics, saying they were a cure for anything from cholera to rheumatism. By the turn of the century the market for devices (tubing, hoses, fluid containers, and the like), laxative pills, and tonics was booming as never before. An endless profusion of remedies, sold in shops and by mail-order enterprises and promising health through regularity of bowel movements, "opened men's purses by opening their bowels." Cleaning colons became big business. It remains so to this day.

The theory of autointoxication was scientifically debunked in the *Journal of the American Medical Association* way back in 1922, and the practice of colon cleansing fell out of favor for a while. However, due to celebrity endorsements, aggressive advertising, and the Internet, colon cleansing and hydrotherapy have again become extremely popular. We are talking a *multi-million-dollar-industry* kind of popular. Reportedly high profile celebs like Princess Diana, Jennifer Aniston, and Madonna were fans of the procedure. *The Daily Mail*, a UK newspaper, reported in 2011 that more than six-thousand Britons were getting colonic irrigations on a monthly basis. Websites and advocates extoll the virtues of colonic irrigations for conditions such as eczema, psoriasis, allergies, fatigue, depression, indigestion, acid reflux, weight loss, gas, bloating, and cancer. The list goes on.

The Impact

Colon cleanse advocates and practitioners often cite the "fact" that most of us are carrying forty to sixty pounds of impacted feces in our colons, which is poisoning our systems, making us sick, and killing people like John Wayne and Elvis Presley. Fecal impaction is dry stool that cannot pass out of the body. I was curious about this "fact-myth" because it is repeated all over the Internet, in blogs, even in videos. I went to Dr. Ira Breite, a board-certified gastroenterologist and clinical professor of medicine at NYU School of Medicine in New York City, and asked him to clear up the confusion. "Although there seem to be many reports of humans having pounds of impacted feces in their colons (Elvis and John Wayne both have stories that they had multiple pounds of fecal material at autopsy), the fact is, it is just not true," Dr. Breite says. So how much poop are we packing on a daily basis? Dr. Breite says that even the largest normal human bowel movement doesn't weigh much more than 250 grams (about half a pound). Repeated use of laxatives, pain medications, poor hydration, and being sedentary can all contribute to constipation, which can in turn lead to fecal impaction. Left untreated, fecal impaction can be dangerous and should be treated by a physician. But Dr. Breite points out that while "impaction can occur, as can constipation, it is still much more about not being able to evacuate rather than an 'excess buildup' of stool." The colon is not functioning properly when it cannot regularly expel stool. It's not true that the majority of people are walking around with pounds of impacted poop in their colons. Dr. Breite sums it up: "If anybody tells you that they you are full of impacted stool, let them know that you think they are full of s**t."

Treating Fecal Impaction

FROM THE NATIONAL CANCER INSTITUTE:
The main treatment for impaction is to moisten and soften the stool so it can be removed or passed out of the body. This is usually done with an enema. Enemas are given only as prescribed by the doctor, since too many enemas can damage the intestine. Stool softeners or glycerin suppositories may be given to make the stool softer and easier to pass. Some patients may need to have stool manually removed from the rectum after it is softened.

Is Colonic Hydrotherapy Good for You?

Does it really detoxify your body? In a word: No. Consider the fact that people have been getting colonics for hundreds of years, and to date there is still no scientific or medical evidence that these procedures offer health benefits except in cases of certain medical conditions such as intractable constipation and other defecation disturbances. In these instances people should be treated by a qualified medical health professional such as a gastroenterologist.

Our bodies are uniquely designed to package and remove waste via the colon and at the same time extract essential nutrients in the process. Perfecting this system has taken thousands of years. Getting regular colonic cleanses is like cutting down the trees in a rain forest. You are wiping out an incredibly complex internal ecosystem that has evolved over eons and affects total body health. Colon cleanses and enemas don't target toxins and leave the good flora behind. The tsunami of fluids and additives blasts away anything in its path. You are quite possibly opening the doors to bacterial pathogens, viruses, and blight by effectively whisking away your body's natural defense systems. In addition, colonic irrigations and enemas can perforate or tear the colon wall. Colonic perforations can cause serious, and sometimes deadly infections. There are reports of gangrene of the pelvic floor, acute water intoxication, colitis, septicemia (systemic infection), and parasites being introduced into the colon from hydrotherapy devices after colonic hydrotherapy.

In 2011 the *Journal of Family Practice* reported: "Most reports in the literature note a variety of adverse effects of colon cleansing that range from mild (e.g., cramping, abdominal pain, fullness, bloating, nausea, vomiting, and soreness) to severe (e.g., electrolyte imbalance and renal failure). Some herbal preparations have also been associated with aplastic anemia and liver toxicity." All of that said, there are people who swear by high colonics. Feelings of wellbeing, euphoria, and better energy and digestion are commonly reported. Why some people get these results is unknown. People may turn to colonic hydrotherapy as a last resort. It is very distressing for patients who suffer from pain, fatigue, constipation, or bowel disorders to be told that there are no medical treatments that can help them. Sometimes the cause of the problem cannot be identified or the symptoms are not responding to medical treatment. It's often at this point that patients seek alternatives for help and relief. This is where things get tricky. On one hand just because a treatment is not evidence based, does not mean it won't be helpful in some patients. The biggest concern is the safety and efficacy of the treatment and the training and skill of the practitioner. Patients need to be very proactive and educated when it comes to their healthcare.

There are angry blogs, articles, and videos reporting that practitioners of colonic hydrotherapy have been bullied by authorities, demeaned by medical professionals, and routinely victimized by the pharmaceutical industry. Supporters believe that drug companies push drugs, and that physicians are uneducated about alternative or complementary healing therapies, all of which is, for the most part, true. However, the real concern from my perspective and on the part of physicians and CAM practitioners with whom I have worked, is the welfare of the patients. As far as the science goes, there is no evidence that colonics cleanse, cure, purify, or detoxify the system.

> " "Colonic cleansing as an adjunct to general health has been around for centuries and will likely continue to be used by uninformed and suggestible individuals, often in response to commercial inducements involving questionable claims of health benefit."
>
> **–AMERICAN JOURNAL OF GASTROENTEROLOGY 2009**

NOTE: *It is not within the scope of this book to examine all of the colonic hydrotherapy training schools (a Google search of "training, colonic hydrotherapy" came up with 7,730,000 hits), their legitimacy, the skill of their practitioners, the licensing of practitioners, or the belief that the medical establishment is on a mission to destroy alternative and complementary practices, including colonic irrigations. So please do not get in a huff if you are a school or a practitioner of colon hydrotherapy. The fact of the matter is licensing requirements for colonic hydrotherapists vary by state in the US and some states do not require licensing at all. Courses require anywhere from only four days to months of training, which may involve online courses and practical training. Associations like The International Association of Colon Hydrotherapy say they are working to set up guidelines for standards of practice and education requirements for colon hydrotherapists.*

Here's Mud in Your Eye

A twenty-two-year-old actress goes on national TV and tells people she is eating clay to "detoxify" her colon and her body. Viewers take her word for it and start buying edible clays. I shouldn't be surprised, yet the legions of celebrities who give out health advice never ceases amaze me. It's also scary that the public believes celebrities simply because they're celebrities. Would you go to a handyman if you needed a brain tumor removed? Clays—and there are many kinds and compositions of clays—have been used medicinally for centuries. On the skin, certain kinds of clays appear to have antibacterial and antimicrobial properties and may help fight infections and absorb secretions, toxins, and contaminants. Cosmetically, clays may help heal blemishes.

But *eating* clay is not so straightforward. The intentional consumption of earth materials, such as clays, by humans and animals is known as geophagy. Proponents claim that edible clay is homeostatic (what?), flushes old fecal matter from the colon, and "pulls" toxins and metals out of the system. Researchers are interested in the antibacterial abilities of certain clays, but at this time there is no scientific evidence in humans to support the safety or efficacy of consuming them. You don't always know what you are getting in a product, either. In 2014 an analysis of nine edible clay samples found that all of the samples had detectable levels of lead and arsenic. The elements in clay—and I am referring to the elements on the periodic table from the wall of your eighth grade chemistry class—could conceivably alter electrolyte balances. Indeed, there have been reports of edible clays both raising and depleting potassium levels, which could have deadly consequences. Eating clay can cause bowel obstructions, mineral imbalances, nutrient excesses, poisoning, and parasitic invasions. For now, I'd skip the edible clays and go for the anti-aging mud mask facial at your favorite spa.

4. Fasting

Fasting
- A Confession
- Reasons People Fast
- What Happens in the Body During Fasts
- Self-Loathing
- The Juicing Thing
- Pros and Cons of Juicing
- Calorie Restriction and Intermittent Fasting

I have a confession to share with you. Many years ago I succumbed to the fasting-is-great rhetoric. Long before I ever took a nutrition course I was living in New York City pursuing a career as a performer. I was in my early twenties, sleeping on my friend Kat's floor (she didn't have a couch), and waiting tables

POINT OF INTEREST

FASTING FOR FAITH-BASED REASONS

*May include an act of dedication, performing pen-
ance for sins, strengthening self-discipline, repenting,
combating temptation, understanding the plight of
the needy, or seeking humility or spiritual connection.*

in New York City. I had little money to buy food, so the only time I could get a good meal was at work. My shift at a restaurant on Madison Avenue and 68th Street, was from four p.m. to midnight. Knowing I was not going to be able to eat again until the following day when I got to work, I'd eat on and off for the whole shift. Of course I gained weight. Of course I was embarrassed about being over-weight (especially when my acting teacher told me I needed to lose weight in order to get work as an actress). Of course I was willing to try anything to lose the weight. While perusing the books in a bookstore—one of my favorite pastimes—I came across a small paperback book enthusiastically espousing the amazing benefits of fasting. It said that by consuming nothing but water and noncaloric fluids I could cleanse my system of vicious poisons and lose weight forever. I was hooked. I stopped eating—for days and days and days. I chewed gum. I drank water and diet soda (which I have always disliked). I was hungry. Really, *really* hungry. I dreamt about food. I felt like a failure because I never experienced the "euphoria" promised by the little paperback book. Instead, I became depressed. I did lose weight. Once I stopped the fast, I regained it all. Then I felt even worse about myself. Sound familiar? I had nightmares about chewing gum for years after that. To this day you will never see me chewing gum.

Fasting, which means voluntarily omitting food or drink or both for an extended period of time, has been around worldwide for centuries. From the Ancient Greeks to Hollywood celebrities, from Egypt to South America, from the Bible to the Quran, fasting has been advocated for spiritual enlightenment, health, mental clarity, and cleansing purposes. People fast for spiritual, personal, medical, political, social, detoxing, or other reasons. The length of the fast varies from a few hours to many days or longer. Some fasts are water only or eliminate certain foods. A fast of a few days should not cause long-lasting physical harm, but longer fasts have been deadly. In 1981, ten prisoners died by going on hunger strikes for political protest when they were in Northern Ireland's Maze Prison. The strike lasted about two months, and according to communications smuggled out of the prison, the deaths were excruciating.

Fasting for weight loss, cleansing, and detoxification purposes has the same seductive, inner purification, quick-fix, aura that colon cleansing does. Proponents vigorously advocate fasting as a way to cure all ills. These kinds of fasts tend to recommend drinking only water, or water and lemon juice with honey and spices, or similar concoctions for days to weeks. They have been promoted by authors, "health providers," clinics, and celebrities for rapid weight loss, detoxification, and even as a cancer cure. The idea of fasting is attractive because it is easy, you don't have to think about what to eat, and there is no learning curve. The truth is there is no scientific evidence to support the practice of fasting for long-term health or weight loss, ridding the body of poisons, or curing any disease. None.

"I see many people who want to embark on fasts out of self-loathing and bowel disgust."
–CHAPLAIN CORMAC LEVENSON

Fasting to detox the body or jumpstart weight loss is a lost cause. Why? Because the weight lost will be regained, and there is no proof that going without food for days at a time helps the body's detoxification systems do their job. In fact, it impairs those processes. Going for long periods of time without food or nutrients begins to scare the body. The body does not know, or care, that you are depriving it of food for weight loss or a "cleanse." It only knows that it's not getting the nutrients it needs to stay alive. The human body perceives the lack of nourishment as an emergent situation and launches a full-out code red response to preserve energy and keep the body functioning.

The brain needs a constant source of glucose (blood sugar) for fuel to maintain basic life-support functions. After a day or so of not eating, the stores of glucose in the liver and muscles, known as glycogen, become depleted. The body then starts to break down muscle and other body proteins and fats for energy. After a week or more the body slows down its metabolic rate to conserve energy. Longer fasts can lead to muscle wasting, depression, lethargy, cognitive decline, nutrient deficiencies, cardiac abnormalities, dehydration, renal failure, gout, and in very long fasts (two months or so), organ failure and death. All the body's energy is diverted toward keeping the brain and body fueled for as long as possible while protecting the protein breakdown in the major organs like the heart. The body's natural detoxification systems rely on food to provide the substrates (basic ingredients) needed to make antibodies and enzymes and support neurological, muscle, and organ health. No food, no substrates=no energy. With no substrates or energy, organ health deteriorates. Tanking organ health means detoxing abilities crash—not to mention other critical physiological functions.

"One must meditate on why they want to fast."
–CHAPLAIN CORMAC LEVENSON

The human body, along with all other life forms on the planet, is in a constant struggle for survival and balance. Forbes.com asked Dr. Marion Nestle, the Paulette Goddard Professor of Nutrition, Food Studies, and Public Health at New York University, about the health concerns associated with fasts. "Fasting induces weight loss and metabolic changes to protect the brain and vital organs against harmful losses. Thin people can usually go about three weeks before the losses become so serious that they are irreversible. Fatter people can last longer." But not much longer. Depriving the body of vital nutrients sends it into a tailspin of desperation to stay alive. The last thing you want to do is freak out your body. For some people fasting for more than a day or two can lead to food insecurity, eating disorders, bingeing, or significant weight gain. Sometimes fasting may be

POINT OF INTEREST

HUNGER

Hunger is the body's way of telling us it needs energy. Hunger is purposely an unpleasant feeling that triggers us to eat food in order to relieve it.

medically necessary, for example to let the gut rest after a stomach flu or bout of diarrhea. In these cases water, nutrient rich broths, nonacidic juices, and other clear fluids are recommended for short periods of time.

Why we Fast

Knowing I was going to write a chapter on fasting, I approached Chaplain Cormac Levenson, MDiv, BCC, Captain of Awesomeness, to seek his guidance with the nonphysiological side of fasting. Cormac is a tall, lean young man whose approach to spirituality, while rooted in theology, also has a good foundation in today's realities. I asked him what his thoughts were about the practice of fasting. His response was shocking: "I see many people who want to embark on fasts out of self-loathing and bowel disgust. One must meditate on why they want to fast." That made me stop and think for a moment. Self-loathing? Bowel disgust? It is true that when we fast for weight loss or "cleansing" purposes it is not a pleasant experience. In fact it can feel downright punitive.

The more I thought about Cormac's comments, the more they made sense to me. So I circled back to ask him to elaborate. "In this culture we are often taught to hate ourselves. We are not good enough, not pretty enough," he says. (For more on this topic see The Only Cleanse discussion on positive and negative self-talk, page 141.) Cormac went on to say, "If you hate your body and want to transcend it by denial, by fasting, you will often end up simply hating your body more— taking hunger pangs not as an invitation into humility gratitude and bodily awareness, but as further proof of the weakness of the body."

I asked Cormac, "What do you advise your patients/clients regarding fasting for weight loss or cleansing purposes?"

His response, "I would happily give my humble opinion that it's a pretty terrible idea." He went on to say, "I would not recommend fasting to most people, but if it is done with intention and is rooted in a [spiritual] tradition, it can be a powerful experience. I recommend seeking the guidance of a spiritual teacher—not a book, but someone they can bring questions to—as well as someone with a strong working knowledge of nutrition."

The Juicing Thing

Juicing is not only a big trend in the US, but for some it has become a status symbol. That's when you know a fad is really sticking. Juicing became popular in the US during the 1990s. The trend came and went—and then returned with a vengeance during the second decade of the twenty-first century. Juicing is the practice of drinking only fruit and/or vegetable juice for a period of time. The purported benefits of juice fasts are quite impressive, including a wide range of claims that it cures cancer, inflammatory bowel diseases, eczema, arthritis and fibroids, that it causes weight loss, that it detoxifies and cleanses the body of heavy metals and poisons, that it reverses the effects of obesity and drinking too much alcohol, that it conveys anti-aging and prosex benefits, and more. What's fascinating is that so many people believe drinking juice can accomplish all of these miraculous deeds.

Alas, juicing does not live up to its reputation. Some adherents of juice fasts say they feel energized and healthy after a juice fast. There are many reasons this may be happening. One obvious reason is they have stopped eating an unhealthy diet. This alone will improve one's energy and help banish malaise relatively quickly. Another reason may be that they are pumping in waves of healthy nutrients from fruits and vegetables. Finally, when people are juicing they're probably getting better hydrated than they were before. Longer juice fasts, however, can spell metabolic trouble because there is little protein or fat to balance the body's energy needs.

A Bowl of Water with a Side of Air

In recent years calorie restriction (CR) for longevity and intermittent fasting (IF) to alleviate certain diseases have gained attention. The CR studies and most IF studies have been done on animals—a practice which I consider animal cruelty. I see no need for IF because we already do it when we sleep at night, a normal and necessary component of the body's cleansing systems. Small studies report that IF or CR may lower blood lipids or blood sugars in some people, but to what end? How long will people be able to periodically starve themselves? Research shows that intermittent fasting for a period longer than a few weeks is difficult for most individuals, since they tend to develop headaches, dizziness, and irritability. People who are obese or have type 2 diabetes, for which IF is being studied, are struggling enough with food choices, portions, weight, and self-image. As a registered dietitian-nutritionist, asking people to basically starve themselves on alternate days or for weeks at a time is practically unethical considering the complex emotional, psychological, and physiological stress they are already experiencing and the possible backlash on all those fronts.

The media, magazines, and Internet articles relating to CR and IF are misleading, and people are already latching on to this newest fad. A wiry gentleman in his mid-sixties approached me after a talk I gave at NYU Langone Medical Center on weight management. He asked me what I thought about intermittent fasting, which I had not addressed in my presentation. The look in his eye told me he already had a very strong opinion about it. I offered my point of view in as scientific and objective a way as possible, and he, feeling defensive nonetheless, offered his opposing, unscientific point of view. I am not sure why he asked my thoughts when he had already made his mind up that he would live longer by barely eating. We do not know, really, what "calorie restriction" means in terms of humans, how much "restriction" is necessary to add a few months or a year onto a life, if cutting all those calories can still provide the nutrients necessary for vigorous physical health and mental well-being . . . the unknowns and questions go on and on. Food, cooking, meals, and celebrations are the cornerstone of many of our daily rituals that offer social interaction, support, family time, pleasure and just happen to provide the nourishment necessary to keep us alive. Life is difficult enough without purposely throwing your body into starvation mode. I see no need to voluntarily deprive oneself of food for unknown and possibly hazardous outcomes.

Gastroenterologists tell me they have "juicing" patients who complain of abdominal pain, constipation, and a general feeling of malaise.

Nowadays people are using their blenders or more expensive options like Vita-Mixers and NutriBullets, to juice. These options are better than the earlier versions of juicing machines, since they include the whole fruit or vegetable—and thus the fiber and pulp. Still, juicing has an undeserved health halo for which even health professionals may fall. Cassie, registered dietitian-nutritionist, joined me on my SiriusXM radio show for a general discussion about nutrition. During my interview with her she confided something I found surprising. "I should probably not tell you this, but I have been doing three-day juice cleanses." She said. I asked her why, since as a registered dietitian-nutritionist she knew better than to believe the juice-cleanse hyperbole. Cassie had two little children under three years old and was struggling to lose her "baby weight." "I thought juicing could help me lose the weight. I have two babies, and I am so busy and exhausted. Juicing is easy because I don't have to think about what I am going to eat. It helps me stop bad habits, and I lose a few pounds." But Cassie, I asked, does it stick? Do the new habits and weight loss stick after the three days when you go back to real life eating? "No," she admitted. "And I know it isn't 'cleansing' me. I was just hoping it would help me get back on track." Even registered dietitian-nutritionists, who feel stuck, look for a quick fix, though we know there isn't any such thing.

Literally *as* I was writing this chapter I received an interview request from a journalist. She wanted me to comment on a whole new bevy of "all-natural" beverages for her story. "Is there any truth to the detoxing, cleansing, or health claims made by the manufacturers of artichoke, birch tree, maple, cactus, watermelon, and coconut juices?" she asked. From what I can see the makers of these beverages are making many unfounded claims, and some are simply not true. Overall if you want to spend the money on these products and like the way they taste, consuming them is probably fine. Just make sure to take into account the additional calories.

But don't expect any miracles. There is no scientific evidence at this time that drinking any kind of juice will rid the body of harmful toxins, "drain" the liver, or otherwise "cleanse the system."

The "juicing thing" bottom line: If you want to drink fresh-pressed juices with their fiber for a few days, it is fine. But don't fall for the hype that says juicing cleanses toxins from the body, cures illnesses or fosters lasting weight loss.

The Smooth-ie Spot

Smoothies come in as juicing's cousin because they are often a combination of fruit and vegetable juices along with yogurt, nuts or nut butters, grains, seeds, and even beans. Smoothie businesses and fitness centers sell smoothies with all kinds of ingredients, including ice cream, sherbet, frozen yogurt, algae, and protein powders. Just because a product is a smoothie, fresh-pressed juice, or "made with whole foods" does not mean it is calorie free. Calories in smoothies can range from two hundred to over eight-hundred calories. Depending on the ingredients, smoothies can be a good option for people on the go or for athletes after a long or intense workout. One mistake I often see with homemade smoothies is that people make them with fruits and vegetables but omit the protein. This leads to getting hungry sooner than later, which means eating more food and calories than intended. Including yogurt, chia seeds, nut butters, soymilk, tofu or even beans can up the protein and satisfaction ante in smoothies.

Pros and Cons of Juicing

Pros

➦ Consume more fruits and vegetables than usual

➦ Increase intake of vitamins, minerals, phytochemicals

➦ A physiological respite from a crummy diet

➦ Better hydration

➦ May be a springboard to eliminating troublesome foods

Cons

➦ **No fiber** (unless you are juicing the whole food in a blender-type apparatus)

➦ **No protein**

➦ **No essential fatty acids**

➦ **Increased risk of renal failure in people with kidney disease**

➦ **Increased risk of oxalate nephropathy and acute renal failure**

➦ **Long-term juice fasts may result in protein calorie malnutrition and other nutrient deficiencies**

➦ **Drinking juice may increase the risk of type 2 diabetes**

➦ **May increase the risk of eating disorders**

➦ **Does not cure anything that we know of at this time**

➦ **Expensive**

➦ **Does not create long-term lifestyle changes to support healthy eating**

5. When Detox Turns Toxic

⟫ **Hidden Drugs in Over-the-Counter Supplements**
⟫ **Invisible Ingredients**
⟫ **Detox Teas Can Cause Problems**
⟫ **Licorice Root**
⟫ **Senna**
⟫ **Casgara Sagrada**
⟫ **Kidney "Cleansers"**
⟫ **What to Avoid**

Let's set the record straight right here: There is no miracle in a bottle that will build muscle, detoxify your system, or cause long-lasting weight loss. At best it is a waste of money. At worst you could die. My recommendation is to avoid over-the-counter (and Internet) cleansing, detox, weight loss, muscle-building, energy-boosting, extreme-anything supplements that make exaggerated claims and promises that sound too good to be true.

"Spike in Harm to Liver Is Tied to Dietary Aids!"

This was the headline splashed across *The New York Times* in December 2013. The article chronicles Christopher Herrera, a seventeen-year-old teen who, when he walked into a Texas emergency room, was bright yellow: a sure sign that something was seriously wrong with his liver. Christopher had been taking an over-the-counter green-tea-extract fat-burning supplement and was suffering from acute liver injury. The liver damage was so severe he was put on a transplant list. Dietary supplements account for nearly twenty percent of drug-related liver injuries that turn up in hospitals. There are multiple reports from emergency rooms of patients with liver, kidney, or heart failure, and some even die from taking bodybuilding, sexual enhancement, extreme energy, weight loss, and detoxing products. Experts say there are likely many more cases that go unreported and untreated. Consumers believe that "all natural" products are safe. But anything, even if it is "all natural" like the green-tea extract in Christopher's supplement, can become a poison in concentrated forms.

Beware of Hidden Ingredients

What's scary is that consumers are buying products they think are safe, but they have been laced with hazardous, banned, or pharmaceutical-grade substances like steroids, hormones, diuretics, and amphetamines.

Examples of Undeclared, Unsafe, or Banned Substances or Drugs Found in Over-the-Counter products:

- *Sibutramine:* appetite suppressant associated with increased risk of heart attack and stroke
- *Phenolphthalein:* a suspected cancer-causing agent
- *Phenytoin:* a prescription-only anti-seizure medication
- *Fenproporex:* a controlled substance similar to amphetamines that can cause arrhythmia (a disorder of your heart rate or rhythm) and possible sudden death

In 2014 alone, the FDA found more than thirty products, including teas, pills, and powders, that contained the banned drug sibutramine. Sibutramine, an appetite suppressant, is a controlled substance that was removed from the market in October of 2010 because it is known to substantially increase blood pressure and may present a significant risk for patients with a history of coronary artery disease, congestive heart failure, arrhythmias, or stroke. These products may also interact in life-threatening ways with other medications.

Invisible Ingredients

In February 2015 the New York Attorney General warned Walmart, Target, Walgreens, and GNC to stop the sale of echinacea, ginseng, and other herbs. DNA testing found 79 percent either had no DNA from the advertised herb or had DNA evidence of material from other plants, such as rice, beans, pine, and other fillers or contaminants. "Consumers already had ample reason to doubt most of the claims made by herbal supplement manufacturers, who have precious little scientific evidence indicating these herbs' effectiveness in the first place," said Center for Science in the Public Interest's senior nutritionist David Schardt. He went on to say that until these products have better oversight and regulation, consumers should stop wasting their money in the herbal supplements aisle.

POINT OF INTEREST

Jesse, a forty-year-old body builder, wanted to get especially lean for an upcoming competition. So she started taking Hydroxycut. Hydroxycut is a brand of over-the-counter, easily obtainable supplements making claims including cleansing properties, "extreme energy," and "hardcore weight loss." These products contain compounds like green tea extract, cascara, and yohimbe, all of which have been associated with liver damage. Within a week of starting to take Hydroxycut Jesse was suffering from abdominal pain, cramps, bloody diarrhea, nausea, vomiting, chills, and fever. It got so bad she was rushed to the emergency room, where she was diagnosed with acute hepatitis (liver inflammation). After an extensive examination and blood tests, the doctors reported that Hydroxycut was the cause of the acute liver injury. Three days after stopping the supplement Jesse's liver calmed down and she was able to go home. There are other reports of Hydroxycut being associated with serious liver injury. In May 2009 the FDA warned consumers to stop taking a whole range of Hydroxycut products because of the risk of liver damage and, as occurred in at least one case, death.

A Spot of Tea

The medicinal effects of tea have a history dating back almost five thousand years. Because tea is known to confer an abundance of health benefits, companies have combined the health halo of teas with various other ingredients, and they sell the concoctions as detox, cleansing, or weight-loss teas. The ingredients, which may or may not contain any real tea, are what can turn a detox product toxic.

Blends of herbs that contain ingredients such as licorice root, wormwood, guarana, mate, and senna populate store shelves and Internet ads. A few cups of these infusions should not cause problems, but there are numerous reports of emergency room visits from people consuming these kinds of mixtures regularly. Hepatotoxocity (toxic liver), hypokalemia (dangerously low potassium levels), renal failure (kidneys start to fail), cardiac arrhythmias (irregular heartbeats), hypertension (high blood pressure) and other serious physical reactions have been linked with people consuming detox/cleansing products.

Licorice Root

Put the licorice down and move away from the candy counter. Whether in candy or teas, black licorice may be hazardous to your health. Licorice (*Glycyrrhiza glabra*) is a common ingredient in drinks, candy, teas, and foods because it adds sweet taste without sugar or calories. Licorice has been used as a medicinal herb for centuries in China, Egypt, Greece, and Rome. The main compound in licorice is called glycyrrhizic acid or glycyrrhizin. This and other chemicals in licorice are thought to be beneficial in treating swelling, coughs, gastrointestinal ulcers, acid reflux, eczema, and upper respiratory infections. Today there are hundreds of products such as teas or herbal blends that contain licorice, claiming it will help cleanse the kidneys, colon, and liver and treat diseases such as cancer and hepatitis.

Common Product Claims for Licorice Tea:
⟫ **Cleanses the body's systems**
⟫ **Strengthens the liver and kidneys**
⟫ **Detoxifies metal and chemical contaminations in the system**
⟫ **Flushes toxins from the liver**

Who would think something as innocent as licorice could cause health problems? Experts are worried that consumers and health professionals are unaware of the potential dangers. There are many reports of serious problems occurring in people who consume excess licorice in teas and licorice-containing foods and candies.

Serious medical problems from consuming
licorice include:

➤ **Hyperaldosteronism (excessive secretion of the hormone aldosterone in the adrenal gland)**
➤ **Pseudo-hyperaldosteronism**
➤ **Hypokalemic myopathy (potassium depletion leading to muscle weakness)**
➤ **Edema (swelling)**
➤ **Thrombocytopenia (abnormally low blood platelet levels)**
➤ **Hypertension (high blood pressure)**

Glycyrrhizic acid in licorice is the primary problem. Glycyrrhizic acid mimics chemicals in the body called mineralocorticoids, which help regulate the balance of water and the electrolytes sodium and potassium. The balance of these electrolytes is critical for muscle, nerve, and organ function and fluid balance. Licorice can cause the body to lose potassium, a condition known as hypokalemia, which can be life threatening. Because of licorice's effects on sodium and potassium levels and kidney function, it can also cause problems with fluid retention, which can lead to high blood pressure, swelling, congestive heart failure, and irregular heartbeats. Licorice may interact with certain medications such as diuretics, ACE inhibitors, laxatives, and diabetes medications.

Deglycyrrhizinated licorice (DGL), where the glycyrrhizin has been removed from the licorice product, is considered to be a safer alternative to whole licorice, but comprehensive safety studies have not been reported on DGL. For now it is best to use DGL products carefully.

A Little Can Go a Long Way

A seventy-six-year-old gentleman reported to the ER with muscle weakness, paralysis, high blood pressure, hypokalemia, and metabolic acidosis, all related to his drinking tea flavored with one hundred grams—about 3.5 ounces—of natural licorice root, for three years. It took two weeks of medical treatment for him to stabilize because of the long half-life of glycyrrhizic acid. I am sure you will be surprised—I know I was—to find that even chewing gum that contains glycyrrhizic acid has been known to make people ill. In one case, a thirty-five-year-old woman ended up in the hospital with high blood pressure, swelling in her limbs, and hypokalemia from chewing three pieces of licorice flavored gum a day. Three weeks after she stopped the gum her symptoms resolved.

There are no specific guidelines for how much licorice tea one should drink. The cleansing and detox tea products I reviewed that listed licorice root or glycrrhizic acid as ingredients did not list the amounts. While some people are more sensitive to glycrrhizic acid than others, it is best for everyone not to overdo licorice. According to the National Institutes of Health, licorice is likely safe for most people when consumed in amounts found in foods. It is possibly safe when consumed in larger quantities when used as medicine, short-term. However, it is unsafe when used in large amounts for more than four weeks.

NOTE: *If you love red licorice you can keep eating it because it does not contain any real licorice.*

In 2013 the FDA issued a warning for people consuming black licorice: If you are over the age of forty and consume multiple two-ounce bags (roughly forty to fifty grams each) of black licorice a day for at least two weeks you could be at risk for heart arrhythmias.

Senna

Senna is a popular herbal laxative, which is why it is often found in "cleansing" teas. Products may combine laxatives such as senna with stimulants like caffeine to compound their laxative effects. People confuse the idea of "cleansing" the body with the normal process of going to the bathroom, which is the body's all-natural way of removing toxins and waste. Any imbalance in this natural process, either constipation or diarrhea, can be a real problem. When someone is constipated, a gentle laxative may be very helpful. Senna is used in many over-the-counter products such as Senekot. It is generally considered safe and is recommended for short-term use (less than one week), though I have seen it prescribed for much longer in patients with cancer or gastrointestinal disorders, those on long-term pain medications, and those with other medically related issues. Some detox teas may contain high amounts of senna. However, since the teas are not regulated by the FDA, the exact amount of senna and its potency is unknown to consumers. Senna, when combined with other laxatives or stimulants, can lead to diarrhea and dehydration. Long term abuse of senna or other stimulant laxatives can lead to "cathartic" colon, which occurs when the colon stops functioning normally. Over uses of these products can cause colonic nerve and muscle injury and in some cases has led to serious liver injury. Eating more plant foods that are high in fiber, increasing fluid intake, and exercising are all great ways to help reduce constipation.

Cascara Sagrada

The herb cascara sagrada is a harsh laxative that has been banned by the FDA since 2002 for use in over-the-counter drugs due to safety concerns. However, cascara can be found in many dietary supplements claiming to cleanse or purify the body. For short-term use cascara may be safe. With longer-term use of high doses of cascara adverse effects have been described, including several cases of clinically apparent liver toxicity. The time to onset of liver injury has varied from a few days to two months of use.

Kidney Cleansers

There are many products claiming they cleanse the kidneys. These are available online and in health food stores. There is no such thing as a kidney-cleansing product, but you wouldn't know that by reading the claims on the labels. Companies claim that their products flush, renew, clean, and detoxify kidneys. Not only will you be wasting money on these products, you could actually be damaging your kidneys. I found two potentially toxic herbs, uva ursi and gravel root, in the same kidney cleanse product online.

Uva Ursi

Sold as a kidney cleansing ingredient, uva ursi is also known as bearberry because bears like eating the fruit. It has been used medicinally since the second century. Uva ursi can be toxic. Hydroquinone, a component of uva ursi, can cause serious liver damage and is a known carcinogen.

Gravel Root

Another kidney cleanse ingredient available over the counter. Gravel root, also known as Joe Pye weed, seems to act as a diuretic, increasing urination. Gravel root contains naturally occurring toxins called hepatotoxic pyrrolizidine alkaloids. Comfrey is another herb that contains these toxic substances. The FDA reports that most cases of pyrrolizidine alkaloid toxicity "result in moderate to severe liver damage, sometimes leading to death." In some cases, the lungs are affected. Pyrrolizidine alkaloids are known carcinogens.

What to Avoid

Products that claim to flush, cleanse, detoxify, or renew the liver, lungs, kidneys, or any other organ.

These herbs have been shown to cause liver toxicity and can be found in "cleansing" or "detoxing" supplements, teas, and other products:

- Pennyroyal
- Glycyrrhizin
- Comfrey
- Cascara
- Yohimbe
- Kamishoyosan
- Kava
- Chaparral
- Skullcap

A review in the *Clinical Journal of the American Society of Nephrology* includes these supplements as having toxic effects on kidneys:

- Cat's Claw
- Chromium
- Germanium
- l-lysine
- Willow Bark
- Yellow oleander
- Chaparral
- Creatine
- Hydrazine
- Thunder god vine
- Wormwood oil
- Yohimbe

Caffeine in normal amounts, as in coffee or tea, is safe for most people. Too much caffeine can make you feel jittery or anxious and make sleeping difficult. Detox and cleansing products may contain caffeine to amplify laxative effects or give an artificial energy boost. You may not know how much caffeine is in a product because the amount is often not listed.

Keep an eye out for these caffeine-containing ingredients:

- Yerba mate
- Guarana
- Caffeine
- Coffee
- Senna
- Cascaras sagrada
- Mate
  - Green tea extract
  - Kola nut
  - Laxative effects
  - Aloe
- Psyllium

6. *The Cleansing Organs*

Our bodies are cleansing and detoxing 24/7. The Only Cleanse focuses on how we can support all the hard work our organs do to keep us healthy. Here is a brief overview of the main cleansing organs, their functions, and what we can do to keep them running at peak performance. You will be amazed and surprised by what you read in this chapter. We look at the liver, kidneys, skin, lungs, mouth, stomach and small intestine, and ears. Ears are not a major cleansing organs, but their ability to self-clean is ingenious, so I included them for fun. Let's start with the liver.

The Liver

If you really want to detoxify and cleanse your body, then focusing on a healthy liver is the place to start. Your liver performs hundreds of essential functions every second of every day, including detoxifying toxins from alcohol, medications, and metabolic byproducts like ammonia. It makes important chemicals, manufactures cholesterol and bile, stores vitamins and minerals, filters and cleans the blood stream of pathogens, contaminants, and other harmful substances, metabolizes nutrients, and regulates immunity.

The liver produces a family of proteins called metallothioneins. Metallothioneins neutralize harmful metals like lead, cadmium, and mercury to prepare for their elimination from the body. The liver is a highly efficient bacterial bounty hunter. Within 0.01 seconds of unwelcome bacteria reaching special liver cells called Kupffer cells, they are trapped, incapacitated, and eventually destroyed. Bam! You are not going to get that kind of pathogen purge from juice cleanses, colonics, or detox teas. Nothing can compare to the body's brilliant and staggering ability to keep you healthy.

Enliven Your Liver
Fat

Eating less fat and being sure to eat the right kind of fat can help optimize liver performance. Unsaturated fats, those that are liquid at room temperature such as olive, canola, peanut, grapeseed, and flax seed oils help keep the liver healthy. Scientists have not pinpointed exactly why unsaturated fats are so liver-friendly. It may be linked with the way the liver processes them. Unsatu-

Liver Actions

- *Detoxifies and removes poisons, toxins, metals, and waste products from the blood stream*
- *Stores vitamins and minerals*
- *Manufactures and recycles cholesterol and triglycerides*
- *Turns glucose into glycogen for storage in the liver and muscle cells*
- *Makes clotting factors to stop excessive bleeding after cuts or injuries*
- *Produces immune factors*
- *Cleanses bacteria from the bloodstream to combat infection*
- *Manufactures bile*
- *Metabolizes, processes, and recycles fats (lipids)*
- *Helps maintain glucose homeostasis*

rated fats reduce the glomming of fat onto organs like the liver and pancreas, and they reduce weight gain. They play key roles in reducing inflammation and lowering cholesterol and triglycerides. Whereas saturated fat, which is solid at room temperature (like butter, lard, bacon, and dairy fats), increases

POINT OF INTEREST

FOR CRUCIFEROUS ENTHUSIASTS

CRUCIFEROUS VEGETABLES:
• *Detoxify by upregulating detoxification enzymes*
• *Prevent oxidative cell and DNA damage*
• *Are chemoprotective against numerous types of cancer*

inflammation and promotes weight gain. Saturated fats may cause excess fat to accumulate around the liver. If the liver is wrapped in a blanket of fat, its essential functions will be impaired. Saturated fat may also increase the storage of visceral fat. You can't see or pinch visceral fat because it lives deep in your belly under your abdominal muscles. Both an excess of visceral fat and a fatty liver are linked with heart disease, cancer, diabetes, and other diseases.

Eat Your Broccoli

Do you know which U.S. president publically admitted disliking broccoli so much that he reportedly banned it from the presidential jet, Air Force One? The story goes that President George H.W. Bush said to the Polish prime minister, "I do not like broccoli…And I haven't liked it since I was a little kid and my mother made me eat it. And I'm President of the United States, and I'm not going to eat any more broccoli!" I have a vision of him stamping his foot like a two-year-old having a tantrum.

Broccoli and its cruciferous cousins got a bad rap from the president. Cruciferous vegetables are especially healthy because they are natural detoxifiers. They contain compounds called glucosinolates, which deactivate and detoxify carcinogens in the liver.

CRUCIFEROUS VEGETABLES
- Broccoli
- Cauliflower
- Cabbage
- Brussels sprouts
- Horseradish
- Watercress
- Turnips
- Radish
- Kale

Along the same lines, apiaceous vegetables (commonly known as the carrot family), including carrots, parsnips, dill, fennel, and celery, contain organic compounds called furanocoumarins. In liver cells furanocoumarins from apiaceous vegetables help inhibit an enzyme called cytochrome P450 1A2, which activates several procarcinogens. A procarcinogen is a substance that can be turned into a cancer-causing chemical in the body.

On the Wagon

Let's cut our liver some slack by supporting its never-ending mission to keep us alive.

Alcohol is a major factor in liver disease, so limiting alcohol consumption is a big step toward supporting a healthy liver. Alcohol has been the most frequently abused drug for centuries, but it was not until the 1960s that it was recognized as a direct hepatotoxin (liver poison). Alcohol and one of its metabolic byproducts, acetaldehyde, are toxic—hence the word "in-toxic-ated." That's why drinking too much alcohol makes you drunk and hungover. The liver uses a lot of energy to quickly metabolize alcohol and neutralize its poisonous effects. Overtime excessive drinking can cause cirrhosis, pancreatitis, and fatty liver disease as well as liver, colorectal, mouth, and throat cancers. Drinking less alcohol means less toxic substances for your liver to handle.

A cleaner diet means ingesting fewer chemicals for your liver to have to neutralize. You can consume fewer chemicals by eating less processed, junk, and fast foods and avoiding unnecessary supplements, over-the-counter (OTC) drugs, or medications. Whether it is vitamins, herbs, or aspirin, the liver is the organ that will be breaking down and metabolizing them.

A Bad Cocktail: Alcohol and Acetaminophen

Drinking alcohol regularly changes the way the liver breaks down certain medications. With acetaminophen, alcohol interferes with how the liver metabolizes it and this creates the accumulation of toxic byproducts that can kill the liver cells. The American College of Gastroenterology reports that people who drink alcoholic beverages regularly are at higher risk of developing severe liver damage from acetaminophen. People who drink alcohol regularly should not take acetaminophen or should speak with their healthcare provider about taking it.

We have all gone into a pharmacy and bought cough medicine, ibuprofen, vitamins, or cold medications. We assume that because we do not need a prescription they are safe to take. Taking high doses of OTC products can cause serious liver problems. My mom was eighty-eight years old and residing in an assisted living community. Though her eyesight was poor, she felt perfectly capable of doling out and taking her own medications. One day she went to the staff nurse, complaining of poor appetite and abdominal pain. A trip to the doctor revealed that Mom had toxic hepatitis. After many questions and blood work, the doctor chalked up the liver inflammation to Mom's accidentally overdosing on Tylenol (acetaminophen), mistaking it for her laxative pills (the pills looked similar). She stopped taking the Tylenol and her symptoms were resolved. From then on the nurses dispensed Mom's medications.

> "I like to have a martini,
> Two at the very most.
> After three I'm under the table,
> after four I'm under my host."
>
> **– DOROTHY PARKER, *THE COLLECTED DOROTHY PARKER***

POINT OF INTEREST

THE METABOLISM OF ALCOHOL
FOR BIOCHEM BUFFS

Most of the alcohol in the body is broken down in the liver by an enzyme called alcohol dehydrogenase (ADH), which transforms it into a highly toxic compound called acetaldehyde (CH_3CHO), a known carcinogen. Acetaldehyde is broken down to a less toxic compound called acetate (CH_3COO) by another enzyme called aldehyde dehydrogenase (ALDH). Acetate then is broken down to carbon dioxide and water.

You can overdose with vitamins, minerals, and other "natural" supplements too. High doses of important vitamins like vitamins D and A, and minerals like iron, can lead to liver injury and other serious health problems. It is best to get the bulk of your vitamins and minerals from food. A few years ago I ran into my friend Aleena at the bank. She told me that her husband, a chiropractor, had just gotten home from the hospital. "Why?" I asked. "What happened?" Aleena said James had been admitted to the ER with acute renal (kidney) failure. For a while doctors could not figure out what was going on. James was healthy, at a good weight. He exercised regularly and had no serious health problems. After reviewing his diet and supplement intake, they pinpointed the problem as toxic hypervitaminosis. Aleena said James had been taking a lot of vitamin, mineral, and herbal supplements. I don't know exactly what he was taking or for how long, but whatever they were, his liver and his kidneys could not handle the overload. Toxic levels of vitamins, minerals, and herbal supplements caused his kidneys to fail and inflame his liver. James stopped taking all the supplements and, thankfully, is fine now.

The Sweet Smell of Success

You can't talk about liver health without addressing sugar, since the liver metabolizes and stores sugar in a number of complex processes.

As far as I am concerned sugar, in the forms of sucrose, honey, maple syrup etc., is not nearly as bad for you as you think. I disagree with "experts" and journalists who use scare tactics to generate media attention, saying sugar is highly toxic and paves the road to the end of civilization. Even water, when consumed in large amounts, can be toxic. Saying sugar is toxic is mixing apples and oranges, so to speak, and clouding the issue. Unlike alcohol, which is toxic all the time, sugar is not toxic when consumed in reasonable amounts, and it is essential for our survival. BUT, and this is a big BUT, we are eating far too much of it and the foods from which we get the most sugar have little or no nutritional value. Our bodies are not designed to handle all the sugar we pump into them.

Carbohydrates break down into sugar in the body. Blood sugar, also known as glucose, is the primary and preferential fuel for your brain, cells, and exercising muscles. We need to have carbohydrates and sugar in our diets to fuel our lives—just a lot less, and preferably from foods such as fruits, vegetables, legumes, and whole grains. That is not to say you can't add some honey or sugar to your tea or favorite cookie recipe or have a piece of chocolate now and again.

Now for the liver part of the equation. Fructose, naturally found in foods like fruits, was once a minor part of our diet. In the early 1900s, the average American took in about fifteen grams of fructose a day (about half an ounce), most of it from eating fruits and vegetables. Today we average almost five times as much, primarily from processed foods, and it is taking a toll on our livers. Fructose is sweeter than glucose, so it is added to many commercial products as fructose or high fructose corn syrup. Fructose is almost entirely biologically managed in the liver. The metabolism of fructose in the liver favors the formation of fat, so an excess of dietary fructose can lead to a fatty liver, high triglycerides, and LDL cholesterol. The easiest thing you can do is to avoid highly processed foods that have added fructose, high fructose corn syrup, and an excess of added sugars. Read the ingredient list on the food package so you know what's in the foods you are eating. Don't worry about fructose naturally found in foods like fruits.

Eat

⇒ **Healthy Fats:** Fats that are liquid at room temperature such as olive, canola, walnut, and grapeseed oils
⇒ **Avocados**
⇒ **Nuts and seeds**
⇒ **Cruciferous vegetables such as broccoli, cauliflower, Brussels sprouts and cabbage**
⇒ **Carrots, celery, parsnips, dill, and parsley**

Avoid

⇒ **High fructose corn syrup**
⇒ **Sugar sweetened beverages:** sodas, presweetened drinks, teas, juices
⇒ **Red and processed meats including beef, lamb, pork, bacon, sausage, and luncheon meats**
⇒ **Butter**
⇒ **Lard**
⇒ **Cheese**
⇒ **Partially hydrogenated oils (trans fats)**—still found in many foods such as breadcrumbs, cake mix, ice cream, crackers, candy, and cereals

Limit

⇒ **Alcohol**
⇒ **Over-the-counter medications, including acetaminophen, aspirin, ibuprofen, naproxen**
⇒ **Highly processed foods such as those with food dyes, artificial sweeteners, fillers, preservatives, chemicals you cannot pronounce, flavor packets, deep fried foods, artificial flavors**

Kidneys

If you have ever had to get a physical exam for a new job you have probably had to pee into a cup for a drug test. How do drugs get into the urine? Via your inner narcotic agents, the kidneys. Along with the liver, your kidneys are top-flight experts at filtering toxic waste and medications from your body.

The Main Functions of the Kidneys

- Controlling blood concentrations and volume by removing selected amounts of water and solutes.
- Helping regulate pH, also known as the body's acid/base balance
- Removing toxic wastes from the blood.

The kidneys' primary jobs are to maintain the body's water and blood volume, balance the pH of the whole body and filter all the blood. We have two kidneys, and each one contains between one to two million nephrons. These tiny nephrons are the functional filters of the kidney. The nephron filtration system removes toxic wastes and knows how much water and which substances, like amino acids, sodium, and potassium, to keep in the body and recycle. The entire volume of blood in the body is filtered, cleansed, and detoxified by the kidneys about sixty times a day.

One of the best ways to keep your kidneys happily cleansing your body is by drinking plenty of water and fluids. The Institute of Medicine recommends women consume about twelve cups of fluids a day, and men sixteen cups. This includes fluids from teas, soups, and juicy fruits and vegetables. No, beer, wine, and tequila do not count.

Sugar-sweetened beverages are one of the biggest contributors to weight gain in the US. They are associated with obesity; type 2 diabetes; and increased risk for cardiovascular disease, nonalcoholic fatty liver disease, kidney disease, and gout.

Protein

Protein and kidneys are inextricably linked. Proteins are made up of building blocks called amino acids. Amino acids are like Legos, the body can build all kinds of structures with them, depending upon the order in which they are stacked. Like the bin of multi-colored, multi-shaped Legos in the toy chest, the kidneys maintain the bin of amino acids to be sure there are enough to fill the body's constantly changing needs. The kidneys maintain this delicate balance through the synthesis, breakdown, filtration, reabsorption, and urinary excretion of amino acids and peptides (two amino acids bonded together).

Healthy protein comes primarily from plant sources such as almonds, pistachios, walnuts, quinoa, lentils, kidney, tofu, edamame, veggie burgers, and red, pinto, and black beans. Your body can only utilize about twenty to thirty-five grams of protein at a time, so you want to spread your protein throughout the day. This also helps manage appetite, blood sugars, energy, and weight and reduces the risk of age-related sarcopenia (muscle loss).

Say No to Paleo and Other High-Protein Diets

The high-protein, no or low carbohydrate fad has taken on a life of its own. Some popular high-protein diets shun virtually all plant foods and focus on foods like beef, cheese, and butter. Still other high-protein diets include fruits and vegetables but forbid foods like whole grains, legumes, and other healthy foods. For one thing, your body needs grains, legumes and other carbohydrates for fuel if for nothing else. Of course, carbohydrates are also brimming with vitamins, minerals, fiber, and a ton of other health-promoting, disease-fighting, body-detoxing compounds. Adherents to the no/low carb-high protein approach can be tenacious in their loyalty. I appeared in a short web video where I was asked to address the Paleo diet. I suggested that current research links increased consumption of animal foods with an increased risk of chronic diseases and that eliminating entire foods groups also eliminates necessary nutrients. I wondered if, for some people, following an extreme kind of diet is easier than one where there are too many decisions to make. Paleo peeps got very upset with that video and started spewing angry Tweets and Facebook posts.

"Get your facts first, then you can distort them as you please."
—MARK TWAIN

High-protein diets are attractive because they are simple, they include foods people like, and initial weight loss happens quickly, even though it is mostly water. The long-term effects of high-protein diets on kidney health are controversial. High-protein diets in people with compromised kidney function may accelerate kidney disease. This is a real concern; of the estimated thirty-one million people in the United States living with chronic kidney disease, nine out of ten don't know they have kidney disease. So people who are trying to lose weight or manage diabetes by going on high-protein diets may end up making matters worse by inadvertently stressing out their kidneys.

The entire volume of blood in the body is filtered, cleansed and detoxified by the kidneys approximately sixty times a day.

Diabetes, high blood pressure, and cardiovascular disease are huge risk factors for kidney disease. Approximately one of three adults with diabetes and one of five adults with high blood pressure has chronic kidney disease. High-protein diets (primarily based in animal foods) raise blood pressure, cholesterol, and inflammation, so they increase the risk for chronic diseases like cancer and cardiovascular disease.

From a scientific standpoint, the evidence is continually mounting against diets rich in animal foods. Eating a diet with a lot of meat and cheese is unhealthy for many reasons. They include the way the body biochemically and physiologically processes these foods, the way they are prepared, and what is being fed to the animals. The reason you don't hear a lot about the unhealthy effects of meat and dairy foods is that the meat and dairy lobbies are very strong in Washington D.C. and work unceasingly to influence federal dietary recommendations. However, the evidence is so convincing that even conservative governmental organizations like the United States Department of Agriculture have to recommend that Americans consume a more plant-based diet.

Do
- Get regular checkups with your MD
- Get checked for high blood pressure and diabetes. If you have these diseases you can reduce the risks associated with them with cleaner living (*The Only Cleanse* is diabetes, heart, and kidney friendly), regular exercise, and healthy eating.
- Skip the crazy diets

Marcia, a soft-spoken artist acquaintance of mine, came over for dinner recently and told me she had "gone Paleo" in the past several months. She is in her early sixties and had an extra twenty-five pounds on her five-two frame. Her doctor told her she had high cholesterol, high triglycerides, and was at risk for heart disease and diabetes. She did not want to take medication so she tried the Paleo diet. "Everyone says it is a good way to lose weight, and you know, our ancestors ate like this," she said.

I always wonder who "everyone" is and why people listen to "everyone." I said nothing because she, like so many people, fell for the ridiculous premise that eating like our ancestors is healthy (of course, the premise is totally wrong on many levels). It's not her fault. Who knows why some wacky trends catch on and stick like gum on a shoe, while others fade away? She went on, "I lost some weight initially, so I was shocked when I went back to the doctor and he said my cholesterol had shot up over fifty points. My blood pressure and triglycerides were up, too." I refrained from commenting and handed her a big bowl of hearty homemade vegetable soup.

With a Grain of Salt

If someone offered you either an ounce of gold or an ounce of salt, which would you choose? If you were living in the kingdom of Ghana back in the ninth century you would have chosen the salt. In West Africa, salt that came down from the Sahara Desert was traded ounce for ounce for gold. Today we can buy salt for as little as three cents per ounce. What a difference a few centuries makes!

Your kidneys use sodium as currency to help maintain fluid balance, which is the amount of water in your cells, tissues, and organs. Sodium is essential because, along with potassium, it creates electrical impulses that keep your brain, heart, muscles, and nervous system functioning. Because sodium affects water and blood volume, it also affects blood pressure. Blood pressure has a direct effect on kidney function. It can either cause or be the result of kidney disease. There are easy ways to keep blood pressure in the range where it's supposed to be. Avoiding processed foods is one. You'd be amazed how much sodium is in some of these foods (see table 92). Regular cardiovascular exercise, limiting alcohol, and loading up on—you guessed it—plants, all lower blood pressure and boost kidney function.

Most of the sodium in our diets comes from restaurant, deli, and processed foods. The American Heart Association recommends 1500-2300 milligrams of sodium a day. You may not think you are eating too much sodium, but consider this: Just *one teaspoon* of table salt has about 2400 milligrams of sodium. Even if you have banned the saltshaker from the table, it's likely you are getting more sodium in your diet than you realize. In fact over eighty percent of the sodium we eat is added to food during processing. Only twenty percent comes from the salt shaker.

Marielle, a forty-two-year-old patient, came to see me. She couldn't believe that at her age she had high blood pressure. "I never use salt when I cook," she said. "I have a healthy diet."

I like to review my patients' diets and look up the nutrient values of the foods they eat with them. They are invariably taken aback when they see, in black and white, what is in the foods they are eating.

First we looked up the Starbucks blueberry scone she has every morning on her way to work. It has an unexpected 510 milligrams of sodium—plus her grande vanilla latte with nonfat milk had 140 milligrams. Later that day she was at a lunch meeting where Panera sandwiches were being served. "I only had half a sandwich, and it was turkey bacon." That half a sandwich has 1460 milligrams of sodium. Plus the requisite 1.5 ounce snack bag of chips with an additional 315 milligrams. Her midafternoon snack was a serving of mini low-fat pretzels for 480 milligrams. Before we even get to dinner Marielle's sodium intake is close to 3000 milligrams. It adds up quickly. On the surface, you can see why she thought her diet was healthy. A closer look revealed that her choices are virtually all highly processed and prepared foods, and very high in sodium.

To eat cleaner and support your body's natural detoxification processes you will need to learn to navigate work, travel, home, and the unexpected potholes in life in a way that involves a lot less processed foods. As you can see, many foods that appear "healthy" have downsides. Marielle defended her work lunch by saying that her usual lunch is a salad. So we reviewed her salad bar choices:

THE ADD-ONS

1 tablespoon of imitation bacon bits	170 mg
1 ounce of shredded cheddar cheese	200 mg
1 pouch of tuna	240 mg
2 tablespoons of sliced black olives	95 mg
3 tablespoons of "lite" Italian dressing	510 mg
Total	1215 mg

Initially she was not very happy and felt frustrated with the food review. But then she realized that with a few easy swaps she could significantly lower the sodium in her diet.

For her salad, I offered simple fixes to save hundreds of milligrams of sodium:

- Use oil and vinegar for salad dressing instead of bottled dressing
- Skip the bacon bits and cheese
- Add tofu or chickpeas instead of pouched tuna

Eat:

- Blueberries
- Strawberries
- Cranberries
- Apples
- Broccoli
- Cauliflower
- Garlic
- Onions
- Olive oil
- Cabbage
- Red, orange, and yellow bell peppers

Limit:

- Restaurant, prepared foods
- Fast food
- Foods with more than 480 milligrams of sodium per serving

Avoid:

- Highly processed foods
- Hot dogs
- Ham and all other luncheon meats
- Fad diets
- Cheese (surprisingly high in sodium)

Table 1: Sodium Saturation

FOODS	SODIUM (milligrams) approximage values)
Smoked ham, three ounces (about three slices)	780
Stouffer's frozen french bread pepperoni pizza	700
Hungry-Man chicken boneless fried frozen dinner	1220
Dunkin' Donuts pretzel salt bagel	3380
Dunkin' Donuts chocolate crumb cake donut	490
McDonald's Premium Grilled Chicken Club	1250
Campbell's Soup on the Go Chicken with Mini Noodles Soup, one container	980
Drake's Ring Ding, two count	260
Three Chips Ahoy cookies	110
4C seasoned bread crumbs, $1/3$ cup (TRANS FATS!)	630
Cap'n Crunch's Peanut Butter Crunch, $3/4$ cup	200
Quaker Oats Instant Oatmeal Weight Control, 1 packet	290
Venti nonfat Frappuccino, Starbucks	300
Starbucks blueberry scone	510
Starbucks Chicken & Greens Caesar Salad Bowl	910

The Diabetes-Kidney Connection

Diabetes refers to a group of conditions where the body has difficulty managing blood glucose (blood sugar) levels for a variety of reasons. Over time, high levels of blood glucose can damage the small blood vessels of the kidneys and weaken the kidneys' nephrons (filters). When the kidneys' blood vessels and filters are damaged, kidney function worsens.

387 million people worldwide have diabetes.

One in two people with diabetes do not know they have it.

Two of the biggest risk factors for type 2 diabetes are being overweight or obese and sedentary. Losing as little as 5 to 7 percent of your body weight can help prevent or delay the onset of diabetes. To start to see positive changes, a two-hundred-pound person could lose as little as ten pounds. If you have diabetes, maintaining a healthy diet and regular physical activity will help you manage the disease and reduce the complications associated with it.

Table 2: Examples of Plant Protein Sources

FOODS	PROTEIN (grams) approximate values
Almond milk, one cup	1
Almonds, one ounce	6
Soy milk, plain, one cup	7
Beans, black, kidney, ½ cup	7
Peanut butter, two tablespoons	8
Tofu, firm, ½ cup	10
Soybeans (edamame), ½ cup	11
Frozen veggie burger, one patty	5-13
Seitan, three ounces	21
One medium bagel	10
Brown rice, one cup cooked	5
Quinoa, one cup cooked	8
Chia seeds, one ounce dried	5
Kidney beans, ½ cup cooked	7
Spinach, ½ cup cooked	3
Oatmeal, one cup, cooked	6
Tahini, one tablespoon	2.6
Hummus, store bought, ½ cup	10

**SUGGESTED WATER AND FLUID INTAKE
(INCLUDES SOUPS, TEA, COFFEE, WATER):**
Women: 12 cups
Men: 16 cups
Athletes need more

The Skin

Your skin is your first line of defense against the outside world and the largest organ in the body. And, like the rest of your body, your skin needs to be fed. Certain foods will bolster the skin's ability to fight disease, detox the body, and slow the process of aging. Skin has to get the vitamins, minerals, amino acids, and fats that it needs to be healthy from the food you eat. Conversely, certain foods and lifestyle choices like smoking or tanning can destroy the skin and damage its ability to protect the body.

When you think of skin as your body's first barrier to invasion, it makes sense that the environment has a significant impact on the health of skin. Skin helps keep our bodies detoxed by acting as a barricade that defends against multiple environmental insults. Free radicals, one form of insult, induce or contribute to adverse effects on the skin, including swelling, wrinkling, photoaging, inflammation, autoimmune reactions, hypersensitivity, pre-cancerous lesions, and skin cancer. Free radicals are molecules that are desperately looking for a mate and will latch on to inappropriate molecules. When there are too many free radicals, they can damage important cellular components such as DNA or the cell membrane. Cigarette smoke, alcohol, pollution, and most importantly sunlight, can damage skin and cause the destruction of collagen fibers, elastin, and skin cells, and they can increase the risk of skin cancers. A primary cause of sunken, wrinkled, scaly skin is inflammation, oxidative stress, and the loss of skin's structural support, flexibility, and elasticity.

Tanned Skin is Damaged Skin.

- In the medical world sunburn is called UV-induced erythema. Sunburn causes responses in the skin (called photochemical reactions) that lead to the stimulation of in ammatory pathways. In a nutshell this means that, as you know, a sunburn really hurts because your skin is actually burned. The heavy-duty inflammation from sunburn can lead to premature aging, drying, wrinkling, and skin cancers.

- There are UVA and UVB rays from the sun. Both cause premature aging to skin and increase the risk of skin cancers. They also suppress the body's immune system. The Skin Cancer Foundation says that UVA damages skin cells called keratinocytes in the epidermis, where most skin cancers occur. (Basal and squamous cells are types of keratinocytes.) UVA contributes to and may even initiate the development of skin cancers.

- UV light is a complete carcinogen, i.e. it causes initiation, promotion, and progression of skin cancer, attributable to its ability to induce both DNA damage and immune suppression.

Toxic Skin

➠ Exposure to ultra violet (UV) light from the sun is the biggest cause of skin aging and pre- and postcancerous skin lesions. When UV rays hit skin, they cause damage and generate radical oxygen species (ROS). ROS can damage cells and DNA, destroy collagen, heighten inflammation, and generally ruin skin at many levels.

➠ Tobacco smoke not only increases your risk for heart disease and cancer, it also destroys the skin's natural detoxing abilities. Tobacco smoke produces oxidative stress and inflammation in skin and impairs collagen resynthesis.

➠ Alcohol use (more than a few drinks a week) is associated with an increased risk for skin cancer, flushing, spider veins, bruising, and an exacerbation of pre-existing skin conditions such as psoriasis and eczema.

➠ Being dehydrated impairs skin's ability to function and lowers immunity.

➠ Poor nutrition saps your immune response, contributes to degradation of structural components such as collagen, and reduces skin's natural ability to take care of itself.

Skin's Super-Detoxing, Protective Powers

Your skin has natural defenses against damaging UV light, which include antioxidant activity by phytochemicals, vitamins C and E, and the anti-inflammatory effects of omega-3 fatty acids. When exposed to external attacks (like second-hand smoke or sun) the skin's natural defenses jump into gear, bringing special compounds like vitamins, fats, and proteins to the area to calm inflammation, repair cell damage, and protect against more death and destruction. Nutrients in foods can act as sponges for UV rays, help protect skin from harmful oxidants, and calm skin responses to environmental insults like heat and pollution. Environmental insults include everything else the world throws at us; smoke, cold, and UV light and stress. If you are not eating the right foods, then your skin will not have the nutritional tools it needs to come to the rescue. Salvation lies in your kitchen. Foods rich in nutrients help maintain the skin's powerful detoxification system and keep skin healthy and vibrant.

Eat Your Carotenoids

When you go to the farmer's market and see the array of bright red, orange, and yellow fruits and vegetables, you are seeing carotenoids in action. These bright colors mean the food is loaded with healthy compounds. You have heard that carrots are good for your eyes. They are. But they are also good for your skin. Carrots are bright orange because they contain a carotenoid called beta-carotene. Beta-carotene is one of five hundred carotenoids that are found in many fruits and vegetables such as kale, tomatoes, sweet potatoes, papaya, and peppers.

Carotenoids

- Work as antioxidants
- Protect cells from damage by free radicals
- Protect skin from UV light
- Are converted in the body to vitamin A
- Stimulate immune response
- Guard against some skin cancers

There are no current dietary reference intake recommendations for carotenoids except to eat plenty of foods high in them. See list below.

Carotenoids That Play Starring Roles in Our Skin and Body Health:

- Beta-carotene
- Beta-cryptoxanthin
- Lutein
- Zeaxanthin
- Lycopene
- Alpha-carotene

These indispensable compounds are not made in the body, so you have to eat them regularly. Carotenoids act as biological antioxidants, protecting cells and tissues from the damaging effects of free radicals. Alpha-carotene, beta-carotene, and beta-cryptoxanthin are provitamin A carotenoids, meaning they can be converted by the body into vitamin A (retinol). In skin, carotenoids act as strong antioxidants that protect skin against photo damage and UV rays. They also stimulate immune response and guard skin against some types of cancers. Include colorful vegetables and fruits loaded with carotenoids in your meals daily to keep your skin's maintenance and defenses at peak performance.

FOR CAROTENOID FANS

There are 563 known carotenoids found in nature. The human body only uses about twenty of them.

Curative Carotenoids

➡ **Vitamin A actions**
➡ **Healthy vision**
➡ **Bone growth**
➡ **Reproduction**
➡ **Cell division**
➡ **Immune system support**
➡ **Strengthening of lymphocytes that fight infection**

Lutein and Zeaxanthin

The retina of the eye loves lutein and zeaxanthin because these antioxidants filter high-energy wavelengths of visible light and help protect eyes from the body's inflammatory response to UVA and UVB rays.

Cancer Protection

A study in the *American Journal of Epidemiology* found that people who eat foods high in alpha-carotene, beta-carotene, beta-cryptoxanthin, and lutein have a lower risk of breast cancer—another good reason to gobble up fruits and vegetables such as collards and tangerines.

Foods High in Carotenoids

Generally these foods contain many carotenoids, but for variety I have put different foods on each list. All are good for you not only because of the carotenoid content but because each has scads of healthy vitamins, minerals, phytochemicals (healthy plant compounds), and fiber. Be creative. For a carotenoid-rich dish add tangerines to your salad, toss some carrots in tomato sauce, or sprinkle chopped pistachios on mango slices.

Beta-Cryptoxanthin:
⇒ **Cooked pumpkin**
⇒ **Papayas**
⇒ **Tangerines**
⇒ **Plums**
⇒ **Peaches**
⇒ **Paprika**

Beta-Carotene
⇒ **Sweet potatoes**
⇒ **Carrot juice**
⇒ **Spinach**
⇒ **Beet greens**
⇒ **Winter squash**
⇒ **Cantaloupes**

Lutein and Zeaxanthin
⇒ **Kale**
⇒ **Collards**
⇒ **Peas**
⇒ **Corn**
⇒ **Brussels sprouts**
⇒ **Boston, romaine and Bibb lettuce**
⇒ **Pistachios**

Lycopene
⇒ **Tomato products: paste, sauce, juice** (get the no-sodium-added products, please)
⇒ **Watermelon**
⇒ **Guava**
⇒ **Pink grapefruit**
⇒ **Salsa**

Tango with Ascorbate and Tocopherols (Translation: Vitamins C and E)

Vitamin C

⇒ Critical for collagen synthesis and support of skin tissues

⇒ Powerful antioxidant.

⇒ Photoprotective

⇒ Has anti-aging properties

⇒ Necessary for wound healing

⇒ Dietary reference intake for adult women: seventy-five milligrams; men: ninety milligrams

Vitamin E

⇒ Works with vitamin C, selenium, and beta-carotene to provide mega antioxidant protection for skin

⇒ Vitamin E works as an antioxidant in the stratum corneum, the first line of defense against external oxidants such as ozone

⇒ Helps protect skin against UV damage.

⇒ An important constituent of skin's natural moisturizer, sebum

⇒ Reduces inflammation

⇒ Lives in cell membranes

⇒ Enhances immune system

⇒ Dietary reference intake for adult women and men: fifteen milligrams (22.4 IU)

Vitamin C

Vitamins C and E work as a team with other micronutrients like selenium to create dynamic anti-oxidant defenses. In skin, vitamin C (listed as ascorbate sometimes), exerts different biologic roles, including participation in collagen synthesis, the regeneration process, and wound healing. Low levels of vitamin C cause collagen to degrade. Without the structural support of collagen, blood vessels, tendons, and skin become fragile and thin. Vitamin C helps reduce inflammation and oxidative stress. Several studies have shown that vitamin C helps protect the skin from damaging UV rays. It may also have anti-aging effects. A study in the *American Journal of Clinical Nutrition* looked at over four thousand women and found that lower intakes of vitamin C were significantly associated with the prevalence of a wrinkled appearance and dry skin as a result of aging. Higher intakes of vitamin C were associated with better skin aging and appearance. That doesn't mean you should go out and megadose with vitamin C. Because vitamin C is a team player, you do not want to over-whelm your system by taking too much of it or any other supplement. If you do, it's like putting a six-four, 275-pound man on one end of a seesaw and a six-pound infant on the other end: totally out of balance. Get your daily supply of collagen-boosting vitamin C from oranges, papayas, peaches, and broccoli.

Foods High in Vitamin C

- Oranges
- Grapefruit
- Kiwi
- Strawberries
- Sweet peppers
- Broccoli
- Spinach
- Tomatoes
- Cantaloupe
- Mangos
- Cauliflower
- Watermelon
- Sweet and white potatoes

Vitamin E

Vitamin E (also known as tocopherols—there is more than one form of vitamin E) actually refers to eight different chemical compounds, all synthesized by plants. Alpha-tocopherol is the form of vitamin E that our bodies use. Vitamin E works best with its friends vitamin C, selenium, and other micronutrients to protect, repair, and heal skin. Vitamin E is found in skin and in hair's natural moisturizer, sebum. It helps protect skin against UV, pollution, and ozone. High ozone levels are found in smog and can strip the skin's protective outer layer of antioxidants like vitamins E and C. The healthier your skin is, the better it will be at combating the deleterious effects of bad air.

Vitamin E Foods:

- Almonds
- Wheat germ
- Hazelnuts
- Sunflower seeds
- Safflower oil
- Spinach

Foot Note

Clean feet are an important part of a cleansed system. Your feet have more than 250,000 sweat glands and produce a pint of sweat each day. It's easy to see why feet get stinky when they sweat so much and are confined in socks and shoes for twelve hours a day.

Use a soft brush to clean your feet and moisturize them after bathing daily. A good foot massage, known as reflexology, always feels good and may stimulate your inner cleansing organs and reduce stress. The theory of reflexology is that certain points on your feet correspond to different parts of the body such as your liver, eyes, spine, intestines, and endocrine glands. The belief is that pressing and massaging these areas can relieve stress, relax muscles, and stimulate the connected organ to function more fully. The National Cancer Institute and the National Institutes of Health have found that reflexology may reduce pain, anxiety, and depression, and enhance relaxation and sleep.

Bonus Section: *The Cocoa Cleanse*

⟫ **Cocoa is heart healthy**
⟫ **Cocoa may be good for skin circulation**
⟫ **Cocoa may have anti-aging effects in skin**
⟫ **Dark chocolate is better than milk chocolate**
⟫ **Chocolate contains healthy chemicals called flavonoids**

The truth is, the few studies that have been done looking at the effects of chocolate or cocoa on skin have been small. But hey, we're taking this ball and running with it. Chocolate makes people happy. Besides, there is compelling research to suggest that chocolate is heart healthy.

Health Benefits of Cocoa:

⟫ **Improves cholesterol**
⟫ **Boosts insulin sensitivity**
⟫ **Lowers blood pressure**
⟫ **Reduces the risk of blood clots**
⟫ **Reduces inflammation**
⟫ **Promotes healthy arteries**

Cocoa improves the flexibility and function of arteries. Healthy blood vessels mean healthy skin (with a healthy diet). Blood whisks away toxins and inflammatory debris and delivers vitamins, minerals, fats, and antioxidants to skin. A few small studies found that drinking or eating flavonol-rich cocoa improved protection from the sun's rays, skin hydration, and circulation. Plump up that skin with good hydration and you'll also be plumping out fine lines and wrinkles. There's more good news: Unlike the saturated fat in red meat and butter, the fat in cocoa does not appear to have unhealthy effects in arteries.

Cocoa contains hefty amounts of minerals such as calcium, magnesium and potassium. It's also loaded with healthy bioactive compounds (these have healthy effects in the body) called flavonoids. There are many types of flavonoids found in fruits, vegetables, tea, wine, and chocolate. Flavonoids are robust antioxidants and reduce inflammation and oxidative stress. The amount of flavonoids in chocolate is dependent on how it is processed. For example the heat and alkalization of cocoa ("Dutch" processing) that helps reduce the bitter taste also significantly reduces the amount of flavonoids. Typically, dark chocolate contains up to three times as many cocoa flavonoids as milk chocolate. Catechins are one of the main flavonoids found in cocoa. Note the big difference in catechin concentrations between cocoa powder and milk chocolate:

- 3.5 ounces of cocoa powder: three hundred milligrams of catechins
- 3.5 ounces of milk chocolate: sixteen milligrams of catechins (not vegan)

Milk chocolate's sixteen milligrams of catechins pales in comparison to dark chocolate's three hundred. Hence the recommendation that we eat dark chocolate that contains a minimum of seventy percent cocoa. Milk chocolate usually has more sugar than dark chocolate, too. Skip the standard candy bars, packaged hot chocolate mix and chocolate milk powder.

- Choose dark chocolate treats containing seventy percent or more cocoa
- Use unsweetened cocoa powder and add your own sweeteners with unsweetened soy, almond, or rice milk for a healthy hot chocolate.
- Chill the above for chocolate milk

NOTE: *Heating hemp milk makes it coagulate, so it is not a good choice for hot chocolate.*

Unsweetened cocoa powder does not dissolve well in cold milk so you will need to heat it up—the microwave is fine—and then chill it for cold chocolate milk. Imagine getting your kids used to a healthy chocolate milk with less sugar.

Just because dark chocolate is a pretty healthy food does not mean you can eat a lot of it. It also has a lot of calories. Just 3.5 ounces of dark chocolate contains about 230 calories and thirteen grams of fat. One little chocolate truffle is seventy-five calories. Enjoy small dark chocolate treats on occasion. You will feel virtuous and healthy.

NOTE: *Dark chocolate contains approximately forty-three to sixty-three milligrams of flavanols per one hundred grams (about three ounces).*

Lungs

Can you imagine doing anything twenty-thousand times in one day, let alone every day? Your lungs can. Every day you breathe in and out nearly twenty thousand times. Each of those twenty-thousand times is an opportunity for unwanted particles and germs to enter your body. Each of those twenty-thousand times your respiratory system launches into its oxygen-absorbing, carbon-dioxide-eliminating, invader-fighting battle plan. The primary function of the lungs is to bring oxygen into the body and remove carbon dioxide. Since the outside world comes directly into our bodies through our mouths and noses, the respiratory tract is also strategically designed to filter and cleanse pathogens and pollutants.

Just Breathe

Air comes in through the nose and mouth, is moistened, warmed, and cleansed by the nasal epithelium (the tissue that lines the nasal cavity), travels down the windpipe (trachea), and enters the bronchial tubes that lead to each lung. From there, the bronchial tubes branch into thousands of smaller, thinner tubes called bronchioles, which end in small bubble-like sacs called alveoli. The lungs have about three hundred million alveoli. Why so many alveoli? To maximize the amount of oxygen inhaled and the carbon dioxide exhaled. The astounding surface area of your lungs, if they were ironed out, would be about the size of a tennis court.

The entire respiratory system, as with the reproductive, digestive, and urinary systems, is lined with mucous membrane that secretes a protective coating of mucus. For most of us, mucus is gross. However, mucus is an essential and complex goo that fights disease and detoxes the body. The respiratory tract produces about two liters of mucus a day from glands called goblet cells and seromucous glands. The consistency of mucus is sticky so it can trap dust, particles, and pathogens. Mucus also contains natural antibiotics, which help to destroy bacteria. Staying well hydrated helps keep mucus in the right consistency—not too thick or too thin—and keeps mucus membranes moist, so they can do their job.

Your Inner HEPA

Fine hairs called cilia inside the nose trap dirt and other large particles that may be inhaled. Smaller particles like pollen or smoke that make it to the lungs are trapped in mucus. The cilia, beating in upward waves, carry the particles up and out of the lungs in a feat of biological engineering called the mucociliary escalator.

Feed Your Lungs

A 2015 study in the *British Medical Journal* of over 120,000 people found that eating a more plant based diet, including whole grains, unsaturated fats, and nuts, and less red and processed meat, refined grains, and sugary drinks, is associated with a lower risk of chronic lung diseases including emphysema and bronchitis. Researchers speculate that a diet high in antioxidants, such as a plant-based diet, may help reduce lung inflammation and the genesis of chronic obstructive lung diseases.

Mold

I was visiting my friend and colleague Dr. Francois Haas, Associate Professor at the NYU School of Medicine's Department of Rehabilitation Medicine. I was telling him about *The Only Cleanse* and asked for his input on lung health. "Mold," he said. "Don't forget to talk about mold." With moist environments or flooding, mold forms can affect people's respiratory systems. "Exposure to mold can cause symptoms ranging from nasal stuffiness, eye or skin irritation, and wheezing to upper respiratory tract symptoms, coughing, lung infections, and asthma," Dr. Haas says.

Detox your home by minimizing mold. Mold growth can be removed from hard surfaces with commercial products, soap and water, or a bleach solution of no more than one cup of bleach in one gallon of water.

The Centers for Disease Control and Prevention recommends these tips for removing mold from your home:
- Never mix bleach with ammonia or other household cleaners. Mixing bleach with ammonia or other cleaning products will produce dangerous, toxic fumes.
- Open windows and doors to provide fresh air.
- Wear nonporous gloves and protective eye wear.

My friend Thomas is the kind of realtor you dream about. He loves his work and does everything he can to make your house-selling or buying experience a positive one. He was getting a house ready to be shown and was cleaning the bathroom, which had some mold in the shower (yes, he was cleaning the house himself). Thomas thought, *If bleach is a good mold killer, then bleach mixed with ammonia would be even better.* The combination of the two volatile chemicals caused the formation of toxic fumes called chloramine gas, which he was inhaling as he scrubbed the bathroom. The fumes seriously inflamed his lungs, and Thomas ended up in the ER. Exposure to chloramine gas can cause serious lung injury and damage mucous membranes. Aggressive medical treatment was required, and Thomas has fully recovered. The lesson here is never mix cleaning products together. And always appreciate your hard working real estate broker.

Mold: *Where It Lives (Everywhere There is Moisture) and How to Handle It*

➤ Check attics and basements, wet walls, window sills, and ventilation systems for mold

➤ Fix leaky plumbing

➤ Wash mold off hard surfaces with detergent and water, and dry completely

➤ Absorbent materials (such as ceiling tiles and carpet) that become moldy may have to be replaced

➤ Moisture control is the key to mold control.

➤ Common sites for indoor mold growth include bathroom tile, basement walls, areas around windows where moisture condenses, and near leaky water fountains or sinks

Avoid

➤ **I don't have to tell you to quit smoking tobacco or avoid second hand smoke.** You know smoking tobacco, whether in the form of cigarettes, e-cigarettes, pipes, hookahs, or cigars is probably the single worst thing you can do to your health.

➤ **Drop the fat:** Being overweight stresses lungs. Studies in obese, asthmatic kids and adults show that weight loss helps people breathe better, reduces inflammation, and lessens asthma symptoms.

➤ **Ditch the processed meats** like bacon, sausage, and pepperoni. I know you love the taste but your lungs and the rest of your body are not so keen on the effects from the sodium and nitrites.

➤ **Reduce or avoid red meat.** Even "grass-fed" meats can

contribute to poor health. Cooking meat creates carcinogenic compounds like heterocyclic amines and polycyclic aromatic hydrocarbons. Scientists think that the minerals in meat (but not in plants) like zinc and iron increase oxidative stress, which can ignite inflammation and lead to serious diseases such as lung and heart disease and cancer. Intrestingly, studies have found a link between high consumption of red and processed meat, and lung cancer, irrespective of smoking status.

Do:

⇒ **Eat whole grains** like wild rice, barley, whole grain cereals (granola, shredded wheat), and whole wheat couscous.

⇒ **Eat nuts** like almonds, walnuts, pistachios, Brazil nuts, and cashews.

⇒ **Eat healthy fats.** Use plant oils in cooking and salads. I love to dip fresh, whole grain bread in unfiltered extra virgin olive oil (the really good stuff). Check for sales because unfiltered EVOO can be expensive.

⇒ **Eat more vegetables and fruits.** Adding more vegetables to your day can be as easy as tossing a bag of frozen broccoli and cauliflower into your pasta or soup. Try topping your hummus on whole wheat pita with shredded carrots and fresh spinach leaves. Have a sliced apple with almond butter as a snack.

⇒ **Stop what you are doing.** Be still. Take slow, deep breaths for several minutes. Studies show that deep breathing for even a short while can improve lung function and lower blood pressure, heart rate, and stress hormones. Not surprisingly, deep breathing increases the lungs' ability to absorb oxygen and remove carbon dioxide.

⇒ **Stay hydrated.** Moist membranes are the defensive linebackers of your respiratory system. If mucous membranes get dried out, they are less able to tackle pathogens and dirt and you are more prone to infections.

⇒ **Get hot and sweaty.** Don't forget that muscles such as those located between your ribs (intercostal), abdominal, and back muscles facilitate breathing. Regular aerobic activity strengthens these muscles and your heart and lungs.

⇒ **Sit up straight. Stand up straight.** You will look years younger and give your lungs the room they need to fully expand. When you slouch, you are smooshing your internal organs together and hobbling their ability to function fully. Pick up your breast bone, drop your shoulders, pull in your abdominals, stack your ribcage over your hips and bring your neck into a neutral position. There, doesn't that feel better?

Out of the Mouths of Babes

Our mouths are the conduits for thoughts, emotions, expressions, songs, speech—and bacteria. Good oral care gives you a healthier body, better breath, and just perhaps, a witty edge. What happens in the mouth is often a reflection of what is happening in the body, and vice versa. A well cared-for mouth helps the body stay clean and healthy. Studies have demonstrated an association between periodontal diseases (those of the gums) and diabetes, cardiovascular disease, stroke, and adverse pregnancy outcomes. Brushing and flossing your teeth regularly cleans away the bacteria in plaque (the sticky, colorless film that constantly forms on your teeth) that causes the gums to become inflamed. Just like in the rest of the GI tract, the oral microbiome needs to be kept in balance. If you neglect your gums and teeth your mouth can be overrun with unwanted pathogens, inflammatory chemicals and infections. I am always surprised at the number of people who do not brush twice a day or floss at all. It's time to step up to the sink, pull out the toothbrush, and floss, folks.

Along with daily oral care, you need to see the dentist twice a year. I know it can be expensive, and personally I find going to the dentist stressful. As nice as my dental hygienist and dentist are, I cannot help but clench my hands into tight fists for the entire experience. Save your teeth, mouth, health and the contents of your wallet by getting regular dental checkups and cleanings. They help prevent infections and catch problems before they turn into dental (and financial) disasters.

Eat

Vitamin C. Vitamin C helps keep gums healthy. Low levels of vitamin C promote gingivitis (gum disease) and bleeding gums.

⇒ **Broccoli**
⇒ **Peppers**
⇒ **Brussels sprouts**
⇒ **Tomatoes**
⇒ **Oranges**
⇒ **Strawberries**

Fiber-Rich Fruits, Vegetables, Grains and Legumes

Foods with fiber have a detergent effect in your mouth, says the American Dental Association. They also stimulate saliva flow, which, next to good home dental care, is your best natural defense against cavities and gum disease.

⇒ **Edamame**
⇒ **Lentils**
⇒ **Prunes**
⇒ **Artichokes**
⇒ **Okra**
⇒ **Quinoa**
⇒ **Shredded wheat**
⇒ **Oats**

Calcium

Calcium is necessary for strong teeth and bones. About twenty minutes after you eat sugary or starchy foods, your saliva begins to neutralize the acids and enzymes attacking your teeth. Because saliva contains traces of calcium and phosphate, it also restores minerals to areas of teeth that have lost them from the bacterial acids.

⇒ **Collard greens**
⇒ **Tofu**
⇒ **Almond butter**
⇒ **Kale**
⇒ **Calcium-fortified plant-based milks like rice and soy milk and cereals**
⇒ **Navy beans**

Swish

Oil pulling is a relatively new fad in the US, but it's a traditional folk remedy that has been practiced for centuries in India and Southeast Asia. It is mentioned in the Ayurvedic text Charaka Samhit and is claimed to cure about thirty systemic diseases, ranging from headaches and migraines to diabetes and asthma. Oil pulling is also touted as a detoxification process for improved oral health and the prevention of gingivitis, plaque, and halitosis (bad breath). The practice involves taking a tablespoon of sesame, coconut, or sunflower oil and swishing it in the mouth for ten to twenty minutes and then spitting it out. The theory is that the oil pulls toxins and bacteria from the teeth, gums and mouth. The act of swishing for such a long time is likely to dislodge particles and possibly bacteria. It does not however, take the place of flossing, brushing, and regular dental checkups. There is no scientific evidence at this time that oil pulling can cure any diseases. A few very small studies suggest that oil pulling may have some beneficial effects, including reducing halitosis or oral plaque.

Dr. Steven Novella, the founder of the website Science-Based Medicine, says: "Oil pulling for general health or any other indication is pure pseudoscience. Detox claims are based on nothing....There is no evidence or plausible rationale to recommend oil pulling for any indication other than as a poor substitute for oral care."

BOTTOM LINE

Oil pulling is time consuming, and there is no evidence that it is beneficial for long-term oral care or that it cures any diseases. If you have bad breath, see your dentist. It could be a sign of periodontal or other disease. To reduce bad breath and oral plaque, try drinking or rinsing your mouth with green tea. Studies show that compounds in green tea deodorize methyl mercaptan, the main cause of halitosis.

Tea

Green and black teas are loaded with plant compounds called polyphenols. Polyphenols in tea have been shown to help reduce bacterial plaque, oral acidity, halitosis, inflammation and cavities.

Limit

Sticky foods like these stick to your teeth so the saliva cannot wash them away.

➡ **Raisins**
➡ **Caramels**

- Jelly beans
- Fruit leathers
- Gum drops
- Peanut brittle
- Sticky buns.
- Sweets.

Mom was right when she told you not to have dessert before dinner, but not for the reason she thought. Bacteria in the mouth feed on sugar and produce acids that affect tooth enamel. When you eat a meal first, your mouth produces more saliva and this helps neutralize acid production and rinse food particles from the mouth.

Avoid

- Tobacco use of any kind and drinking alcohol significantly increase the risk for oral, head, and neck cancers and other oral diseases.
- Diet and sugar-sweetened sodas. The phosphorous and citric acids in both diet and regular soda erode tooth enamel.
- Getting dehydrated. Your mouth needs to stay moist to be healthy. Alcohol and some medications may contribute to a dry mouth. Up your fluid intake and rinse with water during the day.
- Sweets. You know getting cavities sucks. You can limit the risk by curbing sweets.

Ears: *Hear Ye, Hear Ye*

Self-cleaning ears? It's true. Those odd, perfectly shaped structures on the sides of your head are designed to funnel sound—and fight bacteria and detox themselves, too. The ears do this with a unique substance called earwax, or cerumen. Cerumen, secreted by glands in the ear, waterproofs and cleanses the ear canal as it traps microbes and dirt particles, and fights fungus and bacteria. When we speak and eat, the earwax is constantly pushed by the natural movement of our lower jaw toward the outer ear, and from there it falls out naturally, carrying dirt and bacteria with it. Voila! Self-cleaning ears.

It is not uncommon for people to jam a cotton swab or a matchstick in their ears to "clean" them. Experts say sticking anything in your ear smaller than your elbow can be very dangerous. I remember as a child we had

CASE STUDY

A CAUTIONARY OIL PULLING TALE:

A fifty-six-year-old woman was rushed to the hospital in Korea, with a fever and a cough. After an examination she was diagnosed with pneumonia. This was her fourth visit to the ER with pneumonia in only six months. Doctors could not figure out why she kept getting sick. Finally, on this visit they meticulously questioned her about every possible cause of her recurrent pneumonia. She revealed that she had been oil pulling since two weeks prior to her first admission. Bingo! The doctors realized the patient had been aspirating (inhaling into her lungs) some of the oil she had been swishing in her mouth. Aspiration pneumonia occurs when food, saliva, liquid, or vomit is breathed into the lungs or the airways leading to the lungs, causing inflammation and infection. This woman had a double whammy because she was inhaling foreign substances into her lungs that were also loaded with bacteria from her mouth. Once she stopped oil pulling, her bouts with pneumonia stopped, too.

a babysitter we called Tanzy. One day, mom told us Tanzy would not be coming to take care of us for a while. She had been cleaning her ear with a cotton swab as she walked toward her bathroom and punctured her eardrum. Another hazard of sticking things in the ear canal is an increased risk of infection by pushing unwanted pathogens further into the ear. Let your ears cleanse themselves. If you or your children have ear problems, speak with your doctor before putting any object, oil, or drops in your ear.

What you put in your mouth has big effects on your ears. The National Health and Nutrition Examination Survey found that certain foods make a big bang in hearing health. They report that an overall healthy diet reduces hearing loss. Studies show that diets high in cholesterol and saturated fat (e.g., beef, cheese, milk, butter, and refined carbohydrates such as cookies, cakes, and white bread) are associated with hearing loss. This makes sense because, while we rarely associate our food with our ears, foods that increase inflammation, damage arteries, and raise blood pressure will affect tiny arteries and delicate inner ear organs, just as they do the rest of the body.

Polluting Your Ears

Turn down the music! Ongoing loud noise can permanently damage hearing and lead to hearing loss.

Healthy Ear Foods

Vitamin A:

Vitamin A is associated with decreased prevalence of hearing impairment in older individuals.

- Carrots
- Sweet potatoes
- Pumpkin
- Mango
- Black-eyed peas
- Cantaloupe

Vitamin C:

Studies suggest a positive relationship between vitamin C intake and hearing sensitivity.

- Red Peppers
- Strawberries
- Oranges
- Broccoli
- Tomato juice

Ear Candling: Another Dangerous "Cleanse" Fad

Ear candling is a technique that involves placing a lit, hollow, cone-shaped candle into the ear canal; the candle supposedly creates suction to remove earwax. Ear candling is very popular and heavily advertised. Proponents of ear candling claim that it cleanses ears, sinuses, and even the brain. Unfortunately, ear candling can cause serious injury and is not considered an effective treatment for any condition. Doctors warn against ear candling because of potential damage to the ear and eardrum, burns, and potential hearing loss.

Magnesium:

Magnesium reduces development of noise-induced hearing loss, and a positive relationship exists between magnesium intake and hearing sensitivity.

- ⇒ **Spinach**
- ⇒ **Avocado**
- ⇒ **Almonds**
- ⇒ **Cashews**
- ⇒ **Soymilk**
- ⇒ **Shredded wheat**

Vitamin E:

Increased intake of vitamin E has been linked to better hearing.

- ⇒ **Almonds**
- ⇒ **Wheat germ**
- ⇒ **Sunflower seeds**
- ⇒ **Hazelnuts**
- ⇒ **Peanut butter**

Folic acid:

Folic acid may slow the progression of age-related hearing loss.

- ⇒ **Brussels sprouts**
- ⇒ **Asparagus**
- ⇒ **Romaine lettuce**
- ⇒ **Kidney beans**

POINT OF INTEREST

FOR CANCER PREVENTION

*The most important factors thought to be respon-
sible for gastric cancer development are diet and
Helicobacter pylori infection.*

FOR ANATOMY LOVERS

*There are three different sections of the small intes-
tine: the duodenum, jejunum, and ileum.*

The Stomach and Small Intestine

The tour of the body's gastrointestinal detoxing and cleansing systems has taken us into the weird world of the colon and exposed us to entire civilizations living throughout our gut. Now we visit the shores of the stomach and small intestine.

Go Away!

The stomach does not throw out the welcome mat for unwanted visitors. If harmful bacteria try to take a vacay in the stomach they will be burned to death by acid. The stomach secretes many chemicals that help render the foods we eat into absorbable molecules. One of these substances is hydrochloric acid (HCl). HCl is a very strong acid that pounces on and destroys unwanted pathogens that enter the stomach. HCl is secreted by parietal cells that live in the stomach lining. The physiology of the stomach and the mucosal lining is remarkable because it's constructed so that the corrosive action of HCl can burn out the bad guys without eating a hole through the stomach lining. HCl has many other functions as well, including facilitating the absorption of minerals and vitamin B12, activating certain enzymes, and breaking down food into molecules. The stomach mixes and sloshes its contents into a liquid called chyme. Once the food is churned into chyme, it is slowly released from the stomach into the small intestine.

Helicobacter pylori has been in the health news in recent years. It is a bacteria that lives in the stomach, and it's one of the most common bacterial infections worldwide. It is not one of the good guys. *H. Pylori* is a bad guy when it digs in and starts to multiply in the stomach. *H. pylori* infection can lead to rosacea, gastric cancers, and chronic gastritis in adults and children. To help keep *H. Pylori* at bay, eat lots of fruits and vegetables, which studies suggest are protective against *H. pylori* infections, in part due to their high concentrations of vitamin C. On the other hand, hamburgers, sausages, mayo, sodas, and processed meats (e.g., bacon, bologna, and ham) all appear to increase the risk of H. pylori infection.

NOTE: *A high salt concentration in the stomach destroys the mucosal barrier, favors colonization by H. pylori, and leads to inflammation and damage-causing gastritis (inflammation of the GI tract). Processed meats, junk, and fast food are all high in sodium.*

Proton Pump Inhibitors

Experts are concerned about the possible overuse of proton pump inhibitors like Prilosec and Zantac, which decrease the production of HCl. Proton pump inhibitors (PPIs) remain the leading evidence-based therapy for upper gastrointestinal disorders, including gastroesophageal reflux disease, dyspepsia, and peptic ulcer disease. However, overuse of PPIs has been linked with an increased risk of gastrointestinal infections including Clostridium difficile-associated diarrhea, community-acquired pneumonia, bone fracture, nutritional deficiencies, and interference with the metabolism of antiplatelet agents. Speak with your physician to be sure taking PPIs is right for you, and if you have been taking PPIs for a while, revisit whether you still need them. A registered dietitian-nutritionist can help create a food plan that can lessen symptoms of GI issues like reflux.

Sales of PPIs are estimated at over $11 billion annually in the U.S.

The Small Intestine

The small intestine is where most (about 90 percent) of the nutrients from food we eat are absorbed into the body. The small intestine begins where it connects to the stomach and ends at the colon connection. The total length of the intestines is about twenty-five feet (7.6 meters); the small intestine taking up most of the length at about twenty feet. Can you imagine trying to pack twenty-five feet of tubing into an area as small as your abdomen without kinking it? I can't even roll up the garden hose without a struggle. The long length means more surface area for the small intestine to sop up every drop of nutrient rich chyme. In terms of detoxing, the small intestine contains lymph nodes called Peyer's patches that screen out parasites, toxins, and other foreign substances before they can tag along with the nutrients that get absorbed into the body.

Small intestine cancers are rare, comparatively speaking, but what affects the risk seems to jive with the risks of other GI cancers. In 2008 The NIH-AARP Diet and Health Study of 293,703 men and 198,618 women found that people who ate more beans and whole grains (like oats and whole wheat) had a lower risk of small and large intestinal cancers than those who ate less of them. Researchers speculate that the fiber in whole grains and beans decreases transit time in the intestines (which results in less contact between potential carcinogens and the lining of the GI tract) and binds bile acids and carcinogens (see more about bile acids on page 39). The vitamins, minerals, phenols, and phytoestrogens in the plant foods can reduce the formation of cancer cells in both the small and large intestine. Another big study, the Asia Cohort Consortium study of over 500,000 people (a pooled analysis), found that drinking alcohol and being overweight or obese were related to an increased risk of small intestine cancer. Both are also linked with an increased risk colorectal cancer.

For people with celiac disease, the small intestine is where the problems begin. Celiac disease is an autoimmune disorder that can affect genetically susceptible people, whereby eating foods containing gluten causes serious damage to the small intestine. In celiac disease, the feathery projections called villi that line the small intestine and help bring amino acids, fats, glucose, vitamins, and minerals into the blood stream, are attacked by the immune system and stop working. This can lead to serious nutrient deficiencies and other problems. Celiac disease is diagnosed with a blood test and/or a procedure called an endoscopy that looks directly at the small intestine. If you are diagnosed with celiac disease you cannot eat wheat, barley, rye, or any of their relatives. For more on gluten see The Gluten Phenomenon, page 36.

Avoid
- Red and processed meats
- High sodium foods such as highly processed junk and fast food, as well as smoked and cured meats

Limit
- Alcohol

Eat
- Fruits and vegetables high in vitamin C like citrus, broccoli, red and yellow peppers, papaya, strawberries, pineapple, Brussels sprouts, guava, and cauliflower
- Whole grains such as quinoa, whole wheat oats, and buckwheat
- Beans including pinto, split peas, cranberry beans, and black-eyed peas
- Allium vegetables: garlic, onion, leeks, chives, scallions
- Apples
- Tomatoes
- Healthy fats
- Olive oil
- Avocados

The Only Cleanse 14-Day Plan

Intro to the Cleanse

CONGRATULATIONS. You care enough about yourself, your body, and your mind to read *The Only Cleanse*. Now you are ready to take action. We are focusing on the six-phase, 14-Day Plan that can kick start your body into good health and well-being. Why fourteen days? Research shows that in as little as fourteen days healthy lifestyle alterations such as those outlined in *The Only Cleanse* can boost brain, gastrointestinal, heart, and total body health, thus firing up your body's natural ability to cleanse and detoxify itself 24/7. You will need to follow the plan fully for two weeks. One day of eating *The Only Cleanse* way and bouncing back to old behaviors will not do you much good. In the scheme of things, it's only fourteen days. You can do this. Approach *The Only Cleanse Plan* as a fun new adventure in getting healthy and feeling energized.

> "When you are courting a nice girl an hour seems like a second. When you sit on a red-hot cinder a second seems like an hour. That's relativity."
>
> **–ALBERT EINSTEIN**

If fourteen days seems undoable, there is the 7-Day *Only Cleanse* Demi-Plan to help get you started. Follow the first seven days of *The Only Cleanse* 14-Day Food Plan and the full fourteen days of the Space Cleanses, Mindful Moments, Exercise, and Stress Assess Plans.

The Only Cleanse Elements
- ➡ **Food plan**
- ➡ **Foods on the plan**
- ➡ **Foods not on the plan**
- ➡ **Space Cleanses**
- ➡ **Mindful Moments**
- ➡ **Exercise**
- ➡ **Sleep**
- ➡ **Stress Assess**

Are You Ready to Begin The Only Cleanse?
➤ **Assess your motivation**
➤ **Find the Why and Why Not**
➤ **Set realistic goals**
➤ **Personalize your goals**

NOTE: *There is no magical order in which the foods on the plan should be eaten. While there is a 14-Day Plan laid out for you to make the plan easier to follow, it is not set in stone. If you feel you need more calories increase your portions or have an additional snack. You can also add more beans, tofu, nuts and nut butters to dishes. For example, one plan follower added a piece of whole grain toast with almond butter to fill out her chia-oat smoothie breakfast. You can mix and match from the meal lists on page 263. You can also invent your own dishes based on the criteria set forth in this chapter (page 127). We are getting back to basics on the plan. Simple, mostly homemade foods that happen to be vegetarian, with as few processed products as possible.*

The Only Cleanse Support Plan is not about weight loss, though you may lose weight. *The Only Cleanse* helps recalibrate the body and the mind to their natural equilibrium.

You will be eating cleanly and thus "detoxing" from processed foods that are chemically engineered to induce food cravings. Pulitzer-Prize-winning journalist Michael Moss, the "pink slime" whistle blower, explores in depth in his book *Salt, Sugar, Fat* how the giant food companies, using psychologists and food chemists, formulate foods to stimulate the human brain and body to crave those products. Your body is literally being biochemically manipulated to lust after these highly processed foods. *The Only Cleanse* is formulated to purge those chemical cravings by removing them from your diet. The thing about chemical cravings is, physiologically they will go away when the stimulus goes away. Over time you will find that the foods you thought you could not live without actually taste like the synthetic concoctions they really are.

Donna, a thirty-one-year-old administrative assistant in a hospital where I worked, had struggled with weight all her life. She loved McDonald's cheeseburgers, shakes, and fries. I mean, she *really* loved her Micky D's. And she loved ice cream, pepperoni pizza and Cheez Whiz right out of the can. She had tried fad diets before—very low-calorie and low-carb diets—but she could not keep the weight off. This isn't surprising—that is why they're called "fad" diets. We had a few informal chats about healthy foods and eating less fast and junk food as we sauntered though the lunch line in the cafeteria, but Donna was not ready to change her habits. "My job is stressful. I don't have time to cook. Hitting McDonalds or the diner on the way home is easy and takes away the stress of having to shop and prepare meals," she told me.

A few months passed before we crossed paths in the lunch line again. I was amazed at how she had changed. She had lost twenty-five pounds and looked great. I asked her how she did it. She laughed and said "You'll be so pleased. I did it with healthy eating, cutting out junk and fast food, and watching my portions."

I was surprised. "Really? Don't you miss your Micky D's?" I asked.

"You know, I don't," she said with a slightly bewildered expression. "As soon as I stopped eating all that junk I stopped craving it. I don't even want it anymore." She said she never thought that would happen. Donna's leap into a healthy eating plan was spurred by a diagnosis of prediabetes. She had been watching her father battle type 2 diabetes for years and did not want to go down that road. She knew she was dangerously close to doing so. The good thing about prediabetes is that with dietary change, weight management, and exercise you can avoid or significantly delay the onset of type 2 diabetes. For Donna, that diagnosis is what popped her out of complacency and into taking action. "I am really happy that I've lost this weight, and I know I can continue this lifestyle. What I did not expect was how much more energy I have now. I was so focused on losing weight that it never occurred to me that I would feel really good, too."

You will be changing what you are eating to support your body's natural self-cleansing abilities. You will be reorganizing your living space to support behavior change. You will be detoxing your life by cleansing your inner voice of nonstop negativity and reaffirming your positive inner life force. You will be making some simple changes so you sleep better and are less susceptible to the harsh effects of living in a stressful world. But first, you have to ascertain if you are ready to take these steps.

The Only Cleanse helps recalibrate the body and the mind to their natural equilibrium.

The First Step

The first step to making a behavior change is to assess how motivated you are to begin that process. Are you ready to do what it takes to adopt a new, healthier lifestyle? On a scale from one to ten, one being "fuggedaboutit" and ten being "Yes, one thousand percent motivated," where does your motivation fall? If it's below an eight then perhaps this is not the best time for you to begin. That's right. I am saying if you do not really want to do *The Only Cleanse* 14-Day Plan, then don't. Trying to make lifestyle changes when you are not ready is a recipe for failure.

The *Why Not* and the *Why*

What if you are not motivated or ready to make changes? Take a moment to reflect on why you're not motivated. Ask yourself, *Why* don't *I want to feel better, support my body's natural detoxing abilities, or have more energy?* Then ask yourself, *Why* do *I want to be healthier? How will feeling good change my life?* Go deeper and examine any fears that may arise, such as fear of deprivation or failure. Look ahead and ask yourself, *How do I want to feel in six months or a year from now?*

Identifying both the barriers to, and the reasons for, making lifestyle changes gives you a springboard for problem solving. Several years ago I was teaching nutrition classes as part of an ongoing education series in an outpatient cardiac rehabilitation program in New York City. The patients would go to their cardiac exercise session and then come into the conference room for the education classes. Nutrition was an especially prickly topic. People do not like being told that their favorite foods, like roast beef and pizza, are not good for their hearts. This was not a nutrition class they had signed up for. They were only in the class because it was part of the rehab program, so it was not unusual for some patients to be resistant to the nutrition recommendations presented therein.

On a cold February evening, I walked into the conference room, and there sat Barney, a sixty-five-year-old man with a salt-and-pepper beard, his arms folded over his chest. My first class in the series revolved around the different kinds of fats in foods and how they affect the risk of heart disease. About ten minutes into the class, Barney started heckling me. "What do mean hamburgers are unhealthy? Do you expect me to listen to you? What do you know?"

That was just the beginning. I did my best to defuse the situation and finish the class. That one hour class felt like forever that night. I walked back to my office thinking, "Good Lord, how can I help this man?"

To my surprise, Barney called the following day to apologize for being so difficult. He said, "I'm sorry. I'm angry that I had a heart attack. And I took it out on you." From that day on Barney turned a complete 180 degrees. He became my poster-boy. By the end of his three-month cardiac rehab program he was eating a healthier, more plant-based diet (he ditched the hamburgers), exercising regularly, meditating, and feeling better than he had in years. "I thought the fatigue and aches and pains were just because I was sixty-five, and that it was a normal part of aging. Now I feel better than I did at thirty-five." I asked Barney what flipped the switch that motivated him to change. He said he focused on the *why*. "I want to see my granddaughter bat mitzvahed. I want to be here for her." And he was. *The Only Cleanse* begins as a 14-Day plan, but the changes can last a lifetime.

Look ahead and ask yourself how do I want to feel in six months, or a year from now?

If You Are Ready to Experience *The Only Cleanse* Plan, Let's Go!

You may want to enlist family members or friends to join you on *The Only Cleanse* Plan. Research shows that people who have a partner in making changes are more likely to be successful and reach their goals. If you choose to go it alone, that is great, too. Lana, an *Only Cleanse* Plan follower, found it much easier and more fun to do the plan and maintain the changes because her daughter-in-law was on board with her. This was particularly helpful because her husband was revolting against the dietary changes at home. However, once he witnessed Lana's weight loss and the upswing in her energy and mood, he jumped on board, too.

It is time for goal setting. Perhaps you want to have more energy, reach a healthy weight, lower blood sugar or blood pressure, or just feel cleaner and healthier. *The Only Cleanse* is geared to help you reach these kinds of goals. Some goals, like lowering cholesterol or losing a significant amount of weight, will take longer than fourteen days. You can stay on this plan indefinitely by being creative and introducing a variety of plant based foods as you go along. The initial 14-Day Plan is designed to jump-start your detox from processed and less healthy foods and foster healthy habits. Once the fourteen days are done you can liberalize the plan to suit your food preferences and lifestyle, while still maintaining a plant-based, healthy diet. I have no doubt that after the first fourteen days you'll feel a whole lot better than you did when you started.

NOTE: *Do not stop taking prescribed medications during the 14-Day Plan without first consulting your healthcare provider. It is always a good idea to periodically review whatever medications you are on with your healthcare team.*

Take a moment to evaluate how you are feeling. You will do this again at the end of 14-Days. Circle the answer that most applies to you right now:

FATIGUE	Very	Somewhat	A little	None	
ACHY JOINTS, MUSCLES	Very	Somewhat	A little	None	
FEELING FOGGY	Very	Somewhat	A little	None	
ENERGY LEVEL	High	Adequate	Low	Running on Fumes	
GASTROIN-TESTINAL SYMPTOMS (crampy, bloating, constipation, diarrhea, discomfort, etc.)	Constant	Intermittent	Occasional	Not a problem	
SLEEP QUALITY	Great	Good	Adequate	Poor	What is sleep?
MOOD - IN GENERAL	Great	Good	Neutral	Cranky	Sad/depressed

List your goals for the next fourteen days. Be realistic and simple, e.g., get to bed fifteen minutes earlier each night, exercise three or four days a week, eat the plan way for fourteen days, drink two to three more glasses of water each day.

1. _____

2. _____

3. _____

Personalize your plan. Your plan has to be specific to your daily life. Be precise about how you are going to achieve your goals. Add tasks to your to-do list or calendar.

➡ **When will you go shopping?**
➡ **When will you prepare foods for the week?**
➡ **What day will you reorganize your pantry?**
➡ **When, where, and at what time will you be exercising each day?**
➡ **Where will you be eating your meals? At home, work, etc.?**

In terms of what you will be eating, *The Only Cleanse* gives you a 14-Day Food Plan with several options, so that is one thing off your to-do list.

➡ **Plan ahead.** Planning ahead is a key component to changing your habits. *The Only Cleanse* has shopping lists to make life easier for you. You still need to carve out the time to stock the kitchen, prepare the food, exercise, and stress-bust.

➡ **Be Prepared.** Stock your kitchen with healthy foods such as legumes (beans), whole grains, vegetables, fruits, nuts and seeds, condiments, and fun canned things like capers, olives, and tomatoes. Review the shopping lists on pages 267–272.

➡ **Be positive and patient.** Always give yourself a pat on the back for making healthy choices. Do not berate yourself for falling off the wagon. Look at the event as a learning experience and move forward. Remember, changing behaviors you have had for years is a process, and it takes time.

➡ **Practice.** The more you practice your new healthier habits, the easier they become. Take each day step by step, choice by choice, day by day. Revel in the knowledge that you are doing something healthy for yourself and your family.

Plan Details
➡ What can I eat?
➡ Planning on the go
➡ Space Cleanses
➡ Mindful Moments
➡ The beauty of sleep
➡ Stress Assess
➡ Exercise

What Can I Eat?
➡ **Vegan** (except for yogurt and honey)
➡ **All Organic** (if possible)
➡ **If not organic, non-GMO**

What Foods Are on the Plan
➡ **All vegetables:** fresh, plain frozen
➡ **All fruits:** fresh, plain frozen, dried
➡ **All legumes:** plain canned, plain frozen, dried
➡ **All nuts and seeds:** roasted or raw (unsalted, plain), nut butters with no added sugar, salt or palm oil
➡ **All whole grains**
➡ **All unsaturated oils** (liquid at room temperature like olive, canola, peanut and grapeseed oils)
➡ **Plain organic yogurt** (Greek or regular)
➡ **Tea:** black, green, or herbal infusions
➡ **Follow the plan's food plan or make up your own**

What Is NOT on the Plan
➡ **Meat, poultry, fish, processed meats**
➡ **All cheese, milk, dairy** (except yogurt), **eggs**
➡ **Partially hydrogenated oils** (a.k.a. trans fats)
➡ **Deep fried anything**
➡ **Artificial or non-nutritive sweeteners such as stevia, sucralose, aspartame, saccharin, and acesulfame potassium**
➡ **Coffee**
➡ **Soda and other sugar sweetened beverages**
➡ **Diet drinks**

➡ **Alcohol**
➡ **Fast food**
➡ **Junk food**
➡ **Foods with artificial ingredients, flavors, or food dyes**
➡ **Animal products such as chicken or beef broth, gelatin,**
➡ **Worcestershire sauce** (has anchovies)
➡ **Desserts, candy, breakfast pastries**
➡ **Energy, snack, or protein bars**
➡ **Protein shakes, protein powders**

Recipes and Food Lists

The hub of the 14-Day *Only Cleanse* Plan is the Food Plan. The magic of the Food Plan is its simplicity: primarily simple whole foods, totally vegetarian, and mostly vegan.

It is the kind of plan many of us think about doing but don't know how to execute.

You may wonder why going vegetarian is a cleaner way to eat. As we discovered in the chapters on the microbiome and the primary cleansing organs, red and processed meats, dairy foods, saturated fats, junk, and highly processed foods are all linked with chronic diseases and inflammation that affect your health. Research is pretty clear that a more plant-based diet supports a vibrant and healthy human body. A study in 2013 in the *Journal of the American Medical Association* looked at more than seventy thousand Seventh Day Adventists. They found that those individuals who followed a vegetarian diet lived longer and had lower rates of cardiovascular and kidney disease and diabetes than those who were not vegetarians. Scientists love to study the Seventh Day Adventists because they are a very large group of people in the US who can be followed for long periods of time. The philosophy of the Seventh Day Adventists encourages a healthy lifestyle and the consumption of a well-balanced vegetarian diet.

I interviewed Dr. Michael J. Orlich, the lead author of the study, on my SiriusXM radio show. I was curious about the meat eaters in the study. Since the Seventh Day Adventist Church promotes a plant-based diet, did the meat eaters in the study's population eat as much meat as the average American? No, he said, they did not. In this study the "semi-vegetarians" ate meat about once a week. Compare that with the average American, who eats more than 270 pounds of meat every year. That averages out to over a pound of meat a day, per person. This makes the results even more impressive; the study suggests that consuming even small amounts of animal foods regularly increases the risk of chronic disease and death. This is just one of many studies that support the notion that a more plant-based diet, coupled with regular exercise, stress management, and a healthy lifestyle is the way to go for a longer, healthier life.

I'd like you to eat as cleanly as possible for the fourteen days or during the 7-Day Demi-Plan, so you get the full benefits of your efforts. All fruits, vegetables, nuts, seeds, beans, whole grains, herbs, spices, and plant oils (with the exception of palm and coconut) are allowed on the plan. Fresh, plain frozen, and plain canned produce and legumes are all acceptable, too. By "plain" I mean no sauces, added sugar, salt, chemicals, etc.

The plan is created to replace chemically infused, processed, unhealthy foods with tasty, everyday foods that are bursting with nutrients. These foods boost vitality and energize every system in your body.

Nutrition Précis

Carbohydrates: Carbohydrates include starchy carbs like pasta, potatoes, oats, and bread as well as beans, vegetables, fruits, honey, sugar, and milk sugars. Carbohydrates, when digested and molecularly pulled apart, become glucose or fructose molecules. Carbs are the primary and preferential fuel source for all your cells and your brain. People tell me on a daily basis that they have "given up carbs." Please don't do that. Please eat these nutrient rich, healthy foods. A good half of your plate should be nonstarchy carbs like broccoli, spinach, and cauliflower, and a full one-fourth of the plate should be starchy carbs like brown rice, a baked potato (white or sweet), or quinoa. It is fine to have some white pasta or white rice periodically, but most of your grains should be whole.

It is best to buy organic, which by law is non-GMO. If you cannot afford organic products or cannot find them, it's OK. Just do the best you can with what you have available. *The Only Cleanse* 14-Day Food Plan does not include alcohol, junk or fast foods, meat, poultry, fish, or dairy except plain yogurt—no desserts, protein shakes, bars, powders, or pastries. Skipping sweets and the ritual of having dessert regularly for fourteen days will help break the cycle of "dessert expectation." Expecting a sweet after dinner is as much a habit as reaching to answer your phone when it rings. You may find during the plan that you long for that dessert or cocktail. Cravings pass. Habits can be broken and repatterned with healthier habits over time.

Do you eat the same breakfast just about every day? What about lunches? My patients seem to like an eating routine. Or maybe they are just used to having the same cereal or bacon-egg-cheese-sandwich every morning. The plan encourages variety in foods. However, if you want to have the chia-oat smoothie three mornings in a row, that's fine.

NOTE: *Portion size of the meals depends upon your needs. You want to feel satisfied but not stuffed after a meal. Add extra vegetables or a side salad and a bit more protein (beans, tofu, nuts) to meals if you want more food. If you are hungry between meals, drink some tea or water. Then, if you are still hungry, have a snack (snack lists on page 263).*

Whole grains play an important role in lowering the risk of chronic diseases, such as coronary heart disease, diabetes, and cancer, and they also contribute to body weight management and gastrointestinal health. The fiber, protein, healthy fats, vitamins, antioxidants, and minerals in whole grains, along with phytonutrients, synergistically contribute to whole grains' health benefits. Whole grains may help you live longer, too. A 2015 study out of the Harvard T.H. Chan School of Public Health looked at data from more than 74,000 women from the Nurses' Health Study and more than 43,000 men from the Health Professionals Follow-Up Study. Scientists found that eating whole grains reduced mortality by 15 percent. For each serving of whole grains (about one ounce a day), overall mortality dropped by 5 percent and cardiovascular disease-related mortality dropped by 9 percent.

Vegetables, beans, and fruit provide several kinds of fiber that feed the microbiome inhabitants and boost gastrointestinal health. These foods are crammed with phytonutrients, vitamins, minerals, protein, healthy fats, and other compounds that fight disease, reduce inflammation, promote healing, and contribute to the body's vital cleansing abilities.

POINT OF INTEREST

FOR ATHLETES

When you are training hard, a full half of your plate should be starchy whole grain carbohydrates like brown rice, quinoa, oats, and whole grain pastas. The exception here depends on timing. The closer you get to a heavy training session or competition, the less fiber, fat, and protein you eat. Fifteen to thirty minutes before heavy training or a game, choose easily digested carbohydrates such as a rice cake, a handful of cereal, pretzels, juice, or a sports drink.

Fun with Fat

I have great hope that the fat phobia of the 1990s that has hung on through the early 2000s will soon disappear. Fat is essential for life. It tastes good. Fat provides vital physiological functions. There is no reason to shun dietary fats. The prevailing myth that has stoked the fear of fats is that "fat makes you fat." It does not. Eating too much of anything, i.e. more calories than your body needs, whether it is cheese, bread, peanut butter, or broccoli (broccoli is on the theoretical side – because how much broccoli can one really eat in a day?) can make you gain weight. Confusion reigns when it comes to what fats we should be eating. Here is all you need to know: There are good and bad fats. The bad fats are trans fats and saturated fats. The good fats are unsaturated fats. All man-made trans fats are bad and should be avoided. You will know if a product has trans fats if the ingredient list includes "partially hydrogenated oil." You will have to read the labels to discern this (bring your glasses or a microscope. The print can be incredibly small). Fats that are solid at room temperature are saturated (a molecular descriptive), and should be limited. Fats that are liquid at room temperature are unsaturated and can be enjoyed in appropriate portions because, yes, they are high in calories.

Olive, grapeseed, walnut, canola, and peanut oils are liquid at room temperature and thus unsaturated. Foods such as tofu, avocados, and nuts contain unsaturated fats that confer many health benefits. Certain unsaturated fats are essential to the health and well-being of the human body, but we need to eat them because our bodies cannot synthesize them. These include omega-3 and omega-6 fatty acids. These fats play important roles in cell integrity, inflammation, eyesight, mental health, immunity, and brain, cardio-vascular and skin health, plus a lot more. Getting adequate dietary omega-6 fatty acids is usually not a big concern for vegetarians, but getting enough omega-3 fatty acids is. Oily fish is one of the best sources of omega-3s, so if you do not eat fish you need to find alternative omega-3 sources.

Registered dietitian and co-author of *Vegan for Life* Jack Norris rec-ommends that vegetarians and vegans supplement with two to three-hun-dred milligrams of a vegetarian derived omega-3 fat called docosahexae-noic acid (DHA) daily. There are companies that sell vegetarian-derived omega-3 supplements. Norris also recommends including 0.5 grams of un-cooked alpha-linolenic acid (ALA), another omega-3, to your diet daily. This would be the equivalent of 1/5 ounce of walnuts (three halves) or a quarter teaspoon of flaxseed oil. Vegetarian sources of omega-3 fatty acids include walnuts, ground flax seeds or flax meal, flax oil, chia seeds, and soy (tofu, edamame, tempeh).

Why the Fuss Over Saturated Fat?

Saturated fat is not an essential fat. We do not need to eat it. Foods high in saturated fat, much to the dismay of steak, cheese, and bacon lovers, come primarily from animal foods such as meat and dairy. Saturated fat, through complex biochemical processes, increases internal inflammation, serum cho-lesterol, LDL cholesterol (the bad cholesterol), and arterial inflammation and dysfunction. Saturated fat has been associated with an increased risk of ath-erosclerosis, diabetes and nonalcoholic fatty liver disease, and it may increase fat storage in your abdomen. Some mechanisms for saturated fat's unhealthy effects have been identified. For example, it's been determined that saturated fat depresses LDL (bad) cholesterol receptors on hepatic and other cells, lead-ing to an increase in serum cholesterol.

The simplest way to identify a saturated fat is either to look at it (solid at room temperature) or know the source (does the food come from a plant or an animal?). Fats that are solid at room temperature are saturated, and these are primarily found in animal foods. In the plant world, palm and coconut oils are saturated.

Eating more plant foods such as black beans, lentils, quinoa, edamame, spinach, broccoli, apples, and brown rice can help reduce the amount of saturated fat we consume as well as loading us up with heart- healthy vitamins, minerals, anti-oxidants, and fiber.

Protein

High-protein diets have been in and out of the fad-light for decades. Some good has come out of them: We have a better understanding of the role of protein in satiety, blood sugar management, and weight control. On the bad side, people have gotten all kinds of crazy about eating tons of meat, cheese, and bacon, and they've eliminated entire food groups like carbohydrates or fats.

Your body needs all three nutrients—protein, carbohydrates and fat—to be balanced and healthy. The source of these nutrients does make a difference. Plant based proteins such as beans, soy, nuts, and grains are paired with fiber, vitamins, minerals, healthy fats, and anti-oxidants. Organizations such as the American Heart Association, the US Department of Agriculture, and the American Cancer Society, recommend Americans (it is fair to extrapolate this recommendation to people in other countries as well) eat a more plant-based diet because of all the health benefits. Protein is not just for muscles. Amino acids, of which protein is made, play crucial roles in immunity, aid biochemical and neurotransmitter functions, strengthen cell structure, and help transport molecules like hemoglobin. *The Only Cleanse* includes protein sources such as quinoa, corn, kasha, edamame, almond butter, black beans, tofu, soymilk, and chia seeds. Seitan is another great plant-based protein source you can add in to your recipes in place of tofu or beans. Seitan is wheat gluten protein that is often used as "mock meat" in recipes and dishes. Additional plant-based protein sources include: whole wheat pastas and breads, sunflower and pumpkin seeds, and brown and wild rice.

A Note about Beans

There is a persistent myth that beans are high in fat. It's not true. Beans like chickpeas and lentils contain virtually no fat. Beans, also known as legumes, are not only a good source of carbohydrates, but crammed into that little bean are protein, antioxidants, fiber, B vitamins, iron, magnesium, potassium, copper, and zinc.

Tea

For fifty centuries people have known that there is nothing more civilized than having a nice, hot cup of tea to soothe the soul and hydrate the body. Legend has it that Chinese Emperor Shennong (ca. 2700 BCE), discovered tea one day when he was sitting under a camellia tree. He boiled some water to drink. Fortuitously some of the dried leaves of the tree above floated down into the pot of boiling water, and voila, tea was born. Today tea is the most widely consumed beverage in the world next to water, which is great because tea has a lot of health benefits.

"Never trust a man who, when left alone in a room with a tea cosy, doesn't try it on."
–BILLY CONNOLLY

Real tea comes only from the *Camellia sinensis* plant. How the leaves are processed is what differentiates green, black, and oolong teas. Herbal teas do not come from *Camellia sinensis*, so technically they are not teas but are rather infusions of leaves, roots, bark, seeds, or the flowers of other plants.

Tea is loaded with healthy plant chemicals called polyphenols. Polyphenols have been reported to possess antioxidant, antiviral, and anti-inflammatory properties; they modulate detoxification enzymes, stimulate immune function, and decrease platelet aggregation. Tea polyphenols may help reduce the risk of several cancers, including head and neck, urinary tract, digestive, breast, and liver cancers.

The health benefits of tea include:
- Boosting of heart health
- Reduction of arthritis
- Anticancer effects
- Reduced risk of diabetes
- Brain and neuronal health support
- Cavity reduction
- Reduced inflammation

POINT OF INTEREST

FOR TEA FANS

- *Americans drank an estimated 3.6 billion gallons of tea in 2012.*
- *Over 165 million cups of tea are drunk in the UK every single day of the year.*
- *Leading tea-producing countries include Argentina, China, India, Indonesia, Kenya, Malawi, Sri Lanka, Tanzania, and Taiwan.*
- *Panda poo is the newest tea fad. Chinese entrepreneur An Yanshi is using panda dung as a fertilizer for growing tea. For a mere $3547.50, you can buy panda dung tea with hand-painted porcelain containers and a box covered in Shu brocade.*
- *Russians traditionally sweeten their teas with a teaspoon of jam, such as strawberry, cherry, or blackberry.*

The Only Cleanse includes whatever kinds of tea you prefer. Tea naturally contains low amounts of central nervous system stimulants called methylxanthines, including caffeine, theobromine, and theophylline. If you are caffeine sensitive, for late afternoon tea or evening tea you may want to opt for decaf tea or a caffeine-free herbal infusion. Herbal infusions have health benefits as well. For example, peppermint and fennel tea may settle upset stomachs, chamomile tea is commonly believed to calm frazzled nerves, and ginger tea has anti-inflammatory and anti-nausea properties.

Ready-to-Drink Teas

Ready-to-drink tea consumption has grown more than fifteenfold since 2002. In 2012, ready-to-drink sales were conservatively estimated at 4.8 billion dollars. My opinion is that unless the ready-to-drink tea is plain-brewed tea without added sugars, flavoring, colors, or preservatives, you should brew your own tea. All it takes is some boiling water.

The Perfect Cup of Tea

STORAGE: Store tea in an airtight container at room temperature

WATER: Use fresh water for each brew. Tea loves oxygen, and boiling the water more than once reduces the O2 content. Who knew? I've been reboiling the teapot water for years.

WATER TEMPERATURE: Use boiling water for black tea. For green, oolong, and white teas, bring water just to the point where tiny bubbles begin to form, then pour over the tea. The right temp helps avoid bitterness.

STEEP: Steeping tea too long makes it bitter.

- Three to five minutes for black tea, dark oolong, and white teas
- Two or three minutes for light oolong and green teas

The food choices on the plan are unprocessed, or processed with as few chemicals as is realistic. For example, I recommend buying Ezekiel breads or bread from a local bakery because these will have fewer chemicals, preservatives and fillers. Even better, make your own bread. Or, if you are like me and do not have the time or inclination to make bread from scratch, buy a bread maker. I've only just gotten a bread maker, and so I'm in the infatuation phase at the moment. Homemade bread is pretty awesome. Alternatively, you can go to your local grocery store and buy 100 percent whole wheat bread or 100 percent whole grain (gluten free if necessary) bread. Foods such as veggie burgers or crumbles, vegan cheeses, and the like are more processed than the 14-Day Plan allows. After fourteen days, feel free to add them to your diet. I have vegan burgers, "butters," and "mayo" in my refrigerator.

While on the 14-Day Plan, you will probably need to bring your lunch to work or school unless there are good vegan/vegetarian options in nearby eateries and stores. Alison, a young professional living in New York City, said to me, "I'd do *The Only Cleanse*, but I don't cook." For the most part young professionals in New York City don't cook. Actually, it seems to me most people living in NYC don't cook. I certainly did not cook very often when I lived there.

Try cooking at home at least a few days a week. You'll save money and eat a lot healthier. In cities you can always order takeout or have food delivered. This doesn't mean you cannot eat cleanly. Salad bars are a great option for lunches for busy professionals. Load up on all the fresh vegetables and add some avocado slices. Forego the bacon bits, cheese, and croutons and use plain lemon or oil and vinegar for the dressing. Be sure to add beans or tofu to the salad for protein. Vegetarian restaurant soups, though usually high in sodium, are good, too. You do not have to accept what is on the menu. Ask for the chicken hummus salad without the chicken, or request the Mediterranean veggie flat bread without the feta cheese. Most eateries are happy to oblige.

Eating Out Ideas:

➡ **Mexican:** bean, vegetable burrito, guacamole, salsa, (no sour cream or cheese), brown rice
➡ **Indian:** dal, curried vegetables, mulligatawny soup (check to be sure it is vegetarian)
➡ **Chinese:** steamed broccoli, tofu, brown rice with soy sauce
➡ **Middle Eastern:** hummus in whole wheat pita with chopped tomatoes, cucumbers, onions, tahini
➡ **Italian:** pasta primavera (not the one in cream sauce), eggplant parm without cheese, vegetarian pasta e fagioli, escarole with garlic, pizza topped with your favorite vegetables and no cheese (it is surprisingly good)

NOTE: *Sodium is virtually always high in prepared and restaurant foods.*

The plan has meals specifically laid out for each day. There is no specific order in which to have the foods. The plan is organized for ease of preparation and less waste of food (e.g., using leftovers and reinventing last night's dinner), while encouraging variety. If you prefer, there are lists of breakfasts, lunches, dinners, and snacks on pages 263–267, and you can choose what you feel like eating from the lists. Feel free to create your own meals and snacks, following the plan guidelines.

What is Nutritional Yeast?

Nutritional yeast is emerging as a tasty ingredient that ups the umami of your favorite dishes without adding fat or calories. Not to be mistaken for brewer's yeast, nutritional yeast is an inactive yeast made from Saccharomyces cerevisiae, a type of natural fungus. Nutritional yeast adds a cheesy, creamy flavor to vegetables, gravies and soups. Flaked or powdered, nutritional yeast is a good source of protein and B vitamins like vitamin B12. It is an essential ingredient for vegans, whose diets are often deficient in vitamin B12 and low in protein. Sprinkle nutritional yeast on popped corn, or mix with chopped walnuts and sprinkle on pasta as an alternative to Parmesan cheese. Add nutritional yeast to sauces and soups to makes them creamier. 1/4 cup=six grams of protein, daily value=133 percent of vitamin B12, forty-five calories.

For the last four days of the Daily Food Plan you are flying solo. You can repeat previous full day plans or individual recipes. One of the secrets to making lifestyle changes that stick is learning to create healthy choices that take into account your food preferences, budget, schedule, and life's unexpected twists and turns. You are the only one who can do that for you. Patients often ask (some demand) that I hand them a specific diet. "Just tell me what to eat." I don't because it is unrealistic to think that a prewritten utilitarian diet suits everyone's lives. It is best to for you to figure out what works for you. *The Only Cleanse* Food Plan is a guide to help you on your way to a cleaner way of eating. The plan is your training wheels. After a bit of practice you will get the hang of clean eating and soon be well on your way. If you fall back into old habits, the plan is here to help you get back on track.

The Recipes

On my mission to find a registered dietitian-nutritionist to help me out with the recipes I was fortunate to have just had Dana Angelo White as a guest on my SiriusXM radio show. I really hit the jackpot because not only is she a registered dietitian-nutritionist and certified athletic trainer, she also specializes in culinary nutrition. You will find several of Dana's delicious recipes included in the 14-Day *Only Cleanse* Food Plan. The other recipes are my own with the exception of Mollie Katzen's Saladita recipe which I have included with her kind permission, because it is fantastic.

GMOs are a hotly contested and highly political topic these days. There are many concerns associated with mixing and matching DNA from different organisms, including the effects on human and animal health and the far reaching effects on the eco-system.

HERE IS A LIST OF THE MOST COMMON GMO FOODS BY THE NON-GMO PROJECT:

Soy, cotton, canola, corn, sugar beets, Hawaiian papaya, alfalfa, and squash (zucchini and yellow). Many of these items appear as added ingredients in a large amount of the foods we eat. For instance, your family may not eat tofu or drink soy milk, but soy is most likely present in a large percentage of the foods in your pantry. GMOs may be hidden in common processed food ingredients such as: amino acids, aspartame, ascorbic acid, sodium ascorbate, vitamin C, citric acid, sodium citrate, flavorings ("natural" and "artificial"), high fructose corn syrup, hydrolyzed vegetable protein, lactic acid, maltodextrins, molasses, monosodium glutamate, sucrose, textured vegetable protein (TVP), xanthan gum, vitamins, and yeast products.

What is a GMO?

The Non-GMO Project's definition: "GMOs (or 'genetically modified organisms') are living organisms whose genetic material has been artificially manipulated in a laboratory through genetic engineering, or GE. This relatively new science creates unstable combinations of plant, animal, bacteria, and viral genes that do not occur in nature or through traditional crossbreeding methods."

The Plan on the Go

Making healthy choices and sticking to the plan even when you are on the go is doable with some planning. On my SiriusXM radio show many drivers and truckers call in and share their personal tips for healthy eating on the road. In their rigs they have coolers stocked with cut-up vegetables and hummus, PB&J, salads, and water. They know where they can stop to go for a run or walk and which fast food restaurants have healthy-ish options. If you are on the go, bring food with you in insulated coolers. Review your travel plans and find grocery stores and restaurants that can meet the vegetarian criteria set forth in the plan. Many airports have salads, yogurt, and hummus wraps. Choose hotels that have a fitness center or are affiliated with one. Call ahead to see if hotels and local eateries have vegetarian options.

When I first moved to New York City in the early 1980s there were few, if any, vegetarian dishes or restaurants. I often ended up with bread and wine for dinner (which was fine with me but tended to discomfit my dining companions). In the second decade of the 2000s there are tons of vegetarian and vegan selections and full-out vegan restaurants in many cities and towns. A food item does not have to say it is specifically vegetarian to be vegetarian; for example, fruit salad or guacamole and tortilla chips are vegetarian. On the other hand I was at a Japanese restaurant and ordered their "vegetarian" steamed vegetables with garlic sauce. When I asked what was in the garlic sauce I was told it was made with chicken broth. I skipped the garlic sauce and settled for soy sauce. Some restaurants steam vegetables in a chicken or fish broth. Feel free to ask your server or the chef questions about what is in the food you are ordering and how it is prepared. I often call ahead to the restaurant to see what vegetarian options they have.

NOTE: *Because this is a vegetarian plan, it may contain more dietary fiber than you are used to. You need to increase your fluid intake and physical activity to help your body manage the increase in fiber. If beans or certain vegetables make you gassy, you can puree them for easier digestion. Beano, an over the counter de-gassy supplement is helpful for some people. Over time your GI tract should adjust to the extra fiber.*

Space Cleanses and Mindful Moments

The Plan includes Space Cleanses and Mindful Moments. See the section below for the list of Space Cleanses and Mindful Moments. Some are self-explanatory, like the Space Cleanse "Stop using pesticides and herbicides on your garden and lawn," and others involve commentary and elucidation, which you will find here. You may already be practicing some of the Space Cleanses and Mindful Moments, which is terrific, and some of them may not be applicable to you. If so, focus on the Space Cleanses and Mindful Moments that you feel need the most attention. There are Space Cleanses and Mindful Moments, such as **Space Cleanse #2:** *Powering Positivity (Angels & Demons)* and **Space Cleanse #9:** *Cleansing Reactions*, that probably will not be conquered in a week and will require a consistent mindful approach. For example, working to support inner positivity and silence that critical inner voice is something we all need to work on most of the time. Just bringing mindful attention to the issues presented in the Space Cleanses and Mindful Moments can help begin the process of transforming your personal world into a more positive one.

Space Cleanses

Space Cleanses are a series of actions we take to detoxify and cleanse our relationships, thought processes, and personal space. We spend an awful lot of time focusing on what to eat, but we forget that our psychological and emotional well-being are deeply intertwined with our physical and environmental health. Space Cleanses help us identify toxic areas of our lives and offer strategies to help clean them up.

#1 Space Cleanse: *The Kitchen Cleanse*

For details on cleansing the kitchen, see *The Only Cleanse* prep chapter, page 167.

#2 Space Cleanse: *Powering Positivity (Angels & Demons)*

When I was little I saw a cartoon that probably originated in the 1930s. I'm not sure if the animated lead character was human or animal. What I remember about this cartoon was that he had a devil on one shoulder and an angel on the other. The devil was tricky, mischievous, and loud. The angel was always trying to prevent the lead character from falling prey to the devil's seduction. Of course the character was always listening to the devil and getting into buckets of trouble, and the angel had to constantly bail him out. I like this scenario because it is our story in many ways. We have this devil on one shoulder saying the meanest, most disrespectful things to us—about us—and encouraging bad behaviors. We are very familiar and comfortable with this critical inner voice, so most of the time we do not even notice it. Stop and think about it. Don't you say things to yourself that are so unkind that you would never say them to a child, a loved one, or a friend? Yes, I thought so. Then, why is it OK to say such things to yourself? It isn't.

In the world of psychology they call this positive and negative self-talk. We have a constant running dialogue going on in our heads. It's how we think, evaluate our world, make decisions, and function. Part of the ongoing dialogue can be a negative, overly critical voice cloaked in the guise of truthful reality. The negative voice may be an echo of a person who you were (or are) influenced by, a family member, a "friend," or your own insecurities or fears. The voice says things to us like: I am fat, stupid, a failure, ugly or untalented. It takes grains of truth and magnifies and distorts them. For example if you are having difficulty understanding a complicated problem in school or at work, the voice says, *Arrgh! I am so stupid. I will never understand this.*

To cleanse this toxic mental energy we first need to be aware of the negative voice in our heads. Every time that voice chimes in with an unkind, critical, or negative comment, notice it. Acknowledge that it is there. After a few days of this, you start countering the voice with a positive response. Once you open your eyes to this process you will be surprised how integrated that negative voice has become in your daily life.

My dear friend Fiona came to my annual Christmas Eve celebration. Fiona works out a lot and is in terrific shape. She was wearing a green silk wrapped top over gorgeous red contoured pants and heels. I said, "Omigosh, Fiona, you look beautiful!"

She rolled her eyes, and shrugged and said "No. I am not as skinny as you."

"What are you talking about? You look fantastic!" I said. Again, she deflected the compliment. Why do we do that? Why can't we accept a compliment? It is that negative, self-critical, self-defeating, loud, obnoxious voice in our heads. From now on when someone gives you a heartfelt compliment, smile and say thank you. Then make a conscious effort to deny that reflexive self-defeating dialogue and neutralize it with a supportive, kind response to yourself like, "Yes, I do look good!"

You will practice the Space Cleanses to balance your inner dialogues throughout the 14-Day Plan because not only is the negative voice comfortable and familiar, it is habitual. Breaking this habit may feel weird and slightly uncomfortable, like trying to use your left hand to brush your teeth when you are right handed.

Strengthening your positive voice, the angel on your shoulder, is like any skill; it has to be repeated over and over to gain power and agility. Sometimes the truth can feel scary, partly because it's often what we wish to be true and partly because we have not developed a balanced relationship with it. You will be amazed at what a little practice can do. A powerful, positive inner voice gives an unbelievable boost to your outlook on life.

A few years ago Kim, a patient of mine, came to see me after going into a Victoria's Secret dressing room in New York City and trying on undergarments. Looking in the mirror, she said, nearly made her head explode. Bad lighting, three-way mirrors, and seeing angles of yourself you normally do not see can be brutal. As she stood and looked at herself in mirror she could not help but blurt: "Does everyone look this bad in these mirrors?" Fortunately, no one else happened to be in any of the dressing rooms at the time. Kim left the store not buying anything, feeling awful about herself.

> "People have a hard time letting go of their suffering. Out of a fear of the unknown, they prefer suffering that is familiar."
> **–ZEN MASTER THÍCH NHẤT HẠNH**

In reality, did she really look that bad? Of course not. With whom was she comparing herself? The models on the posters all over the store? What good does ripping apart your physical appearance do? It makes you miserable and a lot more likely to engage in unhealthy behaviors like bingeing on sweets or drinking too much alcohol. Instead, counter that negative voice with a positive response. Focus on what a miracle your body is in every facet of its being; how hard it is working to keep you alive and balanced and healthy. If you see aspects that need improvement, then make plans to address them. Come back to *The Only Cleanse* for a reboot, get back on the exercise track, and reinstate your Mindful Moments. Direct your energy toward positive change. Being positive doesn't mean ignoring reality. Being positive is about keeping life in perspective.

NOTE: *From The National Institute of Mental Health: Everyone occasionally feels blue or sad. But these feelings are usually short-lived and pass within a couple of days. When you have depression, it interferes with daily life and causes pain for both you and those who care about you. Depression is a common but serious illness. If you have signs of depression such as persistent feelings of sadness, hopelessness, anxiety, or fatigue, it is a good idea to seek professional help.*

For more information, see: The National Institute of Mental Health: What is Depression? http://www.nimh.nih.gov/health/topics/depression/index.shtml

On Rare Occasions Negative Self-Talk Can Lead to Brilliance:

> **Symptom Recital**
>
> I do not like my state of mind;
> I'm bitter, querulous, unkind.
> I hate my legs, I hate my hands,
> I do not yearn for lovelier lands.
> I dread the dawn's recurrent light;
> I hate to go to bed at night.
> I snoot at simple, earnest folk.
> I cannot take the gentlest joke.
> I find no peace in paint or type.
> My world is but a lot of tripe.
> I'm disillusioned, empty-breasted.
> For what I think, I'd be arrested.
> I am not sick, I am not well.
> My quondam dreams are shot to hell.
> My soul is crushed, my spirit sore;
> I do not like me any more.
> I cavil, quarrel, grumble, grouse.
> I ponder on the narrow house.
> I shudder at the thought of men....
> I'm due to fall in love again.
>
> **–DOROTHY PARKER**

3 Space Cleanse: *Boundaries (Cleansing Our Lives)*

Here we focus on setting boundaries with the toxic people with whom we are close or with whom we must interact regularly, like family members, friends, colleagues or significant others. Toxic people can be negative, angry, sullen, unkind, moody, or just serial complainers. Their dark, gooey vibe feels like it can

POINT OF INTEREST

FOR TREND SETTERS

On my SiriusXM radio show I keep trying to gain momentum for an "I love my cellulite, sags, bags, and wrinkles" movement. So far the response has been, well, nonexistent. I remain hopeful. It is my way of encouraging us all to look at our bodies realistically, accepting them as they are, knowing we are doing the best we can to be healthy. We all struggle with self-criticism. Sometimes the answer can be OK, so I have cellulite. There is nothing I can do about it, so I may as well accept it and love it. I know the last part of that, about loving your cellulite, is a stretch, but it can't hurt to try.

suffocate any positivity you try to muster. As much as you might like to or feel you have to help this person, it is likely you cannot change their inner zeitgeist. It can be a difficult balance between lending an empathetic ear or helping hand and having the life sucked out of you by their vampiric energy.

No matter how hard you try, it is almost impossible to have a healthy relationship with a toxic person—especially a close relationship. Toxic relationships can make you sick. One study in the UK looked at thousands of people and found that those who were in negative close relationships were more likely to have heart disease than those in happier relationships. Our brains perceive unhealthy relationships as stressors and launch the fight-or-flight stress response. The body is flooded with chemicals like cortisol, which are designed to help to you get to safety. Chronic stress, and a continual inner cortisol bath, lead to disease and mental illness in part because of the constant exposure of internal organs and tissues to these chemicals and their byproducts.

Psychologist Dr. Sherrie Bourg Carter offers this explanation of toxic relationships:

"Toxic relationships are characterized by insecurity, abuse of power and control, demandingness, selfishness, insecurity, self-centeredness, criticism, negativity, dishonesty, distrust, demeaning comments and attitudes, and jealousy."

Or, you generally feel sad, depressed, angry, depleted, shamed, or frustrated when you interact with a certain person.

Give your physical and emotional hearts a cleanse by setting boundaries with the toxic people in your life. This may be as simple as not answering the phone or text every time they try to get in touch, or it could be as intense as cutting that person out of your life.

I worked with a physician who I snarkily dubbed "Darth-Vadette" after the evil villain in the Star Wars movies. Whenever she entered the room, Darth's booming, dark, theme music from Star Wars would pulse through my head (at least that made me laugh). She was cold and disrespectful to me and other staff members. When I tried to trade pleasantries with her she would glare at me and blatantly ignore me. Every time I made an effort to relate to her on a professional level, she found some reason to criticize my work. As much as I knew that it was she who had the problem, her invisible punch was tough to dodge. My plan B was to avoid her like the plague, which helped for a while. But having to deal with her was unavoidable. Ultimately, I quit that job and within a few days of leaving I literally felt lighter and happier, and I slept better.

NOTE: *Toxic relationships can come in all shapes and sizes, from mere annoyances to real, physical danger. If you are in physical danger or feel psychologically or emotionally threatened, it is imperative that you seek professional help. You can contact the National Domestic Violence Hotline for more information at http://www.thehotline.org*

4 Space Cleanses: *The Art of Receiving*

From compliments and gifts to an offer to help out, many of us are really bad at receiving. We are so very comfortable in the role of giving and feel so uncomfortable on the other end. Women in particular, being prone to nurturing, suffer from receiving-rejection. Most of us truly enjoy giving, and we would truly enjoy receiving if we got better at it. As with other habit changes in the Space Cleanses, this takes some practice. The discussion earlier in this chapter on compliments is a good place to start. When someone gives you a genuine compliment, receive it. Do not make excuses, deny or deflect it. The compli-menter is offering you a small gift. By refuting their impressions you are calling them a liar and saying their point of view is not valid. By receiving the compliment you are in turn giving them a small gift, while at the same time quelling your inner critic.

Now, about accepting offers of help. We all need help. Some of us need to learn to ask for it, others to receive it. You may want a friend to come to the doctor with you. Ask her. You may need help caring for a loved one. Accept offers from others to bring meals, provide transportation, or give you a much-needed respite. You may want to vent to a friend. Call him. By receiving their aid you are in turn giving them the gift of helping. Give and take is part of the natural rhythm and flow of life. Go with the flow.

NOTE: *With regard to unpaid caregivers, please seek out social services, where you can find important resources to help you with the responsibility of caring for a loved one.*

5 Space Cleanse: *Technology Moratorium*

Put down the phone, tablet, computer, TV, smartwatch, and all other techno-gadgets for at least several waking hours of the day. You need to unplug periodically because too much technology can cause serious cognitive, social, and health problems in adults and kids. Internet addiction is real and spreading quickly. Do you feel anxious, depressed, or irritable when your computer time is shortened or interrupted? Lose track of time when on the computer (doesn't everyone?)? Rely on the computer to cope with negative feelings (sadness, anger, etc.)? These are all signs of Internet addiction. Wrist, neck and back problems are associated with excessive tech use as well as weight gain, depression, and sleep disturbances.

Cognitive and mental functions are affected as well. David Ryan Polgar, digital lifestyle expert and tech ethicist, says we are suffering from "mental obesity" brought on by too much information from the digital world and too little time to process it. "Just like your body needs time to digest food, your mind requires adequate time to reflect," he says. Too much technology results in negative consequences for our ability to move beyond a superficial level of thinking and move toward a deeper, more meaningful, level of thought and process. "Our tech use is going through a similar evolution as our food consumption has; transiting from scarce to plentiful, which in turn leads to overconsumption," Polgar says. Give your mind time to digest the daily onslaught of information by taking a break from tech (which would also be a good time to get in some exercise. I'm just sayin'.).

6 Space Cleanse: *Smudging*

Smudging is an ancient tradition believed to cleanse negative energy from the air, an object, a room, or your body and mind. Smudging is thought to heal and bless, and to attract positive forces. A smudge stick is a bundle of herbs often bound by string. Burning a smudge stick of white sage, cedar, or sweet grass for a short period of time is thought to dissipate dark forces and cleanse negative energies. Smudging is an integral part of Native American purification rituals. Practitioners waft the smudge stick and use the smoke to cleanse their hands or an object, or they trail the smoke through a room for cleansing. You do not want to smudge frequently because inhaling smoke of any kind is not good for your lungs. Smudge your home if negative energies are pervasive. If you have had a difficult experience, are in a dark mood, or were forced to deal with toxic people, light a smudge stick. Place it in a suitable bowl. Bring your hands into the tendrils of smoke to cleanse them; scoop the smoke into your hands and bring it to your forehead to purify negative thoughts. You can buy smudge sticks online or at health food or spiritual stores.

NOTE: *Some smudge sticks can smell a bit like marijuana.*

7 Space Cleanse: *Doing Good Deeds is Good for Your Health and Well-being*

There is nothing more satisfying, cleansing, and loving than doing good deeds for others—whether it is helping a neighbor rake their leaves, donating money to a favorite charity, volunteering at an animal shelter, reading to kids at the library, or visiting residents in nursing homes. Acts of kindness do not have to be heroic. Small acts of daily kindness, like stopping your car to let someone cross the street, holding the door for someone, or calling a friend who is having a tough day, all help fulfill our innate desire to help others and make the world a better place. Many of our random good deeds are daily occurrences. We take care of our children, walk the dog, check on a neighbor, and hug a friend. It's true; these are the right things to do. And we should take a moment to appreciate that we are contributing to a kinder, gentler world.

Opportunities to do good deeds may be planned for or pop up out of nowhere. One day when I was walking into the gym I saw two dogs trotting behind a woman who was crossing the parking lot heading to the gym's front entrance. I assumed they belonged to her and thought it was odd she would bring her dogs to the gym. But as she walked through the front door, the dogs turned around and started trotting back across the parking lot. I realized they were either lost or abandoned. I wrangled them into my car and took them to animal control. They were very sweet dogs and clearly good friends, and I asked the animal control officer to be sure they stayed together. When I called the next day to see if their owners had come to find them I was told no, but there were several people interested in adopting them. I was happy they were safe and would hopefully find a good home, and I left it at that.

About two months later I was rewarded in an unexpected way. I was running in my neighborhood one Sunday morning and saw two young girls, both in their flannel pajamas bottoms, walking two dogs. As I ran by I realized the girls were walking the two dogs I had rescued from the parking lot at the gym. I stopped and asked the girls about the dogs. Yes, they said, we got them at the pound two months ago. We each have one of them and we live next door to each other. It was so cool to see how happy the dogs were with their new families, side by each.

8 Space Cleanse: *Recognizing Good Deeds*

Recognizing someone's good deeds, accomplishments, and talents is another way to dissipate toxic psychic fumes and promote positive outcomes. We all love to witness a good deed, a kind act, thoughtful generosity. In fact scientists have found that viewing others' good deeds inspires us to follow suit. It's like dominoes, in a good way. In one small study researchers split subjects into two groups. One group watched a nature video and the other watched an Oprah Winfrey inspirational story. The people who watched Oprah's video were more likely to volunteer for free for another experiment than the group who watched the nature clip. The Oprah group also gave higher ratings for feeling moved, being optimistic about humanity, and wanting to help others.

Read or watch inspirational stories. Go ahead, tell your son that he did a wonderful job raising money at the car wash for the local animal shelter. Thank a friend who has come to your aid. Acknowledge the nurses who are caring for your loved one (I know for sure that nurses always appreciate chocolate, but don't tell them I told you so). Appreciating the acts of others is uplifting for them and inspiring for you.

People want not simply praise but to be praiseworthy, not simply admiration but to be admirable, according to the values of their group or culture.

---

9 Space Cleanse: *Cleansing Reactions*

Cleansing habitual responses to people, places, or situations helps create a more positive outlook. Review your reactions to common irritants such as getting stuck in traffic, a rude salesperson, or a misbehaving child. Take control and responsibility for your responses. When a habitual response leads to negative consequences, it is time to examine your thoughts and feelings in that situation.

"Every time you are tempted to react in the same old way, ask if you want to be a prisoner of the past or a pioneer of the future."
– DEEPAK CHOPRA

Warren was a financial advisor who lived in New Jersey and worked in Manhattan, on Wall Street. No matter what route he took to drive into the city, he always hit bumper to bumper traffic. He would sit in the car fuming, frustrated and angry, day after day. His high-stress job and daily angry car ride contributed to his high blood pressure and an episode of angina (chest pain) that sent him to the emergency room. Warren realized he needed to make some changes. One change, recommended by a psychologist, was to look at his commute differently. Instead of being angry about the morning ride, Warren learned to expect the traffic. He left earlier and got audio books and music to entertain him in the car while he plodded through the Lincoln Tunnel. His stress levels dropped considerably, and he arrived at work in much better spirits. The same approach applies to people who push your buttons, upset you, or tick you off. Since you cannot change others, it is up to you to reform your negative habitual responses to these folks, to change to responses that do not cause you pain, anger, or agitation.

I often hear stories from friends about their family member's continual bad behavior. What can you do if you are stuck having to deal with this person? Expect the bad behavior. Remove yourself from the line of fire if you can. Maintain appropriate boundaries. Look at the person from a different angle. Maybe they are depressed, ill, or under a lot of stress. Be compassionate. Do not take their behavior personally. Humor is often helpful (maybe not to that person at that time, but to you).

> "We are what we think. All that we are arises with our thoughts. With our thoughts, we make the world."
>
> **–BUDDHA**

10 Space Cleanse: *Detoxify Your Yard*

Stop using herbicides and pesticides on your yard, garden, and woods. They are poisons. Humans and animals are dying because of them. These poisons are drastically altering the ecosystems in the world. Seek out organic, nontoxic, organic gardening and yard products.

11 Space Cleanse: *News Moratorium*

Take a news moratorium one or two days a week. I take regular news moratoriums, not because I like putting my head in the sand—though there are times I wish I could—but because the news is often so distressful and awful that I feel that my heart is shattering into a million pieces. The news can make us want to self-medicate with food, alcohol, or drugs. We act out because we feel helpless to help those in need. Add this to our daily personal dramas, and sometimes it feels overwhelming.

Give yourself a break from toxic news. We can only do the best that we can do. For some of us it is trying to live as kind and respectful a life as we can. For others it is donating to a favorite charity. Taking really good care of yourself is a wonderful place to start. The healthier you are, the better you will feel, the more energy you will have, and the better your mood and coping skills will be. A healthy mind and body mean you can do more to help others, and a healthy mind and body fuel the compassion to care for the planet and all with whom we share it.

My hope and my mission, overall, is this.

#12 Space Cleanse:
Decluttering Your Space
THE STRESS OF MESS

Admit it. One of your guilty pleasures is watching *Hoarders*. You know, that show on cable TV about people with hoarding disorders who are living among mountains of magazines, clothing, toys, appliances, or car parts. Their living spaces are filled to bursting with junk; their lives are filthy, unhealthy, and dangerous. The good part about the show is that it has brought great awareness to a disorder that had previously not been well recognized or addressed. From a nonclinical, less intense perspective, many of us have disorganized work spaces, cluttered cars and messy bedrooms. Psychological studies indicate that cluttered living spaces affect our mental and physical well-being. Humans are genetically wired to collect and keep things. Way back when there was no Amazon, Walmart, or Home Depot, our ancestors stored anything that could be of future use. In this century there is less need to hoard, yet we are collecting more stuff than ever before. Cluttered environments have been linked with stress, weight gain, fatigue, and anxiety.

Decluttering your space is an important part of cleansing your world. The kitchen cleanse was the first step. Now we move on to the rest of your living and working space. Start with one room at a time. Make a cleaning schedule. Bring in (recycled) garbage bags, sponges, boxes, packing tape, Sharpees (to label stuff). Ask family or friends to help if necessary. Donating clothing, books, electronics, and other items is a great way to put your collections of stuff to good use.

Toni is a beautiful, intelligent artist with a warm, infectious laugh that wraps itself around your heart and lights you up. She is ninety-six years old and has known me since I was ten. A bookshelf had broken in her home, so I went over to help fix it. Under her direction, I cleared out a bunch of shelves. Being a visual person, Toni looked carefully at each shelf height, the books, their sizes, and subjects. As we reorganized and cleaned the shelves Toni delighted in looking through books she had forgotten were on the shelf. After we finished, Toni sat there and said "Look what we've done. It's so satisfying." I asked her why reorganizing things felt so good. She thought about it for a minute and said, "Space. We take our space very seriously." She's right. Decluttering and reorganizing your space can be creative and freeing.

> "Stuff is important. You gotta take care of your stuff. You gotta have a place for your stuff. Everybody's gotta have a place for their stuff. That's what life is all about, tryin' to find a place for your stuff."
> **–GEORGE CARLIN**

It may take more than fourteen days to accomplish the decluttering and cleaning of these spaces. You may live in an apartment or condo and not have all this space to clean.

Whatever your circumstance, declutter, reorganize, and cleanse your stuff. Be ruthless.

Clean and reorganize your:

- **Workspace**
- **Living space**
- **Clothing drawers**
- **Junk drawers**
- **Car**
- **Closets**
- **Basement**
- **Attic**
- **Storage spaces**

#13 Space Cleanse: *Cultivate Creativity*

Being creative can have amazing impacts on mental and physical health, as well as unique anti-aging effects. Research shows that cultivating one's creativity helps reduce anxiety and depression, lowers cortisol levels, reduces stress, and improves cognitive function, all of which supports the body's innate cleansing systems and boosts immunity.

Seek out ways to express yourself creatively—for example, playing a musical instrument, dancing, sculpting, cooking, sewing, writing, wood-working, car detailing, or scrapbooking. You need not be artistic in the classical sense. Creativity in science, business, and politics has led to amazing discoveries and changes in the world. Open your mind and heart to new experiences that tap your personal style of creativity. You could learn a new language, take a knitting class, or make up games for children. Listen to new kinds of music. See a live play or musical. Enjoy a concert. Visit a local museum. Read a "real" book (as opposed to one on your tablet or computer). Join a choral group. Surround yourself with beauty. Put fresh flowers in your living room. Buy a piece of artwork to hang on your wall (it need not be expensive). Or, create a piece of art yourself.

From the Medical Journal *Generations*

"William Carlos Williams, known in particular for his poetry, was also a pediatrician. In his early sixties he suffered a stroke that prevented him from continuing to practice medicine. In addition, along with the 50 percent of the population who develop depression following a stroke, Williams developed a severe depression that hospitalized him for a year. But he pulled out of the depression, helped by writing poetry, and ten years later published his work Pictures from Brueghel and Other Poems *(1962), which was awarded a Pulitzer Prize. In his late-life poetry, Williams wrote about "old age that adds as it takes away." It was through his creative expression, his poetry, that he was able to add to his life while aging."*

#14 Space Cleanse: *Get a Massage*

Full disclosure: I have been a licensed massage therapist since 1987 and had a successful private practice in New York City for twenty years. So, I'm a big fan of massage therapy by qualified, licensed practitioners. Back in 1986, when I told people I was in massage school, I got many sniggers, sideways glances, and massage parlor jokes. We've come a long way since then, and medical massage therapy is now part of treatment plans for patients in many hospitals and clinics in the US and around the world. Massage therapists are licensed, as well as certified, in various modalities such as Swedish, sports, deep tissue, pre- and postnatal, Thai, and more. To date there is no evidence that massage breaks up or removes toxins from the body, though devotees may claim that is the case. What massage does do is improve relaxation and circulation, lower blood pressure, aid in pain management, and temporarily reduce pain, fatigue, and other symptoms associated with fibromyalgia. Massage therapy for cancer patients reduces pain, promotes relaxation, and boosts mood and quality of life. In my practice I saw patients' range of motion, muscle spasms, sleep patterns, and sport injuries improve considerably with regular massage therapy. Massage feels really good, and you deserve to feel really good. It can be expensive, so skip the mani-pedi or newest computer gadget and get a massage instead.

Mindful Moments
Don't Worry, Be Happy

Mindful Moments can help us be more positive, and they are an important part of cleansing toxic thought processes. Some of the Mindful Moments in *The Only Cleanse* are tasks, such as counting your blessings. Others are inspirational or humorous quotes to kick-start your day.

Humans have an innate need to maintain self-integrity and an overall sense of adequacy. Everyday life can ding and dent our self-confidence and leave us feeling frustrated or distressed. This can impair our ability to be happy and take a big toll on our health. Research shows that self-affirmations can curb these negative outcomes. Studies show that happier people have more stable marriages, stronger immune systems, higher incomes, and more creative ideas than their less happy peers.

Identifying what is important to you, such as religious beliefs, creativity, relationships with family or friends, kindness, and humor have been shown to help fortify self-confidence and self-image. Psychology experts say that self-affirmations can catalyze people's goals to live a healthier life. *The Only Cleanse* is all about a healthier life.

How Simple Affirmations Can Change Your Life

Margie is fifty years old, athletic, and competitive. She goes to the gym six days a week and takes two or three classes in a row. Susan, a long-time friend of Margie's, is also fifty and exercises regularly. She is not the athlete Margie is, and when they were younger Susan couldn't help but feel inadequate when Margie aced her tennis serves and Susan could barely hit the ball over the net. When they went skiing together Susan was completely humiliated, falling off the pommel lift fifteen times in a row before she made it to the top of the bunny slope, while Margie was shooshing down the black diamond trail. Recently,

POINT OF INTEREST

SELF AFFIRMATIONS

Self-affirmations can reassure people that they have integrity and that life, on balance, is okay in spite of adversity before them.

when they were out to lunch talking about their gym classes and commiserating about the changes their now-middle-aged bodies were going through, Margie said, "When I leave the gym I am thinking I didn't do enough cardio. I should have done heavier weights. I never feel like I have done enough."

Susan told Margie she had been working on her Mindful Moments. "I used to feel so embarrassed about my lack of athleticism, and I was so critical of how my body looked. One day I got to thinking about how unnecessarily miserable I was making myself. I started changing how I thought about me. Now when I finish exercising I say out loud to myself, "I am awesome! It is so great I made time for myself to be healthy today. Yay me!" If you look at Margie and Susan's thought processes, who is going to have the better day? Susan says since she has been doing her Mindful Moments she is happier and healthier than ever. A simple self-affirmation can literally change your life.

#1 Mindful Moment: *Laughter*

"A doctor gave a man six months to live. The man couldn't pay his bill, so he gave him another six months."

–HENNY YOUNGMAN

I chuckled when I read this Henny Youngman joke. Humor is part of our DNA. We all love to laugh. Laughing is not only fun, it's good for your health. Life does not always lend itself to laughter. Stress takes its toll on coping skills, health, and emotional and psychological well-being. It can lower immunity and trigger weight gain, insomnia, depression, and fatigue. We quite literally forget to smile and laugh. Can you remember the last time you had a full-out, hearty laugh?

There are many ways to help reduce stress, including, regular exercise, eating a healthy diet, and laughing. Laughing is one stress buster that is often overlooked. Research suggests that humor may reduce the release of stress hormones such as cortisol and adrenaline. In addition, laughter may boost the immune system. One small study found that people who watched a humorous video and laughed out loud (a term they called "mirthful laughter") experienced reduced stress levels and higher levels of natural killer cells (NK cells). NK cells attack tumor cells and viruses and are important players in the immune system. Intuitively, it makes sense that laughter is healing. It sure feels good. Instinctively, we go to great lengths to ignite a giggle in a baby or a child. There is a whole profession where people do nothing but try to make other people laugh. They are called comedians.

Dave Grotto, M.S. R.D.N., is a registered dietitian-nutritionist and the author of *The Best Things You Can Eat*. He has seen firsthand how humor affects health. "Laughter offers terrific healing effects," Grotto says. He has seen laughter make a real difference in people's perception of pain, mood, and stress levels. Dave first noticed the effects of humor on patients when he was working at the Block Center for Integrative Cancer Treatment in Evanston, Illinois. "I would see patients right after their visit with the doctor, which is not always the best time to be offering nutrition advice. They had just been talking about cancer, were freaked out, and did not want to hear about the benefits of eating broccoli."

So Grotto decided to try to turn that time into a "therapeutic moment." David would warmly embrace his patients, listen to what they had to say, and then try to crack them up. The patients and their families responded so well that David went on to become a Certified Laughter Leader and began incorporating laughter exercises into his treatment plans. "Laughter is contagious" says David. "Studies show the effects of deep, hearty laughter rival those of aerobic exercise, lower blood pressure, and boost the immune system." What if you don't feel like laughing? "That's easy," says David. "Just fake it until you make it." Start with laughter sounds such as "Ha, ha. Ho, ho.

Hee, hee." And repeat. Soon enough you will begin chortling at the silliness of it all, and then you'll really start laughing, he says.

It may feel weird to smile or laugh during difficult times. Allow yourself to experience all your emotions, including joy and laughter. Engage in activities that you enjoy. Watch funny movies or comedians. Hang out with people who amuse you. Keep a sense of humor about yourself. Laugh often. Keep perspective.

#2 Mindful Moment: *Letter of Gratitude*

Spend ten minutes writing a letter of gratitude to someone who has made a difference in your life. A real letter, with paper and pen. You don't have to send it or show it to anyone. Experts say that writing the old-fashioned way stimulates the brain and uses more areas of the brain and more neurological functions than typing on a keyboard.

#3 Mindful Moment: *What Went Well Today*

Write down three things that went well today and why they went well. One study found that people who did this exercise for six months were happier and less depressed .

#4 Mindful Moment: *Counting Blessings*

"When my bankroll is getting small,
I think of when I had none at all.
And I fall asleep
Counting my blessings"

–IRVING BERLIN

Sometimes in life, no matter how hard you try, it is difficult to find a blessing. Most of us at one time or another will go through harsh and heartbreaking experiences. Being appreciative of simple things like having a roof over your head, hot water (a personal favorite), or having access to food or a good friend can give you handholds in stormy seas. Because one thing is awful does not mean everything is. Counting blessings helps keep that in perspective. Focusing on the good and not dwelling on the bad has unexpected benefits, too. In one study people who counted their blessings exercised more than people who listed daily hassles.

#5 Mindful Moment: *Yay Me!*

Give yourself kudos for sticking with the 14-Day Plan. If you have not stuck with the plan, review what is not working for you and create a work-around.

#6 Mindful Moment: *Silly Affirmation*

"A day without sunshine is like, you know, night."

—STEVE MARTIN

#7 Mindful Moment: *Being Present*

Many years ago I went on a silent meditation retreat in Massachusetts. You were not allowed to speak with anyone, make eye contact, or connect in any way with another human for ten days (though some people "cheated," I did not.). It was far more difficult than I had anticipated. In the evenings we attended a dharma, a spiritual talk by the organizers of the retreat. Hungry to hear a human voice, the room was packed every night.

I learned a few things from this experience. One is that there are many kinds of meditation, and not all are for everyone. What I want to introduce here is this: Being in the present moment. Living in the now. I was in my twenties and struggling to get by in New York City. My thought process was often, "At this time tomorrow I will be done with this job. At this time next week maybe I will find a place to live. If I can just get through today, then tomorrow ..." I was not even close to living in the moment. It took some practice to break the habit of avoiding my minute-to-minute reality, but eventually I learned how to stay present, in the moment, and aware. Have you ever driven somewhere and not even remembered having driven there? That is a perfect example of not being present. Dangerous, too.

In daily life, being present includes stopping to appreciate your child's smile, listening to the songs of the birds, flowing with a jazz riff. Not everything in your present moment will be idyllic. Sitting in a crowded New York City subway you may notice the sadness in the face of the man across from you. Being present keeps you healthier and safer than when you are distracted. You will see the guy blow through the red light before you mindlessly step on the accelerator at the green. You will notice the dip in the pavement before you lurch into it and twist your ankle. You will remember to blow out the candle when you leave the room. You will be aware of a subtle pain in your chest and call the doctor. Practice being present, in the exact moment you are in. Right now.

#8 Mindful Moment: *Living Fully*

"Waking up this morning, I smile. Twenty-four brand-new hours are before me. I vow to live fully in each moment and to look at all beings with eyes of compassion."

–THÍCH NHẤT HẠNH

#9 Mindful Moment: *Literary Appreciation*

"The first thing I do in the morning is brush my teeth and sharpen my tongue."

–DOROTHY PARKER

#10 Mindful Moment: *Be Still*

"Wisdom comes with the ability to be still. Just look and just listen. No more is needed. Being still, looking, and listening activates the nonconceptual intelligence within you. Let stillness direct your words and actions."

–ECKHART TOLLE

#11 Mindful Moment: *Thoughts Are Things*

"The way you think, the way you behave, the way you eat, can influence your life by thirty to fifty years."

–DEEPAK CHOPRA

#12 Mindful Moment: *Be Beautiful*

"To be beautiful means to be yourself. You don't need to be accepted by others. You need to accept yourself."

–THÍCH NHẤT HẠNH

Beauty Sleep
  ⇛ **Time management**
  ⇛ **Tips for better sleep**

Sleep is another one of the body's phenomenal, integrated, all-natural detox systems.

A recent study found that when we sleep our brain detoxes itself by flushing out metabolic debris. Granted, the study was done on mice, but the researchers believe that this process is a restorative function that probably applies to humans as well. Brain neurons are very sensitive to their environment, so it is essential that toxins and waste generated during the day be cleared from the brain. Sleep appears to enhance the removal of potentially neurotoxic waste products that accumulate in the brain and central nervous system when we are awake.

The National Sleep Foundation says that most adults should be getting about seven to nine hours of sleep a night. Do you get that much sleep every night? The Centers for Disease Control and Prevention says insufficient sleep is a public health epidemic in the US. Not only does sleep deprivation interfere with the brain's natural detox time, it contributes to obesity, heart disease, diabetes, and other diseases. And let's face it, when we are sleep deprived we become just plain ornery.

I recently had a patient, Elsa, who complained about being exhausted, stressed and not getting enough sleep. She said she went to bed around eleven p.m. or midnight and had to get up early to get her kids on the bus before she went to her full time job at a veterinary clinic. What, I asked, are you doing all that time after dinner? Well, Elsa replied, I am on the computer, reading, playing games, trolling social media. My suggestion: Turn the computer off a good sixty to ninety minutes earlier than usual. The light generated by computers and tablets may make it difficult to get to sleep. Use the extra time to unwind and get to bed at a decent hour. Natural sleep is one of the free, "all-natural" secret ingredients to inner purification and renewal.

Tips for a Good Night's Sleep
1. **Stick to the same bedtime and wake-up time,** even on the weekends. This helps to regulate your body's clock and could help you fall asleep and stay asleep for the night.
2. **Practice a relaxing bedtime ritual.** A relaxing, routine activity right

before bedtime conducted away from bright lights helps separate your sleep time from activities that can cause excitement, stress, or anxiety, which can make it more difficult to fall asleep, remain asleep, or sleep soundly.

3. **Evaluate your room.** Design your sleep environment to establish the conditions you need for sleep: cool, quiet, dark, comfortable, and free of interruptions. Check your room for noise or other distractions, including a bed partner's sleep disruptions, such as snoring. A dry or hot environment, or light from a cable box, computer, or clock can impair sleep. Consider using blackout curtains, eye shades, ear plugs, "white noise," humidifiers, fans, and other devices to mask unwanted noise.

4. **Sleep on a comfortable mattress and pillows.** Make sure your mattress is comfortable and supportive. The one you have been sleeping on for years may have exceeded its life expectancy—about nine or ten years for most good quality mattresses.

5. **Use bright light to help manage your "body clock."** Avoid bright light in the evening and expose yourself to sunlight in the morning and during the day. In the daytime, take walks outside, sit by windows, and keep rooms well lit. This is especially important in the winter months, when daylight is shortened. Light helps regulate a small gland in the brain called the pineal gland. The pineal gland guides our circadian rhythms, sleep cycles, and inner biological clocks.

6. **Avoid alcohol in the evening.** Alcohol and cigarettes can disrupt sleep. Alcohol may help you fall asleep, but it interferes with deep, REM sleep and may cause shallow sleep, multiple awakenings, REM rebound (associated with nightmares or vivid dreams), or sweating.

7. **Wind down.** Your body needs time to shift into sleep mode, so spend the last hour before bed doing a calming activity, such as reading. For some people, using an electronic device such as a laptop can make it hard to fall asleep because the particular type of light emanating from the screens of these devices activates the brain. If you have trouble sleeping, avoid electronics before bed or if you wake up in the middle of the night.

Adapted from the National Sleep Foundation: http://www.sleepfoundation.org/ article/sleep-topics/healthy-sleep-tips

Stress Assess:

⇒ **Taking control of the sympathetic and parasympathetic nervous systems**

⇒ **The benefits of deep breathing**

Your body and mind are intimately connected. The stress reduction piece of *The Only Cleanse* Support System Plan is integral to its success. There are many breathing techniques that have health benefits. In the plan, you will be using a very simple, daily approach that you can engage anywhere, anytime. Periodic slow, deep breathing also known as pranayama, assists the lungs in their detoxification process and as a bonus signals your body to de-stress. Pranayama is the practice of voluntary breath control, consisting of slowly inhaling, pausing for a brief moment, and exhaling. It is often used in conjunction with meditation or physical postures like yoga. Pranayama is known to improve lung function and cardiovascular health, increase neural plasticity (improving neural connections in the brain), and boost the immune system. Deep breathing helps lower blood pressure and pulse rate and helps reduce symptoms of post-traumatic stress disorder.

One way deep breathing works is by stimulating the parasympathetic nervous system. In a sense your body has two nervous systems: the sympathetic and the parasympathetic nervous systems. Your fight or flight system, known as the sympathetic nervous system, is the response you have when you feel threatened. You know that surge of energy you feel when you've just had a near miss on the highway? Your heart races and you are breathing hard, your hands shake and your eyes dilate. This is your body's way of preparing you to either fight for your life or run for it. It is the classic stress response. Your body cannot differentiate between a real life-threatening situation or if you're just upset because your team got trounced in the Super Bowl. Stress is stress. Chronic stress can make us sick. Stress from work, home, kids, school, or whatever can trigger the release of pro-inflammatory compounds such as interleukin-6 and tumor-necrosis-factor alpha, which can contribute to illness and disease and accelerate the aging process. We can't avoid stress, but we can learn to manage it with the help of the second nervous system.

The second nervous system is called the parasympathetic nervous system. This is the chill-out-and-be-cool system. Deliberate deep breathing sends signals to the brain to turn off the sympathetic nervous system and activate the parasympathetic nervous system. When the parasympathetic nervous system is activated, your breathing and heart rate slow down, blood pressure lowers, and neurological changes that calm nerve transmission take place. The release of stress hormones such as cortisol and epinephrine is blunted, and the body literally switches gears. Deep breathing is something you can do periodically throughout the day to reap great stress-busting detox system-support rewards. It's free. You already know how to do it. It is a win-win situation. All you have to do is breathe. Just breathe.

Exercise

If you're already an avid exerciser, keep it up—or maybe now is a good time to mix it up and try something new. For those of you who have slacked off or do not exercise, it's time to take the plunge. You know regular exercise is critical for strong muscles and bones and a healthy heart and brain, and it reduces the risks of diabetes, dementia, cancer, heart disease, and obesity. Exercise also helps reduce stress and anxiety. Physical activity fires up the body's house-cleaning squads and boosts the body's detoxing organs like the kidneys, lungs, and liver.

If you've been sedentary for a while, get your healthcare provider to give you the green light to get on track. Start slowly. Begin by taking a beginner class in Zumba, yoga, spinning, or join a walking program. A brisk twenty-minute walk each day could be enough to reduce the risk of early death, reports a study of over 334,000 European men and women. The study in the *American Journal of Clinical Nutrition* in January of 2015 found that twice as many deaths may be attributable to lack of physical activity, compared to the number of deaths attributable to obesity. The authors estimate that doing exercise equivalent to a twenty-minute brisk walk each day could reduce the risk of dying by up to 30 percent.

Just get off your fanny and go! The benefits of regular exercise manifest pretty quickly. A woman called into my radio show on SiriusXM. Adele said she was so out of shape she could not make her bed without constantly stopping to rest. Once the sheets were changed and blankets spread, she was so exhausted she had to lie down on the newly made bed. Adele said it was scary being unable to accomplish simple household tasks. One day she decided to try a gym membership and began working with a personal trainer. She said that after only six weeks, three times a week, she was able not only to make her bed but to continue with her household chores without stopping. Your body loves to exercise and be healthy. It will reward you with strength, energy, health, and a better mood. There is no downside to regular exercise.

Your Body Doesn't Care

It is not within the scope of *The Only Cleanse* to lay out a personalized exercise plan for you. Your body's adaptations to cardiovascular and resistance exercise are nothing short of miraculous. You have to exercise. You must figure out a way to get moving and keep moving.

⟫ **I don't have time to exercise**
⟫ **I don't like sweating**
⟫ **I was going to take a BodyPump class but had a last-minute meeting**
⟫ **My knees hurt**
⟫ **I am having a bad hair day**

As brilliant as your rationalizations are for not exercising, *your body doesn't care*. Your body doesn't care if you are busy or are in a bad mood. It only knows whether it is moving or not.

HERE'S MY CONVERSATION WITH MYSELF THIS MORNING:

Me: It's really cold out, like in the twenties. I don't feel like running or going to the gym.

Me: Your body doesn't care if it's cold out.

Me: I was up until four a.m., writing.

Me: Your body doesn't care. It only knows if it is moving or not.

Me: Sigh . . . I know. Don't overthink it. Just do it.

Me: Yes. And you will feel really good when you are done. Now let's go.

And I did. And I was really glad I did and so was my body.

Once you start moving, once you get into it, once you see and feel the fantastic results, you will want to continue. Do you need to remotivate and push yourself sometimes? Yes. Will you always be glad you did? Yes. Enlist family and friends to join you. Make an appointment with yourself in your calendar to exercise: day, time and place. If you wait until you "have the time," it will never happen. I am being tough on this. I am tired of people's excuses for not exercising. It is terribly sad when I see people suffering from preventable diseases and disabilities because they did not exercise. Their regret is palpable. They want to turn back the clock. They say to me "I wish I had exercised. I wish this was not happening to me." I do, too. It is never too late, nor too early, to start exercising and making healthy choices.

Health Benefits of Exercise

- Improves sleep
- Has powerful anti-aging effects
- Makes you smarter
- Heightens creativity
- Strengthens the heart
- Improves circulation
- Boosts mood
- Reduces anxiety and depression
- Fires up the immune system
- Enhances the liver, kidneys, lungs, GI tract, and skin's detoxification and cleansing systems
- Reduces the risk for just about every common disease, including cancer, heart disease, diabetes, dementia, obesity, hypertension, stroke, etc.
- Increases your lifespan

This list could go on forever.

Preparing for the Cleanse

It takes about three to four weeks to make a habit and three to four weeks to break one. Be patient. Doing a bit of prep work for the 14-Day *Only Cleanse* Plan will get you ready and psyched to begin.

- ➤ **Prepping for the Kitchen Cleanse**
- ➤ **What food and cleaning chemicals to avoid**
- ➤ **Stock the pantry**
- ➤ **Get grandma's dishes (if she still has them, maybe she'll let you borrow a few)**
- ➤ **Buy new fitness clothing and gadgets**
- ➤ **Track exercise progress**
- ➤ **Keep a daily food record**
- ➤ **Drink hot lemon water**
- ➤ **Ready ... Set ...** *Go!*

"By failing to prepare, you are preparing to fail."

–BENJAMIN FRANKLIN

I. The Kitchen Cleanse

You will be cleaning and rearranging your kitchen, so start planning to spend some time doing this. You do not have to finish it all in one day.

Clean and rearrange the pantry, cupboards, refrigerator, and freezer. Obviously, a clean kitchen has fewer germs and gunk. I'm sure there are nooks and crannies in your kitchen that have not felt the swipe of a sponge in some time. Use as few toxic products as possible.

Help Finding Products with Safe Ingredients

The Environmental Protection Agency (EPA) has a voluntary program that reviews products and allows them to display an EPA "Design for the Environment" (DfE) label if they meet the EPA's criteria. The EPA says that when you see the DfE logo on a product it means that the DfE scientific review team has screened each ingredient for potential human health and environmental effects and that the product contains only those ingredients that pose the least concern among chemicals in their class.

You can check the EPA website for lists of products that meet their criteria: http://www.epa.gov/dfe/index.htm

Great DIY nontoxic cleaning ingredients include white vinegar, baking soda, seltzer, salt, and lemon juice. The "method" company has affordable, nontoxic household products available in stores like Walgreen's, Target, ShopRite, Big Y, and other grocery and drugstore chains. http://methodhome.com

The Good Guide has over 250,000 safe, healthy, green, and ethical products on their searchable website. Products include household, food, and babies' and kids' products. http://www.goodguide.com

The reason we have a kitchen makeover is twofold. First, a clean, well-organized kitchen is a more comfortable place to be, so you will be more inclined to prepare and cook healthy foods. Second, you will be reorganizing the kitchen to create a space that supports your new eating habits. It is easier if less healthy foods or trigger foods are not even on the premises, but it's not always feasible. Keeping them out of sight and in inconvenient places helps reduce consumption. Reorganize your cupboards so the healthy foods are in the front and the less healthy foods in the back or in a different, less convenient cupboard. You are more likely to grab the first box of cookies that greet you when you open the cupboard rather than digging behind them to find the air-popped popcorn.

Researcher Dr. Brian Wansink, author of *Slim By Design*, says that you are three times more likely to eat the first food you see in the cupboard than the fifth one. Wansink also found that by simply having people move their fruits and vegetables from the crisper bins to the top shelves of their refrigerators and move the less healthy foods to the crisper, they ate nearly three times more fruits and vegetables as they did the week before. New habits demand a new environment. Imagine when old habits kick in, and you find yourself standing in front of the cabinet that usually housed the cookies or chips. But now you're faced with whole-wheat crackers or brown rice. What you will do? You will stop and think. You will be more mindful of your choices. You will be creating new habits and patterns. You will continue down the road of awesomeness.

The Environmental Working Group recommends avoiding household products that contain these ingredients: nonylphenol ethoxylates (look for "non-ylphen" or "nonoxynol" within the ingredient name) and 2-butoxyethanol, butoxydiglycol, ethylene- or diethylene glycol butyl ether, diethylene glycol monomethyl ether, or methoxydiglycol.

Tip

You can reduce the amount of arsenic in rice with these tips:
- **Rinse rice before cooking**
- **Cook one cup of rice in six cups of water:** This reduces total and inorganic arsenic content by about 35 and 45 percent respectively, compared to uncooked (raw) rice.

Cleansing the Chemicals

Processed foods contain a lot of chemicals. These compounds affect texture, shelf life, mouth feel, taste, and color, and they act as thickeners or fillers. Some of the chemicals are fine to eat, others are not. The nonprofit organization The Center for Science in the Public Interest (CSPI) has brought toxic food additives to the publics' attention. Here is CSPI's Chemical Kitchen Guide:

CSPI Chemical Kitchen

Chemical Cuisine, Center for Science in the Public Interest
cspinet.org/reports/chemcuisine.htm

ACESULFAME POTASSIUM:
everyone should avoid
Artificial sweetener: *Chewing gum, diet soda, no-sugar added baked goods and desserts, tabletop sweetener (Sunett).*
- Poorly done safety tests in the 1970s suggested that acesulfame potassium may cause cancer. The Food and Drug Administration has refused to require better studies. Acesulfame potassium is often used together with sucralose.

ALGINATE, PROPYLENE GLYCOL ALGINATE: *safe*
Foam stabilizers, thickening agents: *Beer, candy, cheese, ice cream, yogurt.*
- They're made from seaweed (kelp).

ALPHA TOCOPHEROL (VITAMIN E): *safe*
Antioxidant, nutrient: *Oils.*
- Small amounts are added to oils to keep them from going rancid and to other foods to pump up the vitamin E.

ARTIFICIAL AND NATURAL FLAVORING: *certain people should avoid*
- *Breakfast cereal, candy, soda, many other foods.*

- Most of the hundreds of chemicals used to mimic natural flavors also occur in nature and are probably safe. But flavorings are often used in junk foods to mask the absence of natural ingredients (fruit, for example). Flavorings may include additives like MSG or HVP, to which some people are sensitive.

ASCORBIC ACID (VITAMIN C), ERYTHORBIC ACID: *safe*
Antioxidant, color stabilizer, nutrient: *Cereal, cured meat, fruit drinks.*
- It helps maintain the red color of ham, bacon, and other cured foods and it inhibits the formation of cancer-promoting nitrosamines (see Sodium Nitrite). Vitamin C is also used to pump up the vitamin content of foods like "fruit" drinks. Sodium ascorbate is a form of ascorbic acid that dissolves easily. Erythorbic acid is chemically similar to ascorbic acid, but it isn't a vitamin.

ASPARTAME (NUTRASWEET):
everyone should avoid
Artificial sweetener: *Frozen desserts, diet soda, tabletop sweetener (Equal).*
- Disturbing new Italian research in animals indicates that longterm

consumption may increase the risk of leukemia, lymphoma, and breast cancer. Although some people report dizziness, hallucinations, or headaches after drinking diet soda, only one of the controlled studies that looked for a link found one (to headaches). People with the rare disease PKU (phenylketonuria) need to avoid aspartame.

BETA-CAROTENE: *safe*
Coloring, nutrient: *Coffee creamer, margarine, butter, candy.*
• It's an orange pigment that the body converts to vitamin A.

BROMINATED VEGETABLE OIL (BVO): *caution*
Clouding agent, emulsifier: *Soft drinks.*
• It's occasionally used to keep flavor oils in suspension and give a cloudy appearance to citrus-flavored soft drinks. Small residues of BVO remain in body fat, but it's unclear whether they pose any risk.

BUTYLATED HYDROXYANISOLE (BHA): *everyone should avoid*
Antioxidant: *Cereal packages, chewing gum, oil, potato chips.*
• It retards rancidity in fats, oils, and foods that contain oil. According to the federal government's National Toxicology Program, it is "reasonably antici-

pated to be a human carcinogen," based on animal studies.

BUTYLATED HYDROXYTOLUENE (BHT): *caution*
Antioxidant: *Cereal, chewing gum, oil, potato chips.*
• It keeps oils from going rancid. In some animal studies it increased the risk of cancer; in others it decreased the risk.

CAFFEINE: *certain people should avoid*
Flavoring, stimulant: *Added to soft drinks and water. Occurs naturally in coffee, tea, cocoa, and chocolate.*
• It improves alertness and endurance, especially for the sleepdeprived, but can also interfere with sound sleep and make you jittery. If you have those symptoms, consider cutting back. Caffeine is mildly addictive; it causes headaches, irritability, or sleepiness when you go too long without it. High doses (more than 200 mg a day) may increase the risk of miscarriage or rare birth defects. Avoid caffeine if you are pregnant or are trying to become pregnant.

CALCIUM PROPIONATE, SODIUM PROPIONATE: *safe*
Preservative: *Bread, cake, pie, rolls.*
• Calcium propionate prevents the growth of mold on bread and rolls. The calcium is a nutrient and the propionate is safe. Since

calcium interferes with leavening agents, sodium propionate, which is also safe, is used in pies and cakes.

CALCIUM (OR SODIUM) STEAROYL LACTYLATE OR SODIUM STEAROYL FUMARATE: *safe*
Dough conditioner, whipping agent: *Artificial whipped cream, bread dough, cake filling, processed egg whites.*
- They strengthen bread dough so that it can be used in commercial bread-making machinery. They help produce a more uniform grain and greater bread volume. And they act as whipping agents in dried, liquid, or frozen egg whites and artificial whipped cream.

CARRAGEENAN: *safe*
Stabilizing and thickening agent: *Chocolate milk, cottage cheese, ice cream, infant formula, jelly.*
- It comes from seaweed. Large amounts have damaged the colons of test animals, though the small amounts in food are safe.

CASEIN, SODIUM CASEINATE: *certain people should avoid*
Thickening and whitening agent: *Coffee creamer, ice cream, ice milk, sherbet.*
- Casein is the principal protein in milk. Since it's used in some "non-dairy" and "vegetarian" foods,

people who are allergic to milk need to read labels carefully.

CITRIC ACID, SODIUM CITRATE: *safe*
Acid, chelating agent, flavoring: *Candy, soft drinks, fruit drinks, ice cream, instant potatoes, sherbet.*
- Citric acid is used as a tart flavoring and an antioxidant. Sodium citrate is a buffer that controls the acidity of gelatin desserts, jams, ice creams, candies, and other foods.

COCHINEAL OR CARMINE: *certain people should avoid*
Artificial coloring: *Beverages, candy, ice cream, yogurt.*
- Cochineal extract is a red coloring made from the dried and pulverized bodies of insects. Carmine is a more purified coloring made from cochineal. Both have caused rare allergic reactions that range from hives to life-threatening anaphylactic shock.

CORN SYRUP: *cut back*
Sweetener, thickener: *Beverages, cake, candy, cereal, cookies, syrup, yogurt.*
- Corn syrup—which consists mostly of dextrose—is a sweet, thick liquid made by treating cornstarch with acids or enzymes. It is sometimes dried and used as corn syrup solids in coffee creamers and other dry foods. It has no nutritional value

other than calories, it promotes tooth decay, and it is used mainly in foods with little nutritional value.

DEXTROSE (GLUCOSE, CORN SUGAR): *cut back*
Sweetener: *Bread, cookies, soft drinks.*
• When added to foods as a sweetener, it means empty calories and tooth decay.

EDTA: *safe*
Chelating agent: *Canned shellfish, margarine, mayonnaise, processed fruits and vegetables, salad dressing, sandwich spreads, soft drinks.*
• Modern food-manufacturing technology leaves trace amounts of metal in food (from metal rollers, blenders, and containers). EDTA (ethylenediamine tetraacetic acid) chelates the metals— that is, it traps impurities that would otherwise make oils rancid and break down artificial colors.

FERROUS GLUCONATE: *safe*
Coloring, nutrient: *Black olives.*
• It's used to generate a uniform jet-black color in olives and as a source of iron in foods.

FRUCTOSE: *cut back*
Sweetener: *"Health" foods and drinks.*
• Pure fructose is used as a sweetener in a small number of foods. Modest amounts are safe and

don't boost blood sugar levels. But large amounts consumed on a regular basis may raise the risk of heart disease by increasing blood triglyceride levels. They may also contribute to obesity because fructose affects hormones that regulate weight and may not curb appetite as much as an equal amount of glucose or sucrose.

FUMARIC ACID: *safe*
Tartness agent: *Gelatin dessert, pie filling, powdered drinks.*
• It adds tartness and acidity. To help it dissolve faster in cold water, it's often mixed with dioctyl sodium sulfosuccinate (DSS), an additive that appears to be safe.

GELATIN: *safe*
Gelling and thickening agent: *Beverages, cheese spreads, ice cream, powdered dessert mixes, yogurt.*
• It's a protein obtained from animal hides and bones that has less nutritional value than other proteins.

GLYCERIN (GLYCEROL): *safe*
Maintains water content: *Baked goods, candy, fudge.*
• It's a natural component of fat molecules. The body uses it for calories or to make more-complex molecules.

GUMS (ARABIC, FURCELLERAN, GHATTI, GUAR, KARAYA, LOCUST BEAN, TRAGACANTH, XANTHAN): *safe/certain people should avoid*
Stabilizers, thickening agents: *Beverages, candy, cottage cheese, dough, drink mixes, pudding, ice cream, salad dressing.*

- Gums are derived from natural sources (bushes, trees, seaweed, bacteria). Though poorly tested, they're probably safe. In rare instances, tragacanth has caused severe allergic reactions.

HIGH-FRUCTOSE CORN SYRUP (HFCS): *cut back*
Sweetener: *Soft drinks, many other foods.*

- This mixture of two sugars (it's about half fructose, half glucose) has largely replaced table sugar (sucrose) in soft drinks and many other foods because it's cheaper. Despite the urban myth, it's not worse for you than sucrose. Like other sugars, it promotes obesity, tooth decay, and—in people with high triglycerides—heart disease.

HYDROLYZED VEGETABLE PROTEIN (HVP): *certain people should avoid*
Flavor enhancer: *Beef stew, frankfurters, instant soup, sauce mixes.*

- It consists of plant protein (usually from soybeans) that has been chemically broken down into its amino acid components. HVP brings out the natural flavor of food. It contains MSG, and large amounts may cause reactions in sensitive people (see MSG).

INULIN: *safe*
Fat and sugar substitute, source of fiber: *Margarine, baked goods, fillings, dairy foods, frozen desserts, salad dressing.*

- It's a naturally occurring soluble fiber. Inulin doesn't raise blood sugar levels, so it may help people with diabetes. It also stimulates the growth of friendly bacteria in the large intestine.

INVERT SUGAR: *cut back*
Sweetener: *Candy, soft drinks.*

- This 50-50 mixture of two sugars (dextrose and fructose) is sweeter and dissolves better than sucrose (table sugar). It's nothing but empty calories and it contributes to tooth decay.

LACTIC ACID: *safe*
Controls acidity: *Carbonated beverages, cheese, frozen desserts, Spanish olives.*

- It inhibits spoilage in Spanish olives, balances the acidity in cheese, and adds tartness to frozen desserts, carbonated fruit flavored sodas, and other foods.

LACTOSE: *certain people should avoid*
Sweetener: Breakfast pastries, whipped topping mixes.
- Lactose (milk sugar) is nature's way of delivering calories to infant mammals. It's one-sixth as sweet as table sugar and is added to foods as a slightly sweet source of carbohydrates. Some adults have trouble digesting large amounts of lactose.

LECITHIN: *safe*
Antioxidant, emulsifier: *Baked goods, chocolate, ice cream, margarine.*
- It occurs naturally in soybean oil and eggs. It keeps oil and water from separating, retards rancidity, reduces spattering, and helps make cakes fluffier.

MALTITOL, MANNITOL: *cut back*
Sweeteners: *Candy, chocolate, jam, other sugar-free foods.*
- Like other sugar alcohols (sorbitol, xylitol), maltitol and mannitol are not well absorbed by the body, so they have fewer calories than table sugar. And they don't promote tooth decay. Large amounts (above 20 to 30 grams) may have a laxative effect.

MALTODEXTRIN: *safe*
Thickening agent, sweetener: *Canned fruit, salad dressing, instant pudding.*
- It's made from starch. Some maltodextrins are easily digested and absorbed, while others are chemically processed so that they are "resistant"—they can't be broken down by digestive enzymes. That makes them an isolated fiber. These resistant maltodextrins may help lower blood sugar levels, but don't help prevent constipation.

MONO- AND DIGLYCERIDES: *safe*
Emulsifiers: *Baked goods, candy, margarine, peanut butter.*
- They make bread softer, margarine more stable, and caramel less sticky. They also prevent the oil in peanut butter from separating.

MSG (MONOSODIUM GLUTAMATE): *certain people should avoid*
FLAVOR ENHANCER: *Chips, frozen entrées, restaurant food, salad dressing, soup.*
- MSG is the sodium salt of a common amino acid, glutamic acid. It brings out the flavor of foods. In the 1960s, researchers discovered that large amounts fed to infant mice destroyed brain cells. Careful studies have shown that a small number of people are sensitive to large

doses of MSG. Reactions include headache, nausea, weakness, and burning sensations in the back of the neck and the forearms. Other ingredients, like natural flavoring and hydrolyzed vegetable protein (HVP), also contain glutamate.

MYCOPROTEIN: *certain people should avoid*
Meat substitute: *Quorn brand foods.*
• It's made from processed mold (fungus) and is fashioned into imitation meat. A small percentage of people are sensitive to it. Reactions include vomiting, nausea, diarrhea, and, less often, hives and potentially fatal anaphylactic reactions. The FDA has refused to ban the use of mycoprotein or to require foods to bear a warning label about adverse reactions.

NEOTAME: *safe*
Artificial sweetener: *Diet soda, other diet foods.*
• It's chemically related to aspartame, but is used at much lower levels. It's also more stable (unlike aspartame, it can be used in baked foods). Neotame doesn't appear to be a problem for people with PKU (phenylketonuria).

OAT FIBER, WHEAT FIBER: *safe*
Isolated fiber: *Cereal, crackers, bread, muffins.*

• When a food ingredient contains the word "fiber," it's code for an isolated fiber. "Wheat fiber" and "oat hull fiber" are insoluble fibers, which may help prevent constipation but don't lower blood cholesterol or blood sugar. "Oat fiber" can be either insoluble or soluble fiber. Soluble fiber may lower blood cholesterol and blood sugar but doesn't prevent constipation.

OLESTRA (OLEAN): *everyone should avoid*
FAT SUBSTITUTE: *Lay's Light chips, Pringles Light chips.*
• It's a synthetic fat that isn't absorbed as it passes through the digestive system, so it has no calories. It can cause severe and incapacitating diarrhea, loose stools, abdominal cramps, and flatulence.

OLIGOFRUCTOSE: *safe*
Sweetener, bulking agent, emulsifier, prebiotic: *Frozen desserts, cookies, energy and granola bars.*
• It's either synthesized from sucrose or extracted from chicory roots. Like inulin and other soluble fibers, oligofructose is digested by bacteria in the large intestine, but not by human enzymes, and provides only about half the calories of fructose or other sugars. Oligofructose promotes

the growth of beneficial bifidus bacteria.

PARTIALLY HYDROGENATED OIL:
everyone should avoid
Fat: *Baked goods, fried restaurant food, icing, microwave popcorn, pie crust, shortening, stick margarine.*
• Vegetable oil can be made into a semisolid shortening or margarine by chemically adding hydrogen. The process creates trans fats, which raise LDL ("bad") cholesterol and lower HDL ("good") cholesterol, making them worse for your heart than saturated fat.

PHOSPHATES, PHOSPHORIC ACID:
safe
Acidulant, buffer, chelating agent, color stabilizer, emulsifier, nutrient: *Baked goods, breakfast cereal, cheese, cured meat, dehydrated potatoes, powdered food, soda.*
• While excessive consumption of phosphates may contribute to osteoporosis, only a small fraction of the phosphates in the diet comes from additives.

PHYTOSTEROLS OR PHYTOSTANOLS: *safe*
Cholesterol-lowerers: *Margarine (Benecol, Take Control), added to some orange juices and breads.*
• Plant sterols (or stanols) are found naturally in many nuts, seeds, vegetable oils, fruits, vegetables, and other foods. High doses can reduce the absorption of cholesterol from food, which can lower LDL ("bad") cholesterol levels by 10 to 15 percent. They may also slightly reduce the absorption of carotenoids.

POLYDEXTROSE: *cut back*
Bulking agent: *Reduced-calorie salad dressing, baked goods, candies, pudding, frozen desserts.*
• Polydextrose is made by combining dextrose (corn sugar) with the sugar alcohol sorbitol. The result is a slightly sweet, reduced calorie bulking agent. The FDA requires labels of foods that would likely provide more than 15 grams of polydextrose to carry a mild warning: "Sensitive individuals may experience a laxative effect from excessive consumption of this product."

POLYSORBATE 60: *safe*
Emulsifier: *Baked goods, frozen desserts, imitation cream.*
• Polysorbate 60 and its close relatives, polysorbate 65 and polysorbate 80, work like mono- and diglycerides. They keep baked goods from going stale, keep dill oil (a flavoring) dissolved in bottled dill pickles, help coffee creamers dissolve, and prevent oil from separating in artificial whipped cream.

POTASSIUM BROMATE: *everyone should avoid*
Dough strengthener: *White flour.*
- Most bromate rapidly breaks down to form innocuous bromides. However, bromate itself causes cancer in animals, and the tiny amounts that may remain in bread pose a small risk. Bromate was banned in the United Kingdom in 1989 and it isn't used in California (probably because foods made with it would have to carry a cancer warning).

PROPYL GALLATE: *everyone should avoid*
Antioxidant, preservative: *Chewing gum, chicken soup base, meat, potato sticks, oil.*
- It helps prevent fats and oils from spoiling and is often used together with BHA and BHT. The best animal studies hinted that it might cause cancer.

QUININE: *caution/certain people should avoid*
Flavoring: *Bitter lemon, quinine water, tonic water.*
- Quinine has been poorly tested as a food additive, and there's a slight chance that it causes birth defects, so pregnant women should avoid it.

SACCHARIN: *everyone should avoid*
Artificial sweetener: *No-sugar-added foods, tabletop sweetener (Sweet'N Low).*
- Animal studies have shown that it can cause cancer of the bladder, uterus, ovaries, skin, and other organs. It also appears to increase the potency of other cancer-causing chemicals. A National Cancer Institute study found that heavy-saccharin users had higher rates of bladder cancer than people who used smaller amounts.

SALT (SODIUM CHLORIDE): *cut back*
Flavoring, preservative: *Most processed foods.*
- It's probably the single most harmful substance in the food supply. In most people, a diet high in sodium increases blood pressure, which raises heart disease risk.

SODIUM BENZOATE, BENZOIC ACID: *certain people should avoid*
Preservative: *Carbonated drinks, fruit juice, pickles.*
- It appears to be safe, though sensitive people may experience hives, asthma, or other allergic reactions. Sodium benzoate may also exacerbate hyperactivity in some children. When sodium benzoate is used in acidic beverages that also contain ascorbic acid (vitamin C),

the two can form small amounts of benzene, which causes leukemia and other cancers. Under threat of a lawsuit, the leading soft-drink makers recently reformulated their beverages—typically fruit-flavored drinks—to prevent the reaction.

SODIUM CARBOXYMETHYLCELLU-LOSE (CMC): *safe*
THICKENING AND STABILIZING AGENT: *Beer, candy, diet foods, ice cream, icing, pie filling.*
• Among other things, it keeps sugar from crystallizing.

SODIUM NITRATE, SODIUM NITRITE: *everyone should avoid*
Coloring, flavoring, preservative: *Bacon, corned beef, frankfurters, ham, luncheon meat, smoked fish.*
• Sodium nitrite stabilizes the red color in cured meat and adds flavor. Without it, hot dogs and bacon would look gray. It also helps prevent the growth of bacteria that cause botulism. Adding nitrite to food can create small amounts of potent cancer-causing chemicals called nitrosamines, particularly in fried bacon. Companies now add ascorbic acid or erythorbic acid to bacon to keep nitrosamines from forming. While nitrate and nitrite introduce only a small cancer risk, they're still worth avoiding.

SORBIC ACID, POTASSIUM SORBATE: *safe*
Prevents mold: *Cake, cheese, dried fruit, jelly, syrup, wine.*
• Sorbic acid occurs naturally in many plants.

SORBITAN MONOSTEARATE: *safe*
Emulsifier: *Cake, candy, pudding, icing.*
• Like mono- and diglycerides and polysorbates, it keeps oil and water from separating. In chocolate candy, it prevents the discoloration that normally occurs when the candy is warmed up and then cooled.

SORBITOL: *cut back*
Maintains moisture; sweetener, thickening agent:
Diet drinks, no-sugar-added candy and chewing gum.
• It's a sugar alcohol that occurs naturally in fruits and is a close relative of sugar, though it's half as sweet. Because bacteria don't metabolize sorbitol well, it's used in no-sugar-added chewing gum, which doesn't cause tooth decay. Some diabetics use sorbitol-sweetened foods because it's absorbed slowly and doesn't cause blood sugar to increase rapidly. Moderate amounts of sorbitol may have a strong laxative effect, but otherwise it's safe.

STARCH, MODIFIED STARCH: *safe*
Thickening agent: *Baby food, gravy, soup.*

- It's used in many foods as a thickening agent and to keep solids suspended. Chemists can "modify" it with certain chemicals to make it dissolve in cold water. Starch and modified starches sometimes replace nutritious ingredients like fruit. One preliminary study indicated that modified starches can cause diarrhea in infants.

STEVIA: *everyone should avoid*
Natural sweetener,
Dietary supplement:
Diet and no-sugar beverages and foods.

- Small amounts are probably safe. High doses fed to rats reduced sperm production and increased cell proliferation in their testicles, which could cause infertility or other problems. Stevia can only be sold in the United States as a dietary supplement, but several companies are reportedly developing a stevia-derived sweetener and plan to seek approval from the FDA to use it in foods.

SUCRALOSE: *safe*
ARTIFICIAL SWEETENER: *No-sugar-added baked goods, frozen desserts, ice cream, soft drinks, tabletop sweetener (Splenda).*

- Unlike aspartame, sucralose can be used in baked foods. It appears to be the safest artificial sweetener, though no independent tests have been conducted.

SUGAR (SUCROSE): *cut back*
Sweetener: *Sweetened food, table sugar.*

- Sucrose (table sugar) occurs naturally in fruit, sugar cane, and sugar beets. Sugar, corn syrup, and other refined sweeteners make up about 15 percent of the average person's diet, but provide no vitamins, minerals, fiber, or protein. Sucrose and other refined sugars can promote obesity, tooth decay, and—in people with high triglycerides—heart disease.

SULFITES (SODIUM BISULFITE, SULFUR DIOXIDE): *certain people should avoid*
Bleach, preservative: *Dried fruit, processed potatoes, shrimp, wine.*

- Sulfiting agents prevent discoloration (in dried fruit, some fresh shrimp, and some dried, fried, or frozen potatoes) and bacterial growth (in wine). They also destroy vitamin B-1. Sulfites can cause severe reactions in sensitive people, especially those with asthma.

THIAMIN MONONITRATE: *safe*
Vitamin B-1: *Enriched flour, fortified*

cereal.
- It's perfectly safe.

VANILLIN, ETHYL VANILLIN: *safe*
Substitute for vanilla: *Baked goods, beverages, candy, chocolate, frozen desserts, gelatin.*
- Vanilla flavoring is derived from a bean, but vanillin, the major flavor component of vanilla, is cheaper to produce in a factory. A derivative, ethyl vanillin, comes closer to matching the taste of real vanilla.

XYLITOL: *cut back*
Sweetener: *Sugar-free chewing gum, low-calorie foods.*
- Like other sugar alcohols (maltitol, mannitol, sorbitol), xylitol is not well absorbed by the body, so it has fewer calories than table sugar. And it doesn't promote tooth decay. Large amounts may have a laxative effect.

Artificial Colorings

They're used almost exclusively in products with little nutritional value (candy, soda, etc.), so you won't be missing much if you avoid foods that contain them. The presence of colorings usually signals the absence of fruit or other natural ingredients. Colorings contribute to hyperactivity in some children.

BLUE 1. *Baked goods, beverages, candy.*
- Inadequate tests suggested a small cancer risk.

BLUE 2. *Beverages, candy, pet food.*
- The largest study suggested that it caused brain tumors in male mice. Unfortunately, the Food and Drug Administration concluded that there is "reasonable certainty of no harm."

CITRUS RED 2. *Skin of some Florida oranges.*
- Studies indicated that it may slightly increase the risk of cancer, but the coloring doesn't seep through the orange skin into the pulp. Because so little is used, you have only a minuscule increased risk if you eat the peel.

GREEN 3. *Beverages, candy.*
- A 1981 industry-sponsored study showed hints of bladder cancer in laboratory animals, but after the FDA reanalyzed the data, it concluded that the dye was safe. Fortunately, Green 3 is rarely used.

RED 3. *Baked goods, candy, cherries in fruit cocktail.*

- The FDA's recommendation that Red 3 be banned— based on evidence that it caused thyroid tumors in rats—was overruled by pressure from the Reagan Administration.

RED 40. *Candy, gelatin dessert, pastries, pet food, sausage, soda.*
- An FDA review committee acknowledged that the most widely used food dye caused problems in key mouse studies, but said that evidence of harm was not "consistent" or "substantial."

YELLOW 5. *Baked goods, candy, gelatin dessert, pet food.*

- The second most widely used coloring can cause mild allergic reactions, mostly in the small number of people who suffer allergic reactions to aspirin.

YELLOW 6. *Baked goods, beverages, candy, gelatin, sausage.*
- Industry-sponsored animal tests indicated that the third most widely used dye caused tumors of the adrenal gland and kidney. What's more, small amounts of several carcinogens can contaminate Yellow 6. Even so, the FDA concluded that the coloring doesn't endanger humans. Yellow 6 may also cause allergic reactions.

Additive Shopping Guide

SAFE
Alginate
Alpha tocopherol (Vitamin E)
Ascorbic acid (Vitamin C)
Beta-carotene
Calcium propionate
Calcium stearoyl lactylate
Carrageenan
Citric acid
Dioctyl sodium sulfosuccinate
EDTA
Erythorbic acid
Ethyl vanillin
Ferrous gluconate
Fumaric acid
Gelatin
Glycerin (glycerol)
Gums (arabic, furcelleran, ghatti, guar, karaya, locust bean, xanthan)
Inulin
Lactic acid
Lecithin
Maltodextrin
Modified starch
Mono- and diglycerides
Neotame
Oat fiber
Oligofructose
Phosphates
Phosphoric acid
Phytostanols

Phytosterols

Polysorbate 60, 65, 80

Potassium sorbate

Propylene glycol alginate

Sodium ascorbate

Sodium carboxymethyl-cellulose

Sodium citrate

Sodium propionate

Sodium stearoyl fumarate

Sodium stearoyl lactylate

Sorbic acid

Sorbitan monostearate

Starch

Sucralose (Splenda)

Thiamin mononitrate

Vanillin

Wheat fiber

CUT BACK

Corn syrup

Dextrose (corn sugar, glucose)

Fructose

High-fructose corn syrup (HFCS)

Invert sugar

Maltitol

Mannitol

Polydextrose

Salt (sodium chloride)

Sorbitol

Sugar (sucrose)

Xylitol

CAUTION

Artificial colorings (Citrus Red 2, Red 40)

Brominated vegetable oil (BVO)

Butylated hydroxytoluene (BHT)

Quinine

CERTAIN PEOPLE SHOULD AVOID

Artificial colorings (Yellow 5)

Artificial and natural flavoring

Caffeine

Carmine

Casein

Cochineal

Gums (tragacanth)

Hydrolyzed vegetable protein (HVP)

Lactose

MSG (monosodium glutamate)

Mycoprotein (Quorn)

Quinine

Sodium benzoate

Sodium caseinate

Sulfites (sodium bisulfite, sulfur dioxide)

AVOID

Acesulfame potassium

Artificial colorings (Blue 1, Blue 2, Green 3, Red 3, Yellow 6)

Aspartame (NutraSweet)

Butylated hydroxyanisole (BHA)

Olestra (Olean)

Partially hydrogenated oil

Potassium bromate

Propyl gallate

Saccharin

Sodium nitrate, sodium nitrite

Stevia

II. Stock your kitchen.

Use the shopping lists on pages 267–272 to stock the kitchen with the necessary foods and ingredients for the 14-Day Plan. Stock up on the nonperishable items and plan on buying the perishable foods every few days. Chances are you may already have many of the items in your pantry, such as herbs, spices, and condiments.

III. Dig out grandma's dishes.

My grandmother's dinner plates look almost like salad plates next to the su-persized Pier One dinner plates my sister gave me several years ago. Studies show that we eat less and are equally satisfied when we use smaller plates, cups, bowls, and utensils. The opposite is true, also. Bigger dishes and utensils make us eat more than we need. Researchers at Cornell University found that using a large serving spoon instead of a small one increased calories served by 14 percent. Over time this can add up to unwanted weight gain. Terry, a patient of mine, lost twenty pounds just by swapping out her big dishes for smaller ones. A cup of pasta loaded with vegetables looks like a large portion on a nine-inch plate, but like an appetizer on an eleven-inch plate. Simple tricks like these can help us manage portion sizes and weight and help reset our visual expectations.

Tip

⇛ If you are not hungry you can skip the afternoon snack.
⇛ If you do not have a set of smaller dishes, you can always go to a thrift store and pick up a few interesting dishes of smaller size.

IV. Purchase at least one new set of exercise clothing and a pair of appropriate athletic socks and shoes.

I love trying out a new pair of running shoes or yoga pants. My friend Hannah told me that her husband asked her if she wanted a new computer for Christmas. She laughed and said, "I'd really rather spend the money on a new Lululemon outfit." For those of you who are unaware, Lululemon is a trendy, rather expensive line of fitness clothing. The brand is fashionable, but you don't have to buy expensive workout clothing. Buy what you can afford, that is of decent quality in terms of fabric and fit, and it's what you like. Between you and me, I get a kick from the workout clothes I buy at Target.

Our body image affects our motivation and ability to exercise, studies say. What we wear can help us to feel better about ourselves, which in turn spurs us to continue to exercise. Body image is an important factor affecting our self-esteem and our motivation to exercise. We live in a society where feeling good about ourselves and our bodies is discouraged. We feel quite comfortable criticizing our physical appearance with cruel comments such as: *My thighs are huge; my belly is disgusting; I hate my arms,* and on and on. Models, entertainers, celebrities, and other highly visible people we see in the media set ridiculously unreal and unattainable standards of how we are "supposed" to look. Do not be fooled by the photos you see in magazines or online. They are all photoshopped to the nth degree. It is tough not to compare oneself to these images, but we really need to stop doing it. I was chatting with a few colleagues the other day about how we perceive ourselves. Kay, a professor in her midforties, said "I was looking at some old photos of myself in my twenties and I looked great. What was I complaining about back then?" Our bodies are working so hard every second of every day to keep us healthy and alive. We must respect, appreciate and love them. Remember, you deserve to feel fabulous about yourself. Wearing clothes you feel good in is a part of that.

NOTE: *If you feel paralyzed by your concern over how your body looks and are fearful to exercise or wear exercise attire because of this, it is time to seek professional help. http://therapists.psychologytoday.com/rms/? tr=Hdr_Brand*

V. Buy a fun fitness gadget that helps track your workouts.

Tracking your exercise works to keep you motivated in several ways. First, you set goals for yourself such as how many miles a week you want to run or how many days of the week you will be taking a yoga class. Monitoring your progress and achievements is a terrific way to boost motivation and self-confidence. Leigha, a fitness student of mine, uses an app that tracks her running mileage and posts it to her computer calendar. "I get a jolt of satisfaction every time I see how far and how often I run," she says. My friend Ann, an exercise physiologist, uses an old-fashioned wall calendar and puts star or smiley-face stickers on each day she exercises. "The stickers reinforce my good exercise behavior," Ann said. She laughed. "It works for five-year-olds, and it works for me."

Fitness gadgets run from inexpensive pedometers that track your steps to higher tech items that track mileage, pace, sleep, movement, heart rate, and more. Fitness trackers such as fitness wristbands, smartwatches, fitness fobs that clip onto your belt or shoe, and onboard trackers for cyclists are a booming business right now, so there will be many new gadgets to choose from in the coming years.

Pop Quiz

You have thirty seconds to answer this question:
What did you eat two days ago?

BEEEEP: Time's up. Did you remember everything you ate two days ago? Chances are you did not. It is as important to record everything you eat each day as it is to track your exercise activity. Keeping a daily record of your food intake helps you become a mindful eater. We eat mindlessly and often have no memory of what we ate just a few hours ago. The act of having to record your choices makes you stop and think about them. This relates to the process of cleansing because you are replacing mindless, unconscious behaviors with thoughtful, conscious choices. You will be taking control of your decision-making processes, and you are far more likely to make healthier choices when you have to record them. Food records also help you identify trouble spots like parties or nighttime snacking and pin down emotional triggers like boredom, anger, or sadness.

"Every time I see an adult on a bicycle, I no longer despair for the future of the human race."
–H. G. WELLS

Many of the fitness gadgets double as food trackers and upload the information to your computer. You can download apps to your phone or tablet that track your food intake and exercise. Free apps include: LoseIt, MyFitnessPal, or SuperTracker. Old fashioned pen and paper is always an option. Keep track daily.

VI. Join a fitness center

Find a local YMCA, dance or yoga studio, or senior center, hire a qualified personal trainer, and/or enlist someone with whom to walk, run, or go to the gym. Set up a schedule and put it in your calendar. Have a plan B. For example: Plan A might be to take a nine a.m. Tabata class, but your plans are thwarted by a howling blizzard. Plan B is to have exercise DVDs at home you can do instead. Ask friends and fitness instructors what their favorite home exercise DVDs are. You can take many exercise DVDs out of the library and try them before you buy them.

Tip

If you are in charge of the heat in your home, consider purchasing a programmable thermostat. You can have your heat turn on and off at specific times. It saves money and if you are getting up early to exercise, you can program the thermostat to turn on the heat so you can climb out of bed into a warm room. It is very difficult to get up and go to the gym, do an exercise DVD, or go running outside if your house is freezing, or it's pitch dark in the dead of winter. I don't love getting up at the crack o' dark to exercise. Because of my work commitments I was forced into this kind of schedule for several years. The programmable thermostat saved me. Sometimes simple things can make a big difference.

The magazine *Consumer Reports* says that programmable thermostats can trim about 180 dollars a year off your energy bills. In 2014 the prices for these thermostats in the U.S. ranged from thirty-eight dollars to close to eight-hundred dollars. Most live in the midrange.

If you have physical issues that affect your ability to exercise, speak with your healthcare provider about a referral to physical or occupational therapy.

Tip

- **Plan ahead.**
- **Schedule exercise time in your calendar each day.**
- **If something comes up in the middle of the 14-Day period and you have no choice but to veer off the Plan, don't freak out. Stay on track with as much of the plan as you can. For example: Do the Mindful Moments, and hop back on board as soon as you can.**

VII. Each day begins with eight ounces of hot lemon water.

Squeeze half a fresh lemon into eight to ten ounces of hot water (tea temperature). You can pre-squeeze fresh lemon juice and keep it tightly covered in the refrigerator for three or four days, or freeze it in an ice cube tray. You can add small cubes of frozen fresh lemon juice to your hot water. They will melt quickly and bring the hot water to a comfortable drinking temperature. There are no scientific studies showing that this particular beverage directly helps the naturally cleansing support systems in your body, other than to help maintain good hydration. I decided to include this as a part of *The Only Cleanse* because friends from around the globe, including in Greece and China, tell me their parents and grandparents had them drink warm lemon water either to jumpstart the day or when they were ill.

Anecdotally, I am hearing reports of people drinking the lemon water with interesting results. Recently I spoke with Marshall, a twenty-eight-year-old entrepreneur in New York City. He's a go-getter who lives the typical fast-paced New York City lifestyle: working long days, traveling often, going out just about every night. Marshall told me he had been drinking eight or nine large cups of coffee a day. Still, he was fatigued. "I couldn't imagine that drinking that much coffee was healthy for me," he said. So instead of two twenty-four-ounce mega-coffees first thing the in the morning, he opted for a mug of hot lemon water. To his surprise his coffee cravings diminished and he began feeling less stressed and fatigued. Now he says he consumes about two cups of coffee a day, and he is feeling more energized and sleeping better.

Hot lemon water is warm and soothing and a good way to kickstart the day's hydration. Lemons not only contain vitamin C but also a compound called limonene that research suggests may have anti-inflammatory, bactericidal, and anticancer effects.

Each Day Includes:
- ➠ Teeth brushing, two to three times a day
- ➠ Flossing, once a day
- ➠ Mouth rinse with plain water, once or twice a day
- ➠ Cardiovascular exercise, fifteen to sixty minutes, five or six days a week (depending on your fitness level and schedule). This can be a class, exercise DVD, walking, running, dancing, swimming, etc.
- ➠ Strength training, two to four days a week. Outside of a class, this should be initially supervised by a qualified trainer

⮞ **Flexibility:** stretching after each exercise session or participating in classes like yoga

It is essential to keep your skin healthy and properly hydrated so it can do its job in protecting you and keeping you looking your best as well. I asked my colleague, dermatologist Dr. Doris Day, Clinical Associate Professor of Dermatology at NYU School of Medicine and author of *Forget the Facelift*, what we can do on a daily basis to help our skin help us. Here are her special tips, known as "**DDTIPS**," provided exclusively for *The Only Cleanse*:

DDTIPS:

Cleanse properly. Use products that will remove makeup, pollution, and other particles from your skin but won't overstrip your skin or leave it dry and irritated. The days of "squeaky clean" are old news. Now we want soft, supple skin that feels moist and healthy.

Exfoliate on a regular basis. This helps stimulate new, younger skin cells and is great for your skin, but overdoing it will leave your skin irritated and raw. Once a week is good for most people; you may need more or less depending on other products you're using and the sensitivity of your skin.

Moisturize. Most people need a richer moisturizer at night, since you lose more water from your skin at night. Your morning moisturizer should also contain SPF. Men need to moisturize, too, by the way!

Use sunscreen daily. It's so much easier to prevent a problem than to fix it afterward. Chronic sun exposure and sunburns damage the skin and increase risks of premature aging of the skin and skin cancer. But they can also affect water balance and other critical roles of the skin.

Shower or bathe daily. Vegan products are optimal, since in general they do not contain toxic ingredients and are cruelty free.

Here are just a few of the companies who have cruelty-free and/or vegan beauty products. There are many more than are listed here.

➥ **PETA:** Has a searchable database: *http://features.peta.org/cruelty-free-company-search/index.aspx*

➥ **The Beauty Counter:** A company working to eliminate toxic or potentially harmful ingredients from their beauty products. To date they have banned more than fifteen hundred ingredients from their products. *www.beautycounter.com*

➥ **Pangea, The Vegan Store:** Offers a selection of high-quality, completely cruelty-free vegan (non-animal-derived) products. *http://www.veganstore.com/category/vegan-soaps-and-bath*

➥ **Tom's of Maine:** Making cruelty-free, sustainable products with no artificial colors, flavors, preservatives, or fragrances. *http://www.tomsofmainestore.com*

➥ **Lush:** Making effective products from fresh, organic fruit and vegetables, the finest essential oils, and safe synthetics. *http://www.lushusa.com*

➥ **Trader Joe's:** Carries some cruelty-free and vegan products. *http://www.traderjoes.com*

➥ **Aveda:** An environmentally responsible company. Their products are formulated without parabens, phthalates, and sodium lauryl sulfate, and they are cruelty free. *http://www.aveda.com/index.tmpl*

➥ **The Good Guide:** Has over two hundred fifty thousand safe, ethical, green, and healthy product reviews based on scientific ratings. *http://www.goodguide.com*

Ready ... Set ... Go!
Prepare for tomorrow, every day:

If you have children, get them organized, and then focus on your needs.

1. Pack your gym bag or lay out your workout clothes.
2. Prep or plan ahead for tomorrow's lunch.
3. Organize your personal space. Clean out and organize your brief-case, backpack, or purse. Assemble paperwork or other necessities for the following day.
4. Take a shower or bath.
5. Wash/cleanse your face.
6. Brush and floss your teeth.
7. Drink a glass of water.
8. Nighttime affirmation: I will sleep well. I will have pleasant dreams. Repeat.
9. Lie in bed:
   a. Mentally prepare yourself for your workout tomorrow (when, where, etc.) For example: I am getting up and taking the 6:30 a.m. Zumba class tomorrow.
   b. Take a deep breath and exhale stress and negativity. Repeat three times.
   c. Progressive relaxation: Bring your mind into your body and go bit by bit to each part of your body, letting go of any tension. You can go head to toe or vice versa. Relax forehead, jaw, shoulders, neck, arms, hands, etc. If you feel your mind starting to wander, bring it back to your body and start over again.
   d. If you awaken in the night and have trouble going back to sleep, repeat the progressive relaxation.

Let's begin the plan.

The 14-Day Only Cleanse Plan

REMEMBER: You can eat whatever foods fit the criteria set forth in the Intro to the 14-Day Only Cleanse Support System Plan chapter, page 127–128. If you do not like smoothies, then go for the whole grain cereal option or whole grain toast with peanut butter and a banana. If you do not want to forage for chia seeds, skip them. You can mix and match meal options from the lists on page 263–266.

A Note about Portions

The recipes include the number of servings, for example "four to six servings," which suggests portion size. This does not mean you have to eat as much or as little as one-sixth of the dish if it serves six. Your weight, height, and activity level all factor in to how much you need to eat at each meal. If you do not need a midafternoon snack, you can skip it (but don't go for more than three to five hours between meals or snacks, or you will get over-hungry). Eating slowly and mindfully will help you tune in to your body's needs. *The Only Cleanse* wants you to reset your notion of fullness from considering being "stuffed" as normal to feeling satisfied instead.

Prepping for Today's Only Cleanse Support System Plan

Once you begin to integrate *The Only Cleanse* Support System Plan into your daily routine you will find the pieces such as Mindful Moments, food planning, and Stress Assess become a natural part of your day. Set an alarm on your phone to remind you to Stress Assess, drink water, and breathe.

Prepare for tomorrow:

If you have children, get them organized, and then focus on your needs.

1. Pack your gym bag or lay out your workout clothes.
2. Prep or plan ahead for tomorrow's lunch.
3. Organize your personal space. Clean out and organize your briefcase, backpack, or purse. Assemble paperwork or other necessities

for the following day.

4. Take a shower or bath.

5. Wash/cleanse your face.

6. Brush and floss your teeth.

7. Drink a glass of water.

8. Nighttime affirmation: I will sleep well. I will have pleasant dreams. Repeat.

9. Lie in bed:

    a. Mentally prepare yourself for your workout tomorrow (when, where, etc.). For example: I am getting up and taking the 6:30 a.m. Zumba class tomorrow.

    b. Take a deep breath and exhale stress and negativity. Repeat three times.

    c. Progressive relaxation: Bring your mind into your body and go bit by bit to each part of your body, letting go of any tension. You can go head to toe or vice versa. Relax forehead, jaw, shoulders, neck, arms, hands, etc. If you feel your mind starting to wander, bring it back to your body and start over again.

    d. If you awaken in the night and have trouble going back to sleep, repeat the progressive relaxation.

DAY

Space Cleanse #1:
The Kitchen Cleanse, page 167

Mindful Moment #1:
Laughter, page 156

Today and Tomorrow:
Exercise is scheduled. The best time to exercise is when you will do it; make an appointment with yourself to exercise. Put it in your calendar. **Cardio:** minimum ten minutes if you are a beginner. At least forty-five to sixty minutes if you are fit. Flexibility/stretching. If you are listening to music during your workout add a new, upbeat song to your playlist.

Reminder:
Record everything you eat today.

Upon awakening:
Sit quietly. Take three slow, deep breaths.
Say your Mindful Moments.
Mentally review your food and fitness plans for the day (we tend to make better decisions in the morning, so this is a good time to set the tone for the day).
Brush teeth.
Morning shower or bath if you are a morning bather.
Eight ounces hot water with fresh lemon juice.

DAY 1 MENU

BREAKFAST

Get Well Good Morning Smoothie

Tea: green or black

Optional: one or two teaspoons of organic sugar or honey with unsweetened soy, almond, or rice milk

MIDMORNING

Rinse mouth with plain water.

Drink eight ounces water, seltzer, or tea (hot or cold, black, green, herbal).

LUNCH

Lentil Artichoke Soup

Slice of whole grain bread

MIDAFTERNOON

Stand up: March in place, do jumping jacks, or climb stairs for three to five minutes nonstop.

Eight ounces or more of water, tea, seltzer.

LATE AFTERNOON

This only takes a minute or two. You DO have the time.

Stress Assess: Check body for tension; unfurrow brow, relax jaw, drop shoulders, lift sternum, sit/stand up straight. Take three slow, deep breaths.

Stand up: March in place, do jumping jacks, or climb stairs for three to five minutes nonstop. Repeat today's Mindful Moments. Rinse mouth with plain water.

SNACK

¼ cup trail mix

Tea or water

DINNER

One Pot Pasta Primavera

Herbal tea: peppermint, chamomile, or ginger (or another decaffeinated herbal tea you enjoy)

Moment of appreciation: Thank yourself, or whomever, for preparing the food. Appreciate the color, aroma, and texture of the food. Eat slowly, mindfully, appreciatively.

Sit down when eating.

No technology (TV, phone, tablet, etc.) at the dinner table, whether you are eating with others or alone.

Prepare for tomorrow:

If you have children, get them organized, and then focus on your needs.

1. Pack your gym bag or lay out your workout clothes.

2. Prep or plan ahead for tomorrow's lunch

3. Organize your personal space. Clean out and organize your briefcase, backpack, or purse. Assemble paperwork or other necessities for the following day.

4. Take a shower or bath.

5. Wash/cleanse your face.

6. Brush and floss your teeth.

7. Drink a glass of water.

8. Nighttime affirmation: I will sleep well. I will have pleasant dreams. Repeat.

9. Lie in bed:

   a. Mentally prepare yourself for your workout tomorrow (when, where, etc.). For example: I am meeting Pam at the gym at 6:00 a.m.

   b. Take a deep breath and exhale stress and negativity. Repeat three times.

   c. Progressive relaxation: Bring your mind into your body and go bit by bit to each part of your body, letting go of any tension. You can go head to toe or vice versa. Relax forehead, jaw, shoulders, neck, arms, hands, etc. If you feel your mind starting to wander, bring it back to your body and start over again.

   d. If you awaken in the night and have trouble going back to sleep, repeat the progressive relaxation.

DAY

Space Cleanse #2:
Powering Positivity (Angels & Demons), page 141

Mindful Moment #2:
Letter of Gratitude, page 158

Today and Tomorrow:
Exercise is scheduled. The best time to exercise is when you will do it.
   Make an appointment with yourself to exercise. Put it in your
   calendar. **Cardio:** minimum ten minutes if you are a beginner. At
   least forty-five to sixty minutes if you are fit. Flexibility/stretching.
   If you are listening to music during your workout add a new, upbeat
   song to your playlist.

Reminder:
Record everything you eat today.

Upon awakening:
Sit quietly. Take three slow, deep breaths.
Say your Mindful Moments.
Mentally review your food and fitness plans for the day (we tend to
   make better decisions in the morning, so this is a good time to set
   the tone for the day).
Brush teeth.
Morning shower or bath if you are a morning bather.
Eight ounces hot water with fresh lemon juice.

DAY 2 MENU

BREAKFAST

1½ cups of shredded wheat,
¾ cup unsweetened soy milk,
strawberries, ½ banana,
two tablespoons ground
flax seeds, one tablespoon
chopped walnuts

Tea: green or black

Optional: one or two teaspoons
of organic sugar or honey with
unsweetened soy, almond, or
rice milk

MIDMORNING

Rinse mouth with plain water.
Drink eight ounces water, seltzer,
or tea (hot or cold, black, green,
herbal).

LUNCH

Lentil Artichoke Soup
Slice of whole grain bread
Water or tea

MIDAFTERNOON

Stand up: March in place, do
jumping jacks, or climb stairs for
three to five minutes nonstop.
Eight ounces or more of water,
tea, or seltzer

LATE AFTERNOON

This only takes a minute or two.
You DO have the time.

Stress Assess: Check body for
tension; unfurrow brow, relax
jaw, drop shoulders, lift sternum,
sit/stand up straight. Take three
slow, deep breaths.

Stand up: March in place, take a
walk, do jumping jacks, or climb
stairs for three to five minutes
nonstop.

Repeat today's Mindful Moments.
Rinse mouth with plain water.

SNACK

Edamame hummus and carrots,
celery, broccoli crudités
Tea or water

DINNER

Sesame Peanutty Noodles

Herbal tea: peppermint,
chamomile, or ginger (or
another decaffeinated herbal
tea you enjoy)

Moment of appreciation: Thank
yourself, or whomever, for
preparing the food. Appreciate
the color, aroma, and texture of
the food. Eat slowly, mindfully,
appreciatively.

Sit down when eating.

No technology (TV, phone, tablet,
etc.) at the dinner table,
whether you are eating with
others or alone.

Prepare for tomorrow:

If you have children, get them organized, and then focus on your needs.

1. Pack your gym bag or lay out your workout clothes
2. Prep or plan ahead for tomorrow's lunch
3. Organize your personal space. Clean out and organize your briefcase, backpack, or purse. Assemble paperwork or other necessities for the following day.
4. Take a shower or bath.
5. Wash/cleanse your face.
6. Brush and floss your teeth.
7. Drink a glass of water.
8. Nighttime affirmation: I will sleep well. I will have pleasant dreams. Repeat.
9. Lie in bed:
   a. Mentally prepare yourself for your workout tomorrow (when, where, etc.). For example: I am getting up and taking the 6:30 a.m. Cycling class tomorrow.
   b. Take a deep breath and exhale stress and negativity. Repeat three times.
   c. Progressive relaxation: Bring your mind into your body and go bit by bit to each part of your body, letting go of any tension. You can go head to toe or vice versa. Relax forehead, jaw, shoulders, neck, arms, hands, etc. If you feel your mind starting to wander, bring it back to your body and start over again.
   d. If you awaken in the night and have trouble going back to sleep, repeat the progressive relaxation.

DAY

Space Cleanse #3:
BOUNDARIES (CLEANSING OUR LIVES), page 144

Mindful Moment #3:
What Went Well Today, page 158

Today and Tomorrow:
Exercise is scheduled. The best time to exercise is when you will do it.
Make an appointment with yourself to exercise. Put it in your calendar.
Cardio: minimum ten minutes if you are a beginner. At least forty-five to
sixty minutes if you are fit. Flexibility/stretching. If you are listening to
music during your workout add a new, upbeat song to your playlist.

Reminder:
Record everything you eat today.

Upon awakening:
Sit quietly. Take three slow, deep breaths.
Say your Mindful Moments.
Mentally review your food and fitness plans for the day (we tend to
make better decisions in the morning, so this is a good time to set
the tone for the day).
Brush teeth.
Morning shower or bath if you are a morning bather.
Eight ounces hot water with fresh lemon juice.

DAY 3 MENU

BREAKFAST
Blueberry Chia Oat Smoothie
Tea: green or black
Optional: one or two teaspoons
of organic sugar or honey with
unsweetened soy, almond, or
rice milk

MIDMORNING
Rinse mouth with plain water
Drink eight ounces water, seltzer,
or tea (hot or cold, black, green,
herbal)

LUNCH
One Pot Pasta Primavera redux as
pasta salad: drizzle with sherry
or champagne vinegar, pinch
of salt to taste. Add chopped artichoke hearts (canned or jarred).
Water or tea

MIDAFTERNOON
Stand up: March in place, do
jumping jacks, or climb stairs for
three to five minutes nonstop.
Eight ounces or more of water,
tea, or seltzer

LATE AFTERNOON
This only takes a minute or two.
You DO have the time.
Stress Assess: Check body for
tension; unfurrow brow, relax

jaw, drop shoulders, lift sternum, sit/stand up straight. Take
three slow, deep breaths.
Stand up: Take a walk, march
in place, do jumping jacks, or
climb stairs for three to five
minutes nonstop.
Repeat today's Mindful Moments.
Rinse mouth with plain water.

SNACK
Edamame hummus and tortilla
chips (about eight to ten chips)
Tea or water

DINNER
Vegetarian chili
Whole grain crackers
Herbal tea: peppermint, chamomile,
or ginger (or another decaffeinated
herbal tea you enjoy)
Moment of appreciation: Thank
yourself, or whomever, for
preparing the food. Appreciate
the color, aroma, and texture of
the food. Eat slowly, mindfully,
appreciatively.
Sit down when eating.
No technology (TV, phone, tablet,
etc.) at the dinner table,
whether you are eating with
others or alone.

Prepare for tomorrow:

If you have children, get them organized, and then focus on your needs.

1. Pack your gym bag or lay out your workout clothes.
2. Prep or plan ahead for tomorrow's lunch.
3. Organize your personal space. Clean out and organize your briefcase, backpack, or purse. Assemble paperwork or other necessities for the following day.
4. Take a shower or bath.
5. Wash/cleanse your face.
6. Brush and floss your teeth.
7. Drink a glass of water.
8. Nighttime affirmation: I will sleep well. I will have pleasant dreams. Repeat.
9. Lie in bed:
   a. Mentally prepare yourself for your workout tomorrow (when, where, etc.). For example: I am taking the 6:00 p.m. Yoga class tomorrow.
   b. Take a deep breath and exhale stress and negativity.
   c. Progressive relaxation: Bring your mind into your body and go bit by bit to each part of your body, letting go of any tension. You can go head to toe or vice versa. Relax forehead, jaw, shoulders, neck, arms, hands, etc. If you feel your mind starting to wander, bring it back to your body and start over again.
   d. If you awaken in the night and have trouble going back to sleep, repeat the progressive relaxation.

DAY

Space Cleanse #4:
The Art of Receiving, page 146

Mindful Moment #4:
Counting Blessings, page 158

Today and Tomorrow:
Exercise is scheduled. The best time to exercise is when you will do it.
Make an appointment with yourself to exercise. Put it in your calendar.
Cardio: minimum ten minutes if you are a beginner. At least forty-five
to sixty minutes if you are fit. Flexibility/stretching. If you are listening to
music during your workout add a new, upbeat song to your playlist.

Reminder:
Record everything you eat today.

Upon awakening:
Sit quietly. Take three slow, deep breaths.
Say your Mindful Moments.
Mentally review your food and fitness plans for the day (we tend to
make better decisions in the morning, so this is a good time to set
the tone for the day).
Brush teeth.
Morning shower or bath if you are a morning bather.
Eight ounces hot water with fresh lemon juice.

DAY 4 MENU

BREAKFAST

High protein maple brown sugar
oatmeal

Tea: green or black

Optional: one or two teaspoons
of organic sugar or honey with
unsweetened soy, almond, or
rice milk

MIDMORNING

Rinse mouth with plain water.

Drink eight ounces water, seltzer,
or tea (hot or cold, black,
green, herbal).

LUNCH

Vegetarian chili (leftovers)

Water or tea

MIDAFTERNOON

Stand up: March in place, do
jumping jacks, or climb stairs
for three to five minutes
nonstop.

Eight ounces or more of water,
tea, seltzer

LATE AFTERNOON

This only takes a minute or two.
You DO have the time.

Stress Assess: Check body for
tension; unfurrow brow, relax
jaw, drop shoulders, lift sternum, sit/stand up straight. Take
three slow, deep breaths.

Stand up: Take a walk, swing
your arms, march in place, or
do jumping jacks for three to
five minutes nonstop.

Repeat today's Mindful Moments.

Rinse mouth with plain water.

SNACK

Wasa crackers with almond
butter and sliced strawberries,
optional drizzle of honey

Tea or water

DINNER

Sautéed kale and brown rice
(per package directions). For
an added zip substitute vegan
broth, carrot juice, or apple
juice for half the amount of
water. For example: one cup of
dry brown rice with one cup of
water and one cup of broth,
with roasted tofu and roasted
balsamic carrots.

Herbal tea: peppermint, chamomile, or ginger (or another decaffeinated herbal tea you enjoy)

Moment of appreciation: Thank
yourself, or whomever, for
preparing the food. Appreciate
the color, aroma, and texture of
the food. Eat slowly, mindfully,
appreciatively.

Sit down when eating.

No technology (TV, phone, tablet, etc.) at the dinner table, whether you are eating with others or alone.

Prepare for tomorrow:

If you have children, get them organized, and then focus on your needs.

1. Pack your gym bag or lay out your workout clothes.
2. Prep or plan ahead for tomorrow's lunch.
3. Organize your personal space. Clean out and organize your briefcase, backpack, or purse. Assemble paperwork or other necessities for the following day.
4. Take a shower or bath.
5. Wash/cleanse your face.
6. Brush and floss your teeth.
7. Drink a glass of water.
8. Nighttime affirmation: I will sleep well. I will have pleasant dreams. Repeat.
9. Lie in bed:
    a. Mentally prepare yourself for your workout tomorrow (when, where, etc.). For example: I am running 3 miles during my lunch break.
    b. Take a deep breath and exhale stress and negativity. Repeat three times.
    c. Progressive relaxation: Bring your mind into your body and go bit by bit to each part of your body, letting go of any tension. You can go head to toe or vice versa. Relax forehead, jaw, shoulders, neck, arms, hands, etc. If you feel your mind starting to wander, bring it back to your body and start over again.
    d. If you awaken in the night and have trouble going back to sleep, repeat the progressive relaxation.

DAY

5

Space Cleanse #5
Technology Moratorium, page 147

Mindful Moment #5
Yay Me!, page 159

Today and Tomorrow
Exercise is scheduled. The best time to exercise is when you will do it. Make an appointment with yourself to exercise. Put it in your calendar. **Cardio:** minimum ten minutes if you are a beginner. At least forty-five to sixty minutes if you are fit. Flexibility/stretching. If you are listening to music during your workout add a new, upbeat song to your playlist.

Reminder:
Record everything you eat today.

Upon awakening:
Sit quietly. Take three slow, deep breaths.
Say your Mindful Moments.
Mentally review your food and fitness plans for the day (we tend to make better decisions in the morning, so this is a good time to set the tone for the day).
Brush teeth.
Morning shower or bath if you are a morning bather.
Eight ounces hot water with fresh lemon juice.

DAY 5 MENU

BREAKFAST

Tofu Scramble

Tea: green or black

Optional: one or two teaspoons
of organic sugar or honey with
unsweetened soy, almond, or
rice milk

MIDMORNING

Rinse mouth with plain water.

Drink eight ounces water,
seltzer, or tea (hot or cold,
black, green, herbal).

LUNCH

Quinoa Cacophony

Water or tea

MIDAFTERNOON

STAND UP: March in place, do
jumping jacks, or climb stairs for
three to five minutes nonstop.

Eight ounces or more of water,
tea, or seltzer

LATE AFTERNOON:

This only takes a minute or two.
You DO have the time.

Stress Assess: Check body for
tension; unfurrow brow, relax
jaw, drop shoulders, lift sternum, sit/stand up straight. Take
three slow, deep breaths.

Stand up: knee lifts, swing arms,
or climb stairs for three to five
minutes nonstop.

Repeat today's Mindful Moments.

Rinse mouth with plain water.

SNACK

Crunchy rosemary chickpeas

Tea or water

DINNER

Everything but the Kitchen
Sink Stoup

Whole grain crusty bread

Herbal tea: peppermint,
chamomile, or ginger (or
another decaffeinated herbal
tea you enjoy)

Moment of appreciation: Thank
yourself, or whomever, for
preparing the food. Appreciate
the color, aroma, and texture of
the food. Eat slowly, mindfully,
appreciatively.

Sit down when eating.

No technology (TV, phone, tablet,
etc.) at the dinner table,
whether you are eating with
others or alone.

Prepare for tomorrow:

If you have children, get them organized, and then focus on your needs.

1. Pack your gym bag or lay out your workout clothes.
2. Prep or plan ahead for tomorrow's lunch.
3. Organize your personal space. Clean out and organize your briefcase, backpack, or purse. Assemble paperwork or other necessities for the following day.
4. Take a shower or bath.
5. Wash/cleanse your face.
6. Brush and floss your teeth.
7. Drink a glass of water.
8. Nighttime affirmation: I will sleep well. I will have pleasant dreams. Repeat.
9. Lie in bed:
   a. Mentally prepare yourself for your workout tomorrow (when, where, etc.). For example: I am getting up and taking the 8:30 a.m. Kickboxing class tomorrow.
   b. Take a deep breath and exhale stress and negativity. Repeat three times.
   c. Progressive relaxation: Bring your mind into your body and go bit by bit to each part of your body, letting go of any tension. You can go head to toe or vice versa. Relax forehead, jaw, shoulders, neck, arms, hands, etc. If you feel your mind starting to wander, bring it back to your body and start over again.
   d. If you awaken in the night and have trouble going back to sleep, repeat the progressive relaxation.

DAY

Space Cleanse #6:
Smudging, page 148

Mindful Moment #6:
Silly Affirmation, page 159

Today and Tomorrow:
Exercise is scheduled. The best time to exercise is when you will do it. Make an appointment with yourself to exercise. Put it in your calendar. **Cardio:** minimum ten minutes if you are a beginner. At least forty-five to sixty minutes if you are fit. Flexibility/stretching. If you are listening to music during your workout add a new, upbeat song to your playlist.

Reminder:
Record everything you eat today.

Upon awakening:
Sit quietly. Take three slow, deep breaths.
Say your Mindful Moments.
Mentally review your food and fitness plans for the day (we tend to make better decisions in the morning, so this is a good time to set the tone for the day).
Brush teeth.
Morning shower or bath if you are a morning bather.
Eight ounces hot water with fresh lemon juice.

DAY 6 MENU

BREAKFAST
Blueberry Chia Oat Smoothie or Get Well Smoothie

Tea: green or black

Optional: one or two teaspoons of organic sugar or honey with unsweetened soy, almond, or rice milk

MIDMORNING
Rinse mouth with plain water.

Drink eight ounces water, seltzer, or tea (hot or cold, black, green, herbal).

LUNCH
Everything But the Kitchen Sink Stoup

whole grain bread

Tea or water

MIDAFTERNOON
Stand up: March in place, do jumping jacks, or climb stairs for three to five minutes nonstop.

Eight ounces or more of water, tea, or seltzer

LATE AFTERNOON:
This only takes a minute or two. You DO have the time.

Stress Assess: Check body for tension; unfurrow brow, relax jaw, drop shoulders, lift sternum, sit/stand up straight. Take three slow, deep breaths.

Stand up: March in place, do jumping jacks, or climb stairs for three to five minutes nonstop.

Repeat today's Mindful Moments.

Rinse mouth with plain water.

SNACK
5-ingredient roasted tomatillo salsa

Tortilla chips (about ten)

Tea or water

DINNER
Quinoa Cacophany

Herbal tea: peppermint, chamomile, or ginger (or another decaffeinated herbal tea you enjoy)

Moment of appreciation: Thank yourself, or whomever, for preparing the food. Appreciate the color, aroma, and texture of the food. Eat slowly, mindfully, appreciatively.

Sit down when eating.

No technology (TV, phone, tablet, etc.) at the dinner table, whether you are eating with others or alone.

Prepare for tomorrow:

If you have children, get them organized, and then focus on your needs.

1. Pack your gym bag or lay out your workout clothes.
2. Prep or plan ahead for tomorrow's lunch.
3. Organize your personal space. Clean out and organize your briefcase, backpack, or purse. Assemble paperwork or other necessities for the following day.
4. Take a shower or bath.
5. Wash/cleanse your face.
6. Brush and floss your teeth.
7. Drink a glass of water.
8. Nighttime affirmation: I will sleep well. I will have pleasant dreams. Repeat.
9. Lie in bed:
    a. Mentally prepare yourself for your workout tomorrow (when, where, etc.). For example: I am doing a home exercise DVD tomorrow after work.
    b. Take a deep breath and exhale stress and negativity. Repeat three times.
    c. Progressive relaxation: Bring your mind into your body and go bit by bit to each part of your body, letting go of any tension. You can go head to toe or vice versa. Relax forehead, jaw, shoulders, neck, arms, hands, etc. If you feel your mind starting to wander, bring it back to your body and start over again.
    d. If you awaken in the night and have trouble going back to sleep, repeat the progressive relaxation.

DAY

Space Cleanse #7:
Good Deeds, page 148

Mindful Moment #7:
Being Present, page 159

Today and Tomorrow:
Exercise is scheduled. The best time to exercise is when you will do it.
Make an appointment with yourself to exercise. Put it in your calendar.
Cardio: minimum ten minutes if you are a beginner. At least forty-five to
sixty minutes if you are fit. Flexibility/stretching. If you are listening to music
during your workout add a new, upbeat song to your playlist.

Reminder:
Record everything you eat today.

Upon awakening:
Sit quietly. Take three slow, deep breaths.
Say your Mindful Moments.
Mentally review your food and fitness plans for the day (we tend to
    make better decisions in the morning, so this is a good time to set the
    tone for the day).
Brush teeth.
Morning shower or bath if you are a morning bather.
Eight ounces hot water with fresh lemon juice.

DAY 7 MENU

BREAKFAST

1½ cups of shredded wheat,
¾ cup unsweetened soy milk,
strawberries, ½ banana,
two tablespoons ground
flax seeds, one tablespoon
chopped walnuts

Tea: green or black

Optional: one or two teaspoons
of organic sugar or honey with
unsweetened soy, almond, or
rice milk

MIDMORNING

Rinse mouth with plain water.
Drink eight ounces water, seltzer, or
tea (hot or cold, black, green, herbal).

LUNCH

Avocado, tomato, hummus on
whole grain bread with drizzle of
EVOO, salt and pepper to taste

Tea or water

MIDAFTERNOON

Stand up: March in place, do
jumping jacks, or climb stairs for
three to five minutes nonstop.

Eight ounces or more of water,
tea, or seltzer

LATE AFTERNOON:

This only takes a minute or two.
You DO have the time.

Stress Assess: Check body for
tension; unfurrow brow, relax
jaw, drop shoulders, lift sternum,
sit/stand up straight. Take
three slow, deep breaths.

Stand up: Sneak out of work and
take a fun fitness class—OR
take a walk or do knee lifts or
pushups (wall or floor).

Repeat today's Mindful Moments.
Rinse mouth with plain water.

SNACK

¼ cup trail mix

Tea or water

DINNER

Roasted tofu

Balsamic broccoli

Roasted asparagus with lemon,
EVOO

Kasha (prepare per package
instructions)

Herbal tea: peppermint,
chamomile, or ginger (or
another decaffeinated herbal
tea you enjoy)

Moment of appreciation: Thank
yourself, or whomever, for
preparing the food. Appreciate the color, aroma, and
texture of the food. Eat slowly,
mindfully, appreciatively.

Sit down when eating.

No technology (TV, phone, tablet, etc.) at the dinner table, whether you are eating with others or alone.

Prepare for tomorrow:

If you have children, get them organized, and then focus on your needs.

1. Pack your gym bag or lay out your workout clothes.
2. Prep or plan ahead for tomorrow's lunch.
3. Organize your personal space. Clean out and organize your briefcase, backpack, or purse. Assemble paperwork or other necessities for the following day.
4. Take a shower or bath.
5. Wash/cleanse your face.
6. Brush and floss your teeth.
7. Drink a glass of water.
8. Nighttime affirmation: I will sleep well. I will have pleasant dreams. Repeat.
9. Lie in bed:
   a. Mentally prepare yourself for your workout tomorrow (when, where, etc.). For example: I am meeting Laura and Monica and going for a four mile walk today at 2:00 p.m.
   b. Take a deep breath and exhale stress and negativity. Repeat three times.
   c. Progressive relaxation: Bring your mind into your body and go bit by bit to each part of your body, letting go of any tension. You can go head to toe or vice versa. Relax forehead, jaw, shoulders, neck, arms, hands, etc. If you feel your mind starting to wander, bring it back to your body and start over again.
   d. If you awaken in the night and have trouble going back to sleep, repeat the progressive relaxation.

DAY

Space Cleanse #8:
Recognizing Good Deeds, page 149

Mindful Moment #8:
Living Fully, page 160

Today and Tomorrow:
Exercise is scheduled. The best time to exercise is when you will do it. Make an appointment with yourself to exercise. Put it in your calendar. **Cardio:** minimum ten minutes if you are a beginner. At least forty-five to sixty minutes if you are fit. Flexibility/stretching. If you are listening to music during your workout add a new, upbeat song to your playlist.

Reminder:
Record everything you eat today.

Upon awakening:
Sit quietly. Take three slow, deep breaths.
Say your Mindful Moments.
Mentally review your food and fitness plans for the day (we tend to make better decisions in the morning, so this is a good time to set the tone for the day).
Brush teeth.
Morning shower or bath if you are a morning bather.
Eight ounces hot water with fresh lemon juice.

DAY 8 MENU

BREAKFAST

Smoothie of your choice: use fruit, yogurt, soy milk, add nuts, ground flax

Tea: green or black

Optional: one or two teaspoons of organic sugar or honey with unsweetened soy, almond, or rice milk

MIDMORNING

Rinse mouth with plain water.

Drink eight ounces water, seltzer, or tea (hot or cold, black, green, herbal).

LUNCH

Leftover tofu, broccoli, kasha, asparagus

Tomato and watermelon salad

Or

Red cabbage and pistachio salad

Tea or water

MIDAFTERNOON

Stand up: March in place, do jumping jacks, or climb stairs for three to five minutes nonstop.

Eight ounces or more of water, tea, or seltzer

LATE AFTERNOON:

This only takes a minute or two. You DO have the time.

Stress Assess: Check body for tension; unfurrow brow, relax jaw, drop shoulders, lift sternum, sit/stand up straight. Take three slow, deep breaths.

Stand up: March in place, do jumping jacks, or climb stairs for three to five minutes nonstop.

Repeat today's Mindful Moments.

Rinse mouth with plain water.

SNACK

Apple slices with peanut butter

Tea or water

DINNER

Spinach tofu stir fry

Herbal tea: peppermint, chamomile, or ginger (or another decaffeinated herbal tea you enjoy)

Moment of appreciation: Thank yourself, or whomever, for preparing the food. Appreciate the color, aroma, and texture of the food. Eat slowly, mindfully, appreciatively.

Sit down when eating.

No technology (TV, phone, tablet, etc.) at the dinner table, whether you are eating with others or alone.

Prepare for tomorrow:

If you have children, get them organized, and then focus on your needs.

1. Pack your gym bag or lay out your workout clothes.
2. Prep or plan ahead for tomorrow's lunch.
3. Organize your personal space. Clean out and organize your briefcase, backpack, or purse. Assemble paperwork or other necessities for the following day.
4. Take a shower or bath.
5. Wash/cleanse your face.
6. Brush and floss your teeth.
7. Drink a glass of water.
8. Nighttime affirmation: I will sleep well. I will have pleasant dreams. Repeat.
9. Lie in bed:
   a. Mentally prepare yourself for your workout tomorrow (when, where, etc.). For example: I am taking the beginning Boot Camp class today at 5:00 p.m.
   b. Take a deep breath and exhale stress and negativity. Repeat three times.
   c. Progressive relaxation: Bring your mind into your body and go bit by bit to each part of your body, letting go of any tension. You can go head to toe or vice versa. Relax forehead, jaw, shoulders, neck, arms, hands, etc. If you feel your mind starting to wander, bring it back to your body and start over again.
   d. If you awaken in the night and have trouble going back to sleep, repeat the progressive relaxation.

DAY

Space Cleanse #9:
Cleansing Reactions, page 150

Mindful Moment #9:
Literary Appreciation, page 160

Today and Tomorrow:
Exercise is scheduled. The best time to exercise is when you will do it. Make an appointment with yourself to exercise. Put it in your calendar. **Cardio:** minimum ten minutes if you are a beginner. At least forty-five to sixty minutes if you are fit. Flexibility/stretching. If you are listening to music during your workout add a new, upbeat song to your playlist.

Reminder:
Record everything you eat today.

Upon awakening:
Sit quietly. Take three slow, deep breaths.
Say your Mindful Moments.
Mentally review your food and fitness plans for the day (we tend to make better decisions in the morning, so this is a good time to set the tone for the day).
Brush teeth.
Morning shower or bath if you are a morning bather.
Eight ounces hot water with fresh lemon juice.

DAY 9 MENU

BREAKFAST

Oatmeal with soy milk, fruit, drizzle of maple syrup, chopped almonds, dash of cinnamon

Tea: green or black

Optional: one or two teaspoons of organic sugar or honey with unsweetened soy, almond, or rice milk

MIDMORNING

Rinse mouth with plain water.

Drink eight ounces water, seltzer, or tea (hot or cold, black, green, herbal).

LUNCH

Fresh Corn, Black Bean, and Avocado Saladita

Tea or water

MIDAFTERNOON

Stand up: March in place, do jumping jacks, or climb stairs for three to five minutes nonstop.

Eight ounces or more of water, tea, or seltzer

LATE AFTERNOON:

This only takes a minute or two. You DO have the time.

Stress Assess: Check body for tension; unfurrow brow, relax jaw, drop shoulders, lift sternum, sit/stand up straight. Take three slow, deep breaths.

Stand up: Stretch arms up to the ceiling, alternating right and left (breathe). With hips stable and knees bent, twist right and left from the waist.

Repeat today's Mindful Moments. Rinse mouth with plain water.

SNACK

Black bean hummus with carrots, celery, broccoli crudité

Tea or water

DINNER

Leftover spinach tofu stir fry

Steamed green beans

Herbal tea: peppermint, chamomile, or ginger (or another decaffeinated herbal tea you enjoy)

Moment of appreciation: Thank yourself, or whomever, for preparing the food. Appreciate the color, aroma, and texture of the food. Eat slowly, mindfully, appreciatively.

Sit down when eating.

No technology (TV, phone, tablet, etc.) at the dinner table, whether you are eating with others or alone.

Prepare for tomorrow:

If you have children, get them organized, and then focus on your needs.

1. Pack your gym bag or lay out your workout clothes.
2. Prep or plan ahead for tomorrow's lunch.
3. Organize your personal space. Clean out and organize your briefcase, backpack, or purse. Assemble paperwork or other necessities for the following day.
4. Take a shower or bath.
5. Wash/cleanse your face.
6. Brush and floss your teeth.
7. Drink a glass of water.
8. Nighttime affirmation: I will sleep well. I will have pleasant dreams. Repeat.
9. Lie in bed:
   a. Mentally prepare yourself for your workout tomorrow (when, where, etc.) For example: I am cycling with my cycling group today at 7:00 a.m.
   b. Take a deep breath and exhale stress and negativity. Repeat three times.
   c. Progressive relaxation: Bring your mind into your body and go bit by bit to each part of your body, letting go of any tension. You can go head to toe or vice versa. Relax forehead, jaw, shoulders, neck, arms, hands, etc. If you feel your mind starting to wander, bring it back to your body and start over again.
   d. If you awaken in the night and have trouble going back to sleep, repeat the progressive relaxation.

DAY

Space Cleanse #10:
Detoxify Your Yard, page 151

Mindful Moment #10:
Be Still, page 160

Today and Tomorrow:
Exercise is scheduled. The best time to exercise is when you will do
it. Make an appointment with yourself to exercise. Put it in your
calendar. **Cardio:** minimum ten minutes if you are a beginner. At
least forty-five to sixty minutes if you are fit. Flexibility/stretching. If
you are listening to music during your workout add a new, upbeat
song to your playlist.

Reminder:
Record everything you eat today.

Upon awakening:
Sit quietly. Take three slow, deep breaths.
Say your Mindful Moments.
Mentally review your food and fitness plans for the day (we tend to
make better decisions in the morning, so this is a good time to set
the tone for the day).
Brush teeth.
Morning shower or bath if you are a morning bather.
Eight ounces hot water with fresh lemon juice

DAY 10 MENU

BREAKFAST

Smoothie of your choice

Tea: green or black

Optional: one or two teaspoons of organic sugar or honey with unsweetened soy, almond, or rice milk

MIDMORNING

Rinse mouth with plain water.

Drink eight ounces water, seltzer, or tea (hot or cold, black, green, herbal).

LUNCH

Saladita leftovers

Tea or water

MIDAFTERNOON

Stand up: March in place, do jumping jacks, or climb stairs for three to five minutes nonstop.

Eight ounces or more of water, tea, seltzer

LATE AFTERNOON:

This only takes a minute or two. You DO have the time.

Stress Assess: Check body for tension; unfurrow brow, relax jaw, drop shoulders, lift sternum, sit/stand up straight. Take three slow, deep breaths.

Roll shoulders in circles forward and backward; loosen your neck, pull in abs. Go for a walk (long or short).

Repeat today's Mindful Moments.

Rinse mouth with plain water.

SNACK

What sounds good to you?

Tea or water

DINNER

Use up what you have in the fridge. Stuff whole-wheat pitas or flour tortillas with leftover spinach-tofu stir fry.

Herbal tea: peppermint, chamomile, or ginger (or another decaffeinated herbal tea you enjoy)

Moment of appreciation: Thank yourself, or whomever, for preparing the food. Appreciate the color, aroma, and texture of the food. Eat slowly, mindfully, appreciatively.

Sit down when eating.

No technology (TV, phone, tablet, etc.) at the dinner table, whether you are eating with others or alone.

Prepare for tomorrow:

If you have children, get them organized, and then focus on your needs.

1. Pack your gym bag or lay out your workout clothes.
2. Prep or plan ahead for tomorrow's lunch.
3. Organize your personal space. Clean out and organize your briefcase, backpack, or purse. Assemble paperwork or other necessities for the following day.
4. Take a shower or bath.
5. Wash/cleanse your face.
6. Brush and floss your teeth.
7. Drink a glass of water.
8. Nighttime affirmation: I will sleep well. I will have pleasant dreams. Repeat.
9. Lie in bed:
    a. Mentally prepare yourself for your workout tomorrow (when, where, etc.). For example: I am going hiking with Pat today at 1:00 p.m. I am bringing the fruit salad.
    b. Take a deep breath and exhale stress and negativity. Repeat three times.
    c. Progressive relaxation: Bring your mind into your body and go bit by bit to each part of your body, letting go of any tension. You can go head to toe or vice versa. Relax forehead, jaw, shoulders, neck, arms, hands, etc. If you feel your mind starting to wander, bring it back to your body and start over again.
    d. If you awaken in the night and have trouble going back to sleep, repeat the progressive relaxation.

DAY

11

Space Cleanse #11:
News Moratorium, page 151

Mindful Moment #11:
Thoughts are Things, page 160

Today and Tomorrow:
Exercise is scheduled. The best time to exercise is when you will do it. Make an appointment with yourself to exercise. Put it in your calendar. **Cardio:** minimum ten minutes if you are a beginner. At least forty-five to sixty minutes if you are fit. Flexibility/stretching. If you are listening to music during your workout add a new, upbeat song to your playlist.

Reminder:
Record everything you eat today.

Upon awakening:
Sit quietly. Take three slow, deep breaths.
Say your Mindful Moments.
Mentally review your food and fitness plans for the day (we tend to make better decisions in the morning, so this is a good time to set the tone for the day).
Brush teeth.
Morning shower or bath if you are a morning bather.
Eight ounces hot water with fresh lemon juice

DAY 11 MENU
FLYING SOLO! YOU CAN DO THIS.

BREAKFAST

Tea: green or black

Optional: one or two teaspoons of organic sugar or honey with unsweetened soy, almond, or rice milk

Ideas: Smoothie or cereal or oatmeal or whole grain bread with almond butter and banana

MIDMORNING

Rinse mouth with plain water.

Drink eight ounces water, seltzer, or tea (hot or cold, black, green, herbal).

LUNCH

Ideas: Salad, soup, veggie pizza (no cheese)

Tea or water

MIDAFTERNOON

Stand up: March in place, do jumping jacks, or climb stairs for three to five minutes nonstop.

Eight ounces or more of water, tea, or seltzer

LATE AFTERNOON

This only takes a minute or two. You DO have the time.

Stress Assess: Check body for tension; unfurrow brow, relax jaw, drop shoulders, lift sternum, sit/stand up straight. Take three slow, deep breaths.

Side bends, knee lifts, push ups

Repeat today's Mindful Moments.

Rinse mouth with plain water.

SNACK

Ideas: Crudités and hummus or other bean dip, cup of soup, cup of fruit salad with sunflower seeds

Tea or water

DINNER

Reinvent the Quinoa Cacaphony with different vegetables like zucchini, sliced, fresh sliced mushrooms, cucumbers, and grated carrots.

Herbal tea: peppermint, chamomile, or ginger (or another decaffeinated herbal tea you enjoy)

Moment of appreciation: Thank yourself, or whomever, for preparing the food. Appreciate the color, aroma, and texture of the food. Eat slowly, mindfully, appreciatively.

Sit down when eating.

No technology (TV, phone, tablet, etc.) at the dinner table, whether you are eating with others or alone.

Prepare for tomorrow:

If you have children, get them organized, and then focus on your needs.

1. Pack your gym bag or lay out your workout clothes.
2. Prep or plan ahead for tomorrow's lunch.
3. Organize your personal space. Clean out and organize your briefcase, backpack, or purse. Assemble paperwork or other necessities for the following day.
4. Take a shower or bath.
5. Wash/cleanse your face.
6. Brush and floss your teeth.
7. Drink a glass of water.
8. Nighttime affirmation: I will sleep well. I will have pleasant dreams. Repeat.
9. Lie in bed:
    a. Mentally prepare yourself for your workout tomorrow (when, where, etc.). For example: I am taking Sue's jazz dance class at 9:00 a.m.
    b. Take a deep breath and exhale stress and negativity. Repeat three times.
    c. Progressive relaxation: Bring your mind into your body and go bit by bit to each part of your body, letting go of any tension. You can go head to toe or vice versa. Relax forehead, jaw, shoulders, neck, arms, hands, etc. If you feel your mind starting to wander, bring it back to your body and start over again.
    d. If you awaken in the night and have trouble going back to sleep, repeat the progressive relaxation.

DAY
12

Space Cleanse #12:
Decluttering Your Space, page 152

Mindful Moment #12:
Be Beautiful, page 160

Today and Tomorrow
Exercise is scheduled. The best time to exercise is when you will do it. Make an appointment with yourself to exercise. Put it in your calendar. **Cardio:** minimum ten minutes if you are a beginner. At least forty-five to sixty minutes if you are fit. Flexibility/stretching. If you are listening to music during your workout add a new, upbeat song to your playlist.

Reminder:
Record everything you eat today.

Upon awakening:
Sit quietly. Take three slow, deep breaths.
Say your Mindful Moments.
Mentally review your food and fitness plans for the day (we tend to make better decisions in the morning, so this is a good time to set the tone for the day).
Brush teeth.
Morning shower or bath if you are a morning bather.
Eight ounces hot water with fresh lemon juice.

DAY 12 MENU

BREAKFAST

Tea: green or black

Optional: one or two teaspoons of organic sugar or honey with unsweetened soy, almond, or rice milk

Ideas: Smoothie or cereal or oatmeal or whole grain bread with almond butter and banana

MIDMORNING

Rinse mouth with plain water.

Drink eight ounces water, seltzer, or tea (hot or cold, black, green, herbal)

LUNCH

Ideas: Salad, soup, veggie pizza (no cheese)

Tea or water

MIDAFTERNOON

Stand up: March in place, do jumping jacks, or climb stairs for three to five minutes nonstop.

Eight ounces or more of water, tea, seltzer

LATE AFTERNOON

This only takes a minute or two. You DO have the time.

Stress Assess: Check body for tension; unfurrow brow, relax jaw, drop shoulders, lift sternum, sit/stand up straight. Take three slow, deep breaths.

Move your body.

Repeat today's Mindful Moments.

Rinse mouth with plain water.

SNACK

Ideas: Crudités and hummus or other bean dip, cup of soup, cup of fruit salad with sunflower seeds

Tea or water

DINNER

Reinvent the "Everything But the Kitchen Sink Stoup" by swapping the white potato with a sweet potato.

Herbal tea: peppermint, chamomile, or ginger (or another decaffeinated herbal tea you enjoy)

Moment of appreciation: Thank yourself, or whomever, for preparing the food. Appreciate the color, aroma, and texture of the food. Eat slowly, mindfully, appreciatively.

Sit down when eating.

No technology (TV, phone, tablet, etc.) at the dinner table, whether you are eating with others or alone.

Prepare for tomorrow:

If you have children, get them organized, and then focus on your needs.

1. Pack your gym bag or lay out your workout clothes.
2. Prep or plan ahead for tomorrow's lunch.
3. Organize your personal space. Clean out and organize your briefcase, backpack, or purse. Assemble paperwork or other necessities for the following day.
4. Take a shower or bath.
5. Wash/cleanse your face.
6. Brush and floss your teeth.
7. Drink a glass of water.
8. Nighttime affirmation: I will sleep well. I will have pleasant dreams. Repeat.
9. Lie in bed:
   a. Mentally prepare yourself for your workout tomorrow (when, where, etc.). For example: I am playing softball with my team today at noon.
   b. Take a deep breath and exhale stress and negativity. Repeat three times.
   c. Progressive relaxation: Bring your mind into your body and go bit by bit to each part of your body, letting go of any tension. You can go head to toe or vice versa. Relax forehead, jaw, shoulders, neck, arms, hands, etc. If you feel your mind starting to wander, bring it back to your body and start over again.
   d. If you awaken in the night and have trouble going back to sleep, repeat the progressive relaxation.

DAY
13

Space Cleanse #13:
Cultivate Creativity, page 153

Mindful Moments:
Repeat any Mindful Moments that need attention.

Today and Tomorrow:
Exercise is scheduled. The best time to exercise is when you will do it. Make an appointment with yourself to exercise. Put it in your calendar. **Cardio:** minimum ten minutes if you are a beginner. At least forty-five to sixty minutes if you are fit. Flexibility/stretching. If you are listening to music during your workout add a new, upbeat song to your playlist.

Reminder:
Record everything you eat today.

Upon awakening:
Sit quietly. Take three slow, deep breaths.
Say your Mindful Moments
Mentally review your food and fitness plans for the day (we tend to make better decisions in the morning, so this is a good time to set the tone for the day).
Brush teeth
Morning shower or bath if you are a morning bather
Eight ounces hot water with fresh lemon juice

DAY 13 MENU

BREAKFAST

Ideas: Oatmeal: make with soy milk, stir in peanut butter top with a sprinkle of brown sugar and chopped walnuts

Tea: green or black

Optional: one or two teaspoons of organic sugar or honey with unsweetened soy, almond, or rice milk

MIDMORNING

Rinse mouth with plain water.

Drink eight ounces water, seltzer, or tea (hot or cold, black, green, herbal).

LUNCH

Soup, hummus in pita or PB&J

Tea or water

MIDAFTERNOON

Stand up: March in place, do jumping jacks, or climb stairs for three to five minutes nonstop.

Eight ounces or more of water, tea, or seltzer

LATE AFTERNOON:

This only takes a minute or two. You DO have the time.

Stress Assess: Check body for tension; unfurrow brow, relax jaw, drop shoulders, lift sternum, sit/stand up straight. Take three slow, deep breaths.

Move it or lose it.

Repeat today's Mindful Moments.

Rinse mouth with plain water.

SNACK

Orange and mixed nuts

Tea or water

DINNER

Reinvent other Only Cleanse recipes by using different vegetables OR

Idea: Take 15 oz can of white beans, rinsed and drained, saute with 1 clove of chopped garlic, 1 tablespoon of olive oil, slt and fresh pepper to taste. 1 teaspoon of dried rosemary, a splash of white wine venegar. Serve on brown rice or quinoa with any vegetables you have on hand.

Herbal tea: peppermint, chamomile, or ginger (or another decaffeinated herbal tea you enjoy).

Moment of appreciation: Thank yourself, or whomever, for preparing the food. Appreciate the color, aroma, and texture of the food. Eat slowly, mindfully, appreciatively.

Sit down when eating.

No technology (TV, phone, tablet, etc.) at the dinner table, whether you are eating with others or alone.

Woohooo!!!
Prepare for tomorrow:

If you have children, get them organized, and then focus on your needs.

1. Pack your gym bag or lay out your workout clothes.
2. Prep or plan ahead for tomorrow's lunch.
3. Organize your personal space. Clean out and organize your briefcase, backpack, or purse. Assemble paperwork or other necessities for the following day.
4. Take a shower or bath.
5. Wash/cleanse your face.
6. Brush and floss your teeth.
7. Drink a glass of water.
8. Nighttime affirmation: I will sleep well. I will have pleasant dreams. Repeat.
9. Lie in bed:
   a. Mentally prepare yourself for your workout tomorrow (when, where, etc.). For example: I am swimming in the lake this morning before work.
   b. Take a deep breath and exhale stress and negativity. Repeat three times.
   c. Progressive relaxation: Bring your mind into your body and go bit by bit to each part of your body, letting go of any tension. You can go head to toe or vice versa. Relax forehead, jaw, shoulders, neck, arms, hands, etc. If you feel your mind starting to wander, bring it back to your body and start over again.
   d. If you awaken in the night and have trouble going back to sleep, repeat the progressive relaxation.

DAY

Space Cleanse #14:

Get a Massage, page 154

Mindful Moment:

Repeat a Mindful Moment you enjoy.

Today and Tomorrow

Exercise is scheduled. The best time to exercise is when you will do it. Make an appointment with yourself to exercise. Put it in your calendar. **Cardio:** minimum ten minutes if you are a beginner. At least forty-five to sixty minutes if you are fit. Flexibility/stretching. If you are listening to music during your workout add a new, upbeat song to your playlist.

Reminder:

Record everything you eat today.

Upon awakening:

Sit quietly. Take three slow, deep breaths.

Say your Mindful Moments.

Mentally review your food and fitness plans for the day (we tend to make better decisions in the morning, so this is a good time to set the tone for the day).

Brush teeth.

Morning shower or bath if you are a morning bather.

Eight ounces hot water with fresh lemon juice.

DAY 14 MENU

BREAKFAST
Your choice!

Tea: green or black

Optional: one or two teaspoons of organic sugar or honey with unsweetened soy, almond, or rice milk

MIDMORNING
Rinse mouth with plain water.

Drink eight ounces water, seltzer, or tea (hot or cold, black, green, herbal).

LUNCH
Your choice!

Tea or water

MIDAFTERNOON
Stand up: March in place, do jumping jacks, or climb stairs for three to five minutes nonstop.

Eight ounces or more of water, tea, or seltzer

LATE AFTERNOON:
This only takes a minute or two. You DO have the time.

Stress Assess: Check body for tension; unfurrow brow, relax jaw, drop shoulders, lift sternum, sit/stand up straight. Take three slow, deep breaths.

Go! Move!

Repeat today's Mindful Moments.

Rinse mouth with plain water.

SNACK
Yup, it's up to you now.

Tea or water

DINNER
Trust your cooking intuition and try something new for dinner tonight.

SURPRISE! Celebrate with a glass of wine or champagne, or if you don't drink alcohol, a nice piece of dark chocolate.

Herbal tea: peppermint, chamomile, or ginger (or another decaffeinated herbal tea you enjoy)

Moment of appreciation: Thank yourself, or whomever, for preparing the food. Appreciate the color, aroma, and texture of the food. Eat slowly, mindfully, appreciatively.

Sit down when eating.

No technology (TV, phone, tablet, etc.) at the dinner table, whether you are eating with others or alone.

CONGRATULATIONS!

Recipes on the 14-Day Cleanse Plan

NOTE THAT THE NUTRITION INFORMATION IS A GENERAL ESTIMATE.

BREAKFAST

Get Well Good Morning Smoothie

SERVES 2

You can make this a nondairy smoothie by using soy or coconut yogurt. If you want to be decadent you could use a vanilla soy ice cream, but that will up the calories. The flax (sold as ground flax or flax meal) and walnuts provide some anti-inflammatory omega-3 fats. The banana is a good source of fiber and potassium, and the berries provide fiber, vitamin C, and powerful anti-oxidants such as ellagic acid and anthocyanidins. The yogurt gives your microbiome a boost with live active cultures. And the soy milk adds staying power with nine grams of protein. Sweeten with honey if desired.

INGREDIENTS

½ cup sliced strawberries - any berries such as blueberries, raspberries, black raspberries. Fresh or frozen are good.

1 banana, sliced

1 tablespoon chopped walnuts

1 tablespoon ground flax seeds or flax meal

½ cup plain nonfat Greek or regular yogurt

1 cup unsweetened soy milk

Honey to taste

OPTIONAL:

Dash of vanilla extract

Dash of cinnamon

Mint garnish

Blend all ingredients together in a blender or with an immersion blender.

NUTRITION INFO PER SERVING:
CALORIES: 239; TOTAL FAT: 6 GRAMS; SATURATED FAT: 1 GRAM; TOTAL CARBOHYDRATES: 30 GRAMS; PROTEIN: 18 GRAMS; SODIUM: 97 MILLIGRAMS; CHOLESTEROL: 0 MILLIGRAMS; FIBER: 4 GRAMS

Blueberry Chia Oat Smoothie

SERVES 1-2

This has a thicker texture by the next day because of the oats and chia. This smoothie has a nice kick of fiber and protein. Adjust the ingredients to your taste and texture preferences. Make the night before.

INGREDIENTS

¼ cup old-fashioned rolled oats

1-2 teaspoons chia seeds

1 cup unsweetened soy milk (you can use unsweetened almond, hemp, rice or coconut milk)

½ cup silken or soft tofu

½ cup frozen or fresh blueberries (any berries will work)

½ cup banana

Honey to taste

Dash of vanilla extract (optional)

Put oats and chia seeds in the blender and blend until almost powdery.

Add the remaining ingredients and blend until smooth.

Keep in the fridge overnight (so the oats soften and chia seeds absorb the fluid).

In the morning, add additional milk or ice and blend to adjust consistency.

NUTRITION INFO PER SERVING:
CALORIES: 160; TOTAL FAT: 5 GRAMS; SATURATED FAT: 0.5 GRAMS; TOTAL CARBOHYDRATES: 24 GRAMS; PROTEIN: 9 GRAMS; SODIUM: 50 MILLIGRAMS; CHOLESTEROL: 0 MILLIGRAMS; FIBER: 6 GRAMS

High-Protein Maple Brown Sugar Oatmeal Dana White, MS RDN

SERVES: 4

Oatmeal is high in beta-glucan, the kind of soluble fiber that helps lower cholesterol and may help lower blood pressure.

INGREDIENTS

2 cups rolled oats

¼ teaspoon kosher salt

2 tablespoons light brown sugar

4 cups soy milk

1 cup 2% plain Greek yogurt

8 teaspoons maple syrup

Topping suggestions: sliced banana, pumpkin seeds, granola, raisins, chopped apple

In a medium saucepan combine oats, salt, brown sugar, and milk. Bring to a simmer, reduce heat, and cook for five minutes, stirring frequently until thick and creamy. Add yogurt, stir well. Transfer to four bowls and serve topped with two teaspoons of maple syrup and other toppings if desired.

NUTRITION INFO PER SERVING:
CALORIES: 331; TOTAL FAT: 5 GRAMS; SATURATED FAT: 2 GRAMS; TOTAL CARBOHYDRATES: 56 GRAMS; PROTEIN: 18 GRAMS; SODIUM: 219 MILLIGRAMS; CHOLESTEROL: 9 MILLIGRAMS; FIBER: 4 GRAMS

Tofu Scramble

SERVES 4-6

You will love the Tex-Mex flavors of this dish. The turmeric creates a yellow, eggy color and contains an anti-inflammatory and anticancer compound called curcumin. Serve the scramble in warm, whole-wheat pitas or with whole grain toast.

INGREDIENTS

2 tablespoons olive oil

1 green bell pepper, chopped

1 sweet red bell pepper, chopped

3 scallions, trimmed and sliced

½ teaspoon ground cumin

1½ teaspoons turmeric

2 14-ounce blocks extra-firm tofu, drained and mashed with a fork

Kosher salt to taste

1 15-ounce can black beans, rinsed, drained

3 tablespoons chopped fresh parsley or cilantro

¼ cup quartered fresh grape or cherry tomatoes

Freshly ground pepper

In a large nonstick, deep skillet, heat oil on medium. When hot but not sizzling, add the peppers and cook for about four or five minutes.

Add the scallions, cumin and turmeric and cook for another minute.

Stir in the crumbled tofu, pinch of salt, and cook for five or six minutes, until the liquid has evaporated.

Add beans; cook, stirring gently with a spatula, one or two minutes.

Stir in all except one teaspoon of the parsley or cilantro.

Serve in warmed medium size whole wheat pita or with toast. Top with fresh diced grape tomatoes or salsa. Add salt and fresh pepper to taste.

Garnish scramble and plate edges with remaining parsley.

NUTRITION INFO PER SERVING:
CALORIES: 370; TOTAL FAT: 18 GRAMS; SATURATED FAT: 2.5 GRAMS; TOTAL CARBOHYDRATES: 27 GRAMS; PROTEIN: 27 GRAMS; SODIUM: 450 MILLIGRAMS; CHOLESTEROL: 0 MILLIGRAMS; FIBER: 12 GRAM

LUNCH

Lentil Artichoke Soup

MAKES: 4 TO 6 SERVINGS (MAYBE A LITTLE MORE)

This is a hearty soup your mouth will savor and your microbiome will love. The artichokes and lentils offer a hefty dose of gut-friendly fiber along with protein, vitamin C, antioxidants, and more.

INGREDIENTS

2 tablespoons olive oil

½ yellow onion diced

1 carrot sliced or diced

3 cloves garlic minced

1 tablespoon dried basil

1 tablespoon dried oregano

2 cups water

¼ teaspoon crushed red pepper flakes (optional)

1 teaspoon kosher salt

1 bay leaf

1 cup dried red lentils

2 28-ounce cans fire roasted chopped tomatoes with juices

1 15-ounce can quartered artichoke hearts, drained, dice the edible portions

½ bunch kale. Cut out ribs and julienne the leaves. I roll them up and make thin slices across the roll.

In a three-quart pot over medium heat, add the olive oil.

Add the onion and sauté until fragrant and just translucent.

Add the carrot and cook three or four minutes, stirring occasionally

Add the garlic, basil, and oregano, and cook for about one minute. You do not want to burn the garlic.

Add the water, pepper flakes, salt, bay leaf, and red lentils. Stir.

Bring to a boil then turn down to a simmer and add the tomatoes with their juices, artichokes, and kale.

Simmer for twenty minutes, until the lentils are tender but not mushy.

Remove the bay leaf

Salt to taste

Serve with a drizzle of extra virgin olive oil.

Variation: Add one tablespoon of sherry or wine vinegar just before serving.

NUTRITION INFO PER SERVING FOR 6:
CALORIES: 280; TOTAL FAT: 6 GRAMS; SATURATED FAT: 1 GRAM; TOTAL CARBOHYDRATES: 48 GRAMS; PROTEIN: 15 GRAMS; SODIUM: 400 MILLIGRAMS; CHOLESTEROL: 0 MILLIGRAMS; FIBER: 14 GRAMS

Quinoa Cacophony

SERVES 6-8

Quinoa is a high-protein grain and a good source of fiber. A versatile grain that takes only twelve minutes to cook, it can be used in porridges, pancakes, in cold salads or as a hot entrée. The apple cider adds a subtle sweet taste which is a nice counterpoint to the lime and spices in the dressing. This dish can be served warm or at room temperature. You can make this the day before serving.

INGREDIENTS

1½ cup water

½ cup apple cider

1 cup uncooked red or tricolor quinoa, rinsed

3-4 tablespoons EVOO

Fresh lime juice from one lime

¼ teaspoons ground cumin

¼ teaspoons ground coriander

1 garlic clove finely minced

¼ teaspoons salt

¾ cup shelled, cooked edamame

1 cup cooked corn kernels (frozen, thawed, drained, or fresh)

1 orange bell pepper, diced

1 cup grape tomatoes halved

1 10-ounce can artichoke hearts, chopped (leave off prickly, fibrous parts)

Red pepper flakes to taste or 1 diced jalapeno pepper (seeds removed) optional

Salt and freshly ground pepper to taste

In a saucepan bring water and apple cider to a boil. Add the rinsed quinoa, cover. Lower heat and simmer for twelve to fourteen minutes. Drain, fluff with a fork, let cool.

In a medium bowl whisk together the olive oil, lime juice, cumin, coriander, garlic, and salt. Set aside.

In a large bowl, gently toss the remaining ingredients together with the cooled quinoa. Stir in the dressing and combine thoroughly. Add salt and pepper to taste. Refrigerate for one or two hours or overnight before serving. Adjust taste if necessary before serving by adding more lime juice, a pinch of salt, or drizzle of EVOO.

NUTRITION INFO PER SERVING FOR 6:
CALORIES: 250; TOTAL FAT: 10 GRAMS; SATURATED FAT: 1.5 GRAMS; TOTAL CARBOHYDRATES: 36 GRAMS; PROTEIN: 8 GRAMS; SODIUM: 125 MILLIGRAMS; CHOLESTEROL: 0 MILLIGRAMS; FIBER: 7 GRAMS

Edamame or Black Bean Hummus

SERVES ABOUT 4

Hummus is a protein-packed, high-fiber dip, spread, and sauce. You can make hummus with many kinds of beans. This recipe does not use tahini, but feel free to add a tablespoon or two if you like. You can turn the dip into a sauce by adding additional water or broth and pouring over pasta or rice or salad.

1 bag of shelled frozen edamame or 1 15-ounce can of white beans rinsed (add a sprinkle of dried rosemary) or 1 15-ounce can of black beans (rinsed) (add ½ minced jalapeno pepper or dash of hot sauce).

2-3 tablespoons EVOO

2-3 tablespoons fresh lemon juice

1 clove garlic, minced

½ teaspoons ground cumin

Splash of unseasoned rice vinegar (optional)

Kosher salt to taste

Cook the edamame per package directions. Add all the ingredients to a food processor and blend until smooth. Add water if necessary to adjust the consistency.

NUTRITION INFO PER SERVING FOR 4:
CALORIES: 170; TOTAL FAT: 11 GRAMS; SATURATED FAT: 1.5 GRAMS; TOTAL CARBOHYDRATES: GRAMS; PROTEIN: 9 GRAMS; SODIUM: 5 MILLIGRAMS; CHOLESTEROL: 0 MILLIGRAMS; FIBER: 4 GRAMS

Tomato and Watermelon Salad

SERVES 4 TO 6

An unexpected combo, the tomatoes and watermelon make a great pair. Both contain lycopene, a powerful antioxidant. This is a terrific summer salad. You can cut the watermelon into fun shapes with a cookie cutter. If you can't find watermelon off-season, then go with the cabbage pistachio salad.

INGREDIENTS

1-2 cups of grape or cherry tomatoes halved (heirloom tomatoes are fun too because of their variety of colors)

1 medium cucumber, seeded, and cut into ¾-inch cubes

1 cup yellow or red seedless watermelon, cubed or cut into shapes

1 Hass avocado, cut in large dice

1 tablespoon of a mix of fresh basil, cilantro and dill

¼ teaspoons ground coriander

3 tablespoons extra virgin olive oil

3 tablespoons balsamic vinegar

Kosher salt and freshly ground black pepper to taste

In a bowl, combine the tomatoes, cucumber, watermelon, and avocado.

Add the herbs and coriander and toss gently

For the dressing, whisk together the olive oil and balsamic vinegar in a small bowl. Add salt and pepper to taste. Pour evenly over the salad and gently toss.

NUTRITION INFO PER SERVING FOR 4:
CALORIES: 200; TOTAL FAT: 18 GRAMS; SATURATED FAT: 2.5 GRAMS; TOTAL CARBOHYDRATES: 12 GRAMS; PROTEIN: 2 GRAMS; SODIUM: 160 MILLIGRAMS; CHOLESTEROL: 0 MILLIGRAMS; FIBER: 4 GRAMS

Everything But the Kitchen Sink Stoup

SERVES 4 -6

This is hearty stoup (soup + stew) that is a meal in itself. One secret ingredient is the pumpkin puree. It adds a depth of flavor and a bonus of beta-carotene. The lemon and soy sauce take this stoup to a whole new level of deliciousness. To save time you can pull out the food processor, put in the slicing blade, and slice the carrot, parsnip, celery, potato, and peppers (as opposed to hand chopping). You can use almost any vegetables in this stoup. It is a great way to use up vegetables in the crisper. To increase the protein, add an additional fifteen-ounce can of beans (rinsed)—cannellini, kidney, or chickpeas would be nice, or cubed tofu, or both. I've doubled this recipe by adding two each of the potatoes, carrots, celery, parsnips, and sweet bell peppers and whatever other vegetables I happened to have in the kitchen, concomitantly increasing the water or stock and herbs, lemon and soy sauce to taste. This will give you enough to freeze for days when cooking just isn't in the cards.

2 tablespoons olive oil

2 garlic cloves, minced

1½ cups stemmed, quartered Brussels sprouts

1 large carrot chopped

1 parsnip chopped

1 stalk of celery chopped

1 large potato chopped

¾ teaspoon salt

1 16-ounce can pureed pumpkin

1 16-ounce can sodium free chopped tomatoes

1 15 ounce can of no-sodium added cannellini or kidney beans

2-3 cups vegan stock or water

1 sweet red bell pepper chopped

1½ teaspoons dried dill

½ teaspoon marjoram

1 teaspoon basil

freshly ground black pepper to taste

2-3 teaspoons low sodium soy sauce

1 tablespoon fresh lemon juice, more to taste

½ cup of plain Greek or soy yogurt sour cream*

2 teaspoons minced fresh parsley (for garnish)

In a large pot add one tablespoon of the olive oil and sauté the garlic until it becomes fragrant, about one minute.

Add the rest of the oil and the next six ingredients and cook over moderate heat (covered) for ten to fifteen minutes, stirring intermittently.

Stir in pumpkin puree and tomatoes with their juice, plus stock or water, and peppers. Bring to boil, lower to a simmer. Cover and simmer until all the vegetables are tender (twenty minutes).

Add herbs, soy sauce, and lemon juice and continue to simmer another five minutes.

Serve topped with a dollop of yogurt sour cream (optional) and a sprinkle of chopped parsley. Serve with warm, crusty, whole-grain peasant bread.

*Yogurt sour cream: ½ cup plain Greek, soy or coconut yogurt, plus ⅛ teaspoon of powdered garlic and a tiny pinch of salt.

NUTRITION INFO PER SERVING FOR 4:
CALORIES 340 ; TOTAL FAT: 8 GRAMS; SATURATED FAT: 1.5 GRAMS; TOTAL CARBOHYDRATES: 52 GRAMS; PROTEIN: 4 GRAMS; SODIUM: 550 MILLIGRAMS; CHOLESTEROL: 0 MILLIGRAMS; FIBER: 17 GRAMS

Red Cabbage and Pistachio Salad

SERVES ABOUT 8

Purple cabbage and pistachios are an unusual but really tasty pairing. Cabbage is a particularly healthy vegetable because it is loaded with disease fighting compounds like anthocyanins. Anthocyanins provide fruits and vegetables with their bright blue, purple, and red colors. They help fight cancer and boost brain and heart health. There are over thirty-six kinds of anthocyanins in purple cabbage, and it's loaded with vitamins K and C.

INGREDIENTS

One small purple cabbage—
   discard wilted outer leaves,
   wash, drain, core and slice
   into ¼-inch ribbons
      1 tablespoon kosher salt

⅓ cup unseasoned rice
   vinegar or sherry vinegar

1 tablespoon toasted
   sesame oil

2 tablespoons EVOO

2 tablespoons canola oil

Ground black pepper

1-1½ cups shelled, unsalted,
   roasted pistachios (walnuts
   or macadamia nuts would
   work well, too)

Place cabbage in a large bowl and toss with salt. Mix well but gently to be sure all the pieces have a coating of salt. If necessary add more salt.

Shift the salted cabbage to a sieve or strainer and place over a bowl for about half an hour to drain.

DRESSING

In a small bowl, whisk together vinegar, sesame oil, EVOO, and canola oil.

When cabbage has drained, squeeze handfuls of the cabbage to remove excess water and salt.

Put prepared cabbage in a large salad bowl.

Pour dressing over the cabbage and toss well.

Sprinkle with pistachios and add fresh ground pepper to taste

NUTRITION INFO PER SERVING FOR 8:
CALORIES: 230; TOTAL FAT: 19 GRAMS; SATURATED FAT: 2 GRAMS; TOTAL CARBOHYDRATES: 12 GRAMS; PROTEIN: 6 GRAMS; SODIUM: 460 MILLIGRAMS; CHOLESTEROL: 0 MILLIGRAMS; FIBER: 4 GRAMS

Fresh Corn, Black Bean, and Avocado Saladita

Adapted from Mollie Katzen's "Vegetable Dishes I Can't Live Without"

ABOUT 6-8 SERVINGS

I make recipes from this cookbook all the time. Mollie was nice enough to let me include this recipe in The Only Cleanse. This dish requires no cooking and minimal chopping. It is a big favorite at my parties. You can make it up to two days ahead of time, if you keep it tightly covered in the refrigerator. Serve as an entree or an appetizer. Serve with tortilla chips, whole-wheat pita toasts, or on its own.

INGREDIENTS

2 ears sweet corn—about 2 cups; place fresh corn on the cob in boiling water for about 2 minutes. Remove and rinse with cool water. When cool, cut the corn off the cob (frozen or canned corn are OK).

3-4 tablespoons fresh lime juice

3 tablespoons extra-virgin olive oil

1 15-ounce can (1¾ cups) black beans, rinsed and drained

1½ cup diced halved cherry or grape tomatoes

½ cup minced orange or yellow bell pepper

3 tablespoons very finely minced Poblano chile

¼ teaspoon minced garlic

3 tablespoons finely minced red onion

Kosher salt to taste, about ⅓ teaspoon

⅓ cup minced cilantro

2 medium firm-but-ripe avocados, carefully diced

Freshly ground black pepper

In a medium-large bowl, combine all the ingredients except the avocados and black pepper, and mix well. Cover and let marinate for at least an hour or more before serving.

Gently stir in the avocado dice about fifteen minutes or so before serving. Add black pepper to taste.

Serve cold or at room temperature.

NUTRITION INFO PER SERVING FOR 6:
CALORIES: 320; TOTAL FAT: 17 GRAMS; SATURATED FAT: 2.5 GRAMS; TOTAL CARBOHYDRATES: 36 GRAMS; PROTEIN: 10 GRAMS; SODIUM: 240 MILLIGRAMS; CHOLESTEROL: 0 MILLIGRAMS; FIBER: 13 GRAMS

SNACKS

Crunchy Rosemary Chickpeas

Dana White, MS RDN

MAKES ABOUT 1½ CUPS

A simply amazing crunchy snack! These magically delish beans are also high in protein and fiber.

INGREDIENTS

1 15-ounce can chickpeas, rinsed and drained

1 tablespoon EVOO

Sprinkle with kosher salt to taste

1 teaspoon finely chopped rosemary

Preheat oven to 350° F.

Drain chickpeas and dry well with a paper towel.

Place on a baking sheet and season with olive oil, kosher salt, and rosemary; toss well to coat.

Bake for about forty to fifty minutes, turning periodically, until crisp and sizzling. Remove from oven and sprinkle with kosher salt.

Allow to cool and serve at room temperature. Store in an airtight container for up to two days.

NUTRITION INFO PER 1/4 CUP SERVING:
CALORIES: 203; TOTAL FAT: 5 GRAMS; SATURATED FAT: 0 GRAMS; TOTAL CARBOHYDRATES: 30 GRAMS; PROTEIN: 10 GRAMS; SODIUM: 206 MILLIGRAMS; CHOLESTEROL: 0 MILLIGRAMS; FIBER: 9 GRAMS

5-Ingredient Roasted Tomatillo Salsa

Dana White, MS RDN

MAKES ABOUT 3 CUPS

INGREDIENTS

6 large tomatillos (about 1½ pounds), quartered

1 clove garlic

½ medium white onion, chopped

2 teaspoons olive oil

¾ teaspoon salt & pepper

¾ cup fresh cilantro

Juice of ½ lime

Preheat oven to 400° F.

Place tomatillos, garlic, and onion on a sheet pan. Drizzle with two teaspoons olive oil and season with ¾ teaspoon salt and black pepper to taste.

Roast for twenty minutes, until tomatillos are tender, then set aside to cool slightly.

Place roasted vegetables, cilantro, and lime juice in a food processor and pulse until smooth. Serve chilled or at room temperature.

NUTRITION INFO PER TABLESPOON:
CALORIES: 5; TOTAL FAT: 0 GRAMS; SATURATED FAT: 0 GRAMS; TOTAL CARBOHYDRATES: 1 GRAM; PROTEIN: 0 GRAMS; SODIUM: 18 MILLIGRAMS; CHOLESTEROL: 0 MILLIGRAMS; FIBER: 0 GRAMS

DINNER

One Pot Pasta Primavera

SERVES 4-6

You can use any vegetables you have on hand. Experiment with herbs such as ¼ cup chopped cilantro or parsley, two tablespoons chopped fresh tarragon, or one tablespoon finely minced fresh rosemary or oregano. Many herbs have antioxidant and anti-inflammatory properties

INGREDIENTS:

3 tablespoons olive oil

1-2 tablespoons garlic, minced

1 teaspoon grated lemon zest (use the lemon for fresh lemon juice)

2 small zucchini, halved and cut into ½-inch-thick slices

1 carrot, cut in thin rounds

1 medium red bell pepper, diced

3 cups of broccoli florets

2 cups cauliflower florets

1 15-ounce can cannellini beans rinsed

8 ounces whole-grain pasta of your choice

2 cups halved grape tomatoes

½ cup thinly sliced scallions

½ cup chopped fresh basil leaves (more if you love fresh basil), roll basil leaves and slice thinly

Salt and fresh ground pepper to taste

Combine oil, garlic, and lemon zest in small bowl. Set aside.

Bring a large pot of water to boiling. Blanch the all the vegetables, except the tomatoes and scallions, by adding them to the boiling water. Cook for 2 minutes. Using a slotted spoon remove the vegetables put in a sieve, rinse with cold water and let drain. Add the pasta to the same pot of boiling water and cook for about twelve minutes, until al dente. Drain pasta, reserving half a cup of cooking water.

Return pasta to the pot, add in the blanched vegetables and stir in tomatoes, scallions, basil, oil mixture, and reserved cooking water. Heat over medium-low heat until tomatoes and vegetables are hot. Add salt and pepper to taste.

NUTRITION INFO PER SERVING FOR 6:
CALORIES: 320; TOTAL FAT: 8 GRAMS; SATURATED FAT: 1 GRAM; TOTAL CARBOHYDRATES: 52 GRAMS; PROTEIN: 11 GRAMS; SODIUM: 440 MILLIGRAMS; CHOLESTEROL: 0 MILLIGRAMS; FIBER: 12 GRAMS

Sesame Peanutty Noodles

SERVES ABOUT 8

Visually, cutting vegetables into strips is pretty, but I tend to chop everything. Play with the amounts of soy sauce, vinegar, and honey. Sesame oil has a strong flavor. If you love it add more sesame oil and less EVOO. You can reinvent last night's pasta noodles by whisking together this sauce the next day for lunch or dinner. Try adding edamame, tofu cubes, or snow peas.

1 pound whole wheat capellini spaghetti or brown rice noodles

½ cup smooth natural peanut butter (no salt or sugar added)

¼ cup low sodium soy sauce

1 teaspoon salt (to taste)

¼ cup rice vinegar (unseasoned)

2 teaspoons toasted sesame oil

2 teaspoons of finely minced or grated fresh ginger

2 tablespoons fresh lime juice

1 tablespoon EVOO

1 tablespoon honey (more or less to taste)

2 cloves garlic, minced

½ teaspoon red pepper flakes

1 red bell pepper, cut into long, thin strips

2 tablespoons water chestnuts, sliced

1 carrot, thinly sliced

1 cucumber, seeded, (or an English cucumber) cut into slices

3-4 scallions, minced

1 tablespoon toasted sesame seeds

In a large pot of boiling water cook noodles until al dente. Drain and rinse with cold water. Note that rice noodles cook very quickly.

In a medium bowl, whisk together peanut butter, soy sauce, salt, vinegar, sesame oil, ginger, lime juice, EVOO, and honey. Taste. Add warm water to adjust the consistency. Stir in garlic, and red pepper flakes (optional).

In a large bowl, gently toss pasta with red bell pepper, water chestnuts, and carrots, and (if using) add the snow peas, tofu, or edamame (shelled, cooked). With more vegetables you may need more sauce.

Plate the noodle mixture. Ladle the peanutty sauce on top. Top with cucumber slices and sprinkle with sesame seeds.

Serve chilled or at room temperature

NUTRITION INFO PER SERVING FOR 8:
CALORIES: 320; TOTAL FAT: 12 GRAMS; SATURATED FAT: 2.5 GRAMS; TOTAL CARBOHYDRATES: 45 GRAMS; PROTEIN: 12 GRAMS; SODIUM: 570 MILLIGRAMS; CHOLESTEROL: 0 MILLIGRAMS; FIBER: 8 GRAMS

Vegetarian Chili

Dana White, MS RDN

SERVES: 6

Who doesn't love chili? This nutrient-packed recipe by registered dietitian Dana Angelo White is nothing short of mega-nutrition in a bowl. With a little cutting and chopping and a flourish of can opening, this is an easy, hearty meal.

1 tablespoon olive oil

½ cup chopped red onion

½ cup chopped red bell pepper

1 finely chopped jalapeno pepper (optional)

½ cup chopped celery

¼ teaspoon kosher salt

1 clove minced garlic

1 teaspoon ground cumin

½ cup vegetable broth or water

1 teaspoon soy sauce

1 cup dark beer

2 28-ounce cans crushed tomatoes

1 15-ounce can tomato sauce

¼ teaspoon cayenne pepper

3 tablespoons chili powder

½ teaspoon celery salt

2 teaspoon dried tarragon

1 15-ounce can garbanzo beans, rinsed and drained

1 15-ounce can red kidney beans, rinsed and drained

1 15-ounce can black beans, rinsed and drained

¾ cup frozen corn kernels

1 sweet potato, peeled and cubed

Heat oil in a large pot or Dutch oven over medium heat.

Sauté onion, peppers, and celery for three to five minutes until tender, then season with salt.

Add garlic and cumin, cook for one minute, stirring gently to toast cumin.

Stir in vegetable broth, soy sauce, beer, crushed tomatoes, and tomato sauce. Add in the spices.

Stir in beans, taste to adjust seasoning (add more salt or chili powder, if desired).

Bring to a simmer and cook uncovered for twenty minutes, stirring occasionally.

Add corn and sweet potato, cook for an additional fifteen minutes or until sweet potato is tender.

NUTRITION INFO PER SERVING:
CALORIES: 312; TOTAL FAT: 4 GRAMS; SATURATED FAT: 0.5 GRAMS; TOTAL CARBOHYDRATES: 56 GRAMS; PROTEIN: 14 GRAMS; SODIUM: 500 MILLIGRAMS; FIBER: 15 GRAMS

Sautéed Kale and Brown Rice

Dana White, MS RDN

SERVES: 4

Kale has made it to the big time. It is one of the best vegetables for healthy eyes because it is brimming with the retina-friendly antioxidants lutein and zeaxanthine.

INGREDIENTS

1 tablespoon extra virgin olive oil

2 bunches kale, trimmed and chopped

2 cloves garlic, minced

Sea salt and freshly ground black pepper to taste

1 tablespoon balsamic vinegar

Heat oil in a large skillet over medium-high heat.

Add kale, season with salt and pepper, and sauté for two or three minutes.

Add garlic; reduce heat to medium, and cook, turning frequently for an additional five minutes.

Add vinegar and continue to cook until kale is just tender, about five minutes more.

For an additional zip, substitute vegan broth, carrot juice, or apple juice for ¼-½ the amount of water

NUTRITION INFO PER SERVING:
CALORIES: 103; TOTAL FAT: 3 GRAMS; SATURATED FAT: 0 GRAMS; TOTAL CARBOHYDRATES: 15 GRAMS; PROTEIN: 3 GRAMS; SODIUM: 125 MILLIGRAMS; CHOLESTEROL: 0 MILLIGRAMS; FIBER: 3 GRAMS

Roasted Tofu

Dana White, MS RDN

SERVES 4

INGREDIENTS

1 package extra-firm tofu

2 tablespoons canola oil

2 teaspoons rice vinegar

2 teaspoons honey

2 teaspoons soy sauce

1 teaspoon sesame oil

1 teaspoon chili sauce (such as Sriracha)

Slice tofu into pieces approximately half an inch thick and two inches long (domino-sized pieces). Place pieces in a bowl lined with paper towels and refrigerate for fifteen or twenty minutes to remove excess water.

Preheat oven to 425° F. In a large bowl whisk canola oil, vinegar, honey, soy sauce, sesame oil, and chili sauce.

Add tofu and gently toss to coat. Transfer to a sheet pan and bake for twenty or twenty-five minutes (turning once), until golden brown.

NUTRITION INFO PER SERVING:
CALORIES: 105; TOTAL FAT: 5 GRAMS; SATURATED FAT: 1 GRAM; TOTAL CARBOHYDRATES: 4 GRAMS; PROTEIN: 10 GRAMS; SODIUM: 172 MILLIGRAMS; CHOLESTEROL: 0 MILLIGRAMS; FIBER: 1 GRAM

Roasted Balsamic Carrots

SERVES 4-6

This is a really easy dish that brightens up any meal. Balsamic vinegar adds a richly flavored, almost-sweet aura to the roasted carrots. For variation use parsnips alone or mix with the carrots. Add fresh thyme or a squeeze of fresh lemon juice.

INGREDIENTS

Olive oil

4-5 medium carrots sliced into sticks

Balsamic vinegar

Salt to taste

Preheat oven to 425° F. Line a sheet pan with tin foil and lightly coat with olive oil. Toss the sliced carrots in the pan in a single layer. Roast, turning once or twice, for about twenty minutes. Remove pan from oven. Drizzle balsamic vinegar over the carrots and toss to coat. Return to the oven for another three to five minutes, until most of the vinegar has evaporated. Remove from the oven and sprinkle with kosher salt. Serve hot, warm, or at room temp.

NUTRITION INFO PER SERVING FOR 4:
CALORIES: 60; TOTAL FAT: 3.5 GRAMS; SATURATED FAT:0 GRAMS; TOTAL CARBOHYDRATES: 7 GRAMS; PROTEIN: <1 GRAM; SODIUM: 45 MILLIGRAMS; CHOLESTEROL: 0 MILLIGRAMS; FIBER: 2 GRAMS

Balsamic Broccoli

SERVES 4

This is such a quick and easy side dish to prepare. Broccoli is a powerhouse vegetable, high in vitamin C and fiber.

INGREDIENTS

1 tablespoon canola oil

3 cloves of garlic, thinly sliced

2 tablespoons balsamic vinegar

2 teaspoons soy sauce

1 teaspoon brown sugar

1 pound broccoli florets, about 4 cups

Heat oil in a small saucepan over medium heat.

In a large pot, boil plenty of water.

Blanch the broccoli by dropping it into boiling water for one or two minutes.

Drain in a colander and rinse with cold water. Let the broccoli continue to drain in the sink for a few minutes (you can use the broccoli-infused water for cooking pasta or rice).

In the meantime, sauté the garlic on medium heat until fragrant, about one minute.

Whisk in the vinegar, sugar, and soy sauce. Lower the heat. Whisking continuously, cook until the mixture reaches a syrup-like consistency, about two or three minutes.

Drizzle the dressing over the broccoli. Serve warm, cold, or at room temperature.

NUTRITION INFO PER SERVING (1 CUP):
CALORIES: 80; TOTAL FAT: 4 GRAMS; SATURATED FAT: 0 GRAMS; TOTAL CARBOHYDRATES: 9 GRAMS; PROTEIN: 4 GRAMS; SODIUM: 120 MILLIGRAMS; CHOLESTEROL: 0 MILLIGRAMS; FIBER: 3 GRAMS

Roasted Asparagus

SERVES 4

Asparagus is high in vitamin K and folate. It also contains inulin, a favorite meal of your gut microbiota.

EVOO

2 pounds of fresh asparagus, trim off woody ends

Salt to taste

1-2 tablespoons fresh lemon juice

Preheat oven to 425° F. Line a sheet pan with tin foil. Lightly coat with olive oil.

Lay asparagus in pan in a single layer.

Roast for about fifteen minutes, until tender but still al dente.

Remove from oven, sprinkle with kosher salt and fresh lemon juice. Toss lightly with tongs.

Serve hot, warm, or at room temperature

NUTRITION INFO PER SERVING:
CALORIES: 80; TOTAL FAT: 3.5 GRAMS; SATURATED FAT: 0.5 GRAMS; TOTAL CARBOHYDRATES: 9 GRAMS; PROTEIN: 5 GRAMS; SODIUM: 300 MILLIGRAMS; CHOLESTEROL: 0 MILLIGRAMS; FIBER: 5 GRAMS

Spinach Tofu Stir-Fry

SERVES 4

A great intro to stir frying and tofu. Serve over brown rice, brown rice noodles, or quinoa.

INGREDIENTS

2 cups of cooked brown rice

1 tablespoon grapeseed oil

1 block of extra firm tofu, cut into small blocks

2 garlic cloves, minced

1 teaspoon grated or minced fresh ginger

¼ teaspoon red chili flakes

1 tablespoon soy sauce to taste

1 10-ounce bag baby spinach, stemmed, rinsed, patted dry with a paper towel

2 tablespoons toasted sesame seeds

2 teaspoon sesame oil

In a medium pot boil two cups of water. Rinse the rice in a sieve and add to the boiling water. Lower the heat and cover. Simmer for thirty-five to forty minutes (check package directions).

When the rice is about halfway done, heat the canola oil over medium-high heat in a large nonstick skillet or wok. Add the tofu. Stir periodically and cook for three to five minutes until the tofu is golden.

Stir in the garlic and ginger and cook another minute until the garlic is fragrant but not burned.

Add one tablespoon of soy sauce

Stir in the spinach and stir-fry until the spinach is wilted, about two minutes. Remove from heat.

Plate a portion of brown rice. Top with the spinach-tofu mixture. Sprinkle with sesame seeds and a drizzle of sesame oil. Add soy sauce to taste.

NUTRITION INFO PER SERVING OF THE VEGETABLE MIXTURE:
CALORIES: 310; TOTAL FAT: 15 GRAMS; SATURATED FAT: 2 GRAMS; TOTAL CARBOHYDRATES: 29 GRAMS; PROTEIN: 17 GRAMS; SODIUM: 200 MILLIGRAMS; CHOLESTEROL: 0 MILLIGRAMS; FIBER: 5 GRAMS

Meals listed by Day of The Only Cleanse Plan

YOU CAN MIX AND MATCH MEALS IN WHATEVER ORDER YOU DESIRE.

DAY 1

BREAKFAST	Get Well Good Morning Smoothie
LUNCH	Lentil Artichoke Soup Slice of whole grain bread
SNACK	¼ cup trail mix
DINNER	One Pot Pasta Primavera

DAY 2

BREAKFAST	Shredded wheat, unsweetened soy milk, strawberries, ½ banana, two tablespoons ground flax seeds, one tablespoon chopped walnuts
LUNCH	Lentil Artichoke Soup Slice of whole-grain bread
SNACK	Edamame Hummus and carrots, celery, broccoli crudités
DINNER	Sesame Peanutty Noodles

DAY 3		
BREAKFAST	Blueberry Chia Oat Smoothie
LUNCH	One Pot Pasta Primavera redux, as pasta salad: *drizzle with sherry or champagne vinegar, pinch of salt to taste. Add chopped artichoke hearts, sliced olives.*
SNACK	Edamame Hummus, and tortilla chips
DINNER	Vegetarian Chili Whole grain crackers

DAY 4		
BREAKFAST	High Protein Maple Brown Sugar Oatmeal
LUNCH	Vegetarian Chili (leftovers)
SNACK	Wasa crackers with almond butter and sliced strawberries, honey
DINNER	Sautéed Kale and Brown Rice

DAY 5		
BREAKFAST	Tofu Scramble
LUNCH	Quinoa Cacophony
SNACK	Crunchy Rosemary Chickpeas
DINNER	Everything but the Kitchen Sink Stoup Whole grain crusty bread

DAY 6	**BREAKFAST**	Blueberry Chia Oat or Get Well Smoothie
	LUNCH	Kitchen Sink Stoup Whole-grain bread
	SNACK	5-ingredient Roasted Tomatillo Salsa Tortilla Chips (about ten)
	DINNER	Quinoa Cacophony
DAY 7	**BREAKFAST**	Shredded wheat, soy milk, berries, ½ banana, ground flax seeds, one tablespoon chopped walnuts,
	LUNCH	Avocado, tomato, hummus on whole grain bread with drizzle of EVOO, salt and pepper to taste
	SNACK	¼ cup trail mix
	DINNER	Roasted Tofu Balsamic Broccoli Roasted Asparagus with Lemon, EVOO Kasha (prepare per package instructions)
DAY 8	**BREAKFAST**	Smoothie of your choice
	LUNCH	Leftover tofu, broccoli, kasha, asparagus Tomato Watermelon Salad *(summer)* Cabbage Pistachio Salad *(winter)*
	SNACK	Apple slices with peanut butter
	DINNER	Spinach Tofu Stir Fry

DAY 9		
	BREAKFAST	Oatmeal with soy milk, fruit, drizzle of maple syrup, chopped almonds, dash of cinnamon
	LUNCH	Fresh Corn, Black Bean, and Avocado Saladita
	SNACK	Black Bean Hummus with carrots, celery, broccoli crudité
	DINNER	Spinach Tofu Stir Fry Steamed green beans

DAY 10		
	BREAKFAST	Smoothie of your choice
	LUNCH	Saladita leftovers
	SNACK	Up to you
	DINNER	Use up what you have in the fridge. Stuff whole-wheat pitas or flour tortillas with leftover spinach-tofu stir fry.

DAYS 11-13: USE YOUR IMAGINATION

DAY 14: SURPRISE!

The Only Cleanse Basic Shopping List

Here is the basic shopping list for recipes listed in the 14-Day Daily Food Plan. The amounts are estimates. Check the food plan chart on page 263 and the recipes on page 235 to see what you will need for the week if you choose to follow the Day by Day Meal Plan. While there are three or four zucchini on the list, you may only need two zucchini the first week of the plan. This list is to give you an overview of what you will need. Stock up on nonperishables such as the beans, dried spices, and canned and jarred foods for ease of shopping and preparing foods during the week.

The List

Organic Greek plain or regular plain yogurt (32-ounce containers)

Almonds, 16-ounce bag, sliced or slivered
Almond butter, no added salt, sugar, or palm oil
Apples
Apricots, dried, 1 package
Artichoke hearts, 2-3 15-ounce cans or jars
Asparagus, 1 bunch
Avocado, 3-4. Buy one to two days before you need them so they will be ripe.

Balsamic vinegar
Bananas, 1 bunch
Basil, fresh
Basil, dried, 1 jar
Bay leaves

Beer, dark, one bottle (to cook with)
Black beans, 5 cans
Blueberries, frozen, unsweetened, 1 or 2 12-15 ounce bags
Broccoli, 1-2 bunches
Brown rice, 16-ounce bag (or more)
Brown sugar, light
Fresh Brussels sprouts, 16- or 12-ounce bag

Cabbage, 1 small red cabbage
Cannellini beans, 2-4 cans
Canola oil
Carrots, a few bags
Cayenne pepper, 1 jar
Celery, 1 bag
Celery salt, 1 jar
Chia seeds, 1 small bag
Chickpeas, 2-3 cans
Chili powder, 1 jar
Chili sauce (e.g., Sriracha), one bottle

Cilantro bunches, as needed

Cinnamon, 1 jar

Coriander, ground, 1 jar

Coriander, seed, 1 small jar

Corn kernels, 2-4 fresh ears and/or 1-2 16-ounce packages, frozen

Cucumber, 3-4

Cumin, ground, 1 jar

Curry powder, 1 jar

Dill, dried, 1 jar

Edamame, 2-3 12-ounce bags, shelled, frozen

EVOO, a few bottles. Look for unfiltered

Fennel, ground, small jar

Flax seeds, ground, 16-ounce bag (I keep it in the freezer because flax tends to get rancid quickly)

Garlic, lots of fresh garlic!

Garlic powder, 1 small jar

Grape tomatoes, 1-2 pints

Green bell pepper, 2-3

Ginger, fresh

Honey

Hot sauce (optional)

Jalapeno, 3-4 whole (optional)

Kale, 2-3 bunches

Kasha

Kidney beans, 2-3 cans

Kosher salt

Lemon, 5-6 whole fresh

Lime, 2-3 whole fresh

Lentils, red, dried, 1 cup

Maple syrup

Marjoram, dried

Mustard, Dijon

Nectarines, 3

Nutmeg, ground, small jar

Oats, rolled, 18-ounce container

Oats, steel-cut, 1 cup

Onion, red, 2

Onion, yellow, 1 small

Onion, white, roasted, 1 or 2

Oregano, fresh

Oregano, dried, 1 jar

Parsley bunches as needed

Parsnips, 1 bag or 1 or 2 parsnips

Peanut butter, "natural," no added salt, sugar, or palm oil

Pepper, black, to grind fresh

Peppers, roasted, red, 1 jar

Pistachios, unshelled, unsalted, roasted

Potato, white, 1

Pumpkin puree, 1 16-ounce can

Quinoa

Radish, a bunch

Rosemary, fresh

Red bell peppers, 2-4

Red pepper flakes, 1 jar

Rice vinegar, unseasoned

Salsa 1 16-ounce jar (check ingredi-
    ents. Avoid added chemicals)

Scallions, 1-2 bunches

Sesame oil

Sesame seeds, 1 small jar, or buy in
    bulk, which costs less

Soba noodles, 1 package

Soy milk, unsweetened, 2-3
    32-ounce cartons (refrigerate
    after opening)

Soy sauce

Spinach, 6-7 ounce bag of baby
    spinach

Strawberries

Sugar, granulated

Summer squash, 2 or more

Sweet potato, 1 or 2

Tarragon, dried, 1 jar

Trail mix, mixed nuts, (dried fruit
    optional)

Thyme

Tomatillos, 6 large [1½ pounds]

Tomatoes, a few ripe

Tomatoes, grape, cherry, or heir-
    loom variety

Tomatoes, 2-3 28-ounce cans,
    chopped or crushed, no sodi-
    um added

Fire-roasted tomatoes, 4 28-ounce
    cans e.g., Muir Glen

Tomato sauce, 1 15-ounce can (no
    added sodium)

Tofu, firm or extra firm, several
    packages

Tofu, silken (this has a very soft
    texture for smoothies or sauces)

Turmeric, 1 jar

Vegan vegetable broth, 2-3
    32-ounce boxes

Walnuts

Small seedless watermelon

Zucchini 3-4

Whole-grain pita chips

Whole-grain pasta

Whole-wheat pita

Whole-wheat tortillas, 4-6

100% whole-grain bread, such as
    Ezekiel

The Only Cleanse General Shopping List

ADD OR SUBTRACT HEALTHY CHOICES DEPENDING ON YOUR PREFERENCES

This, as the title suggests, is a general list to get you started. There are many more healthy, vegetarian, and vegan foods in the stores. Read the ingredient labels on packages and choose the products that have the fewest, if any chemicals. For example, at the grocery store I see hummus with all kinds of additives, and on the same shelf another brand of hummus with no additives. Food additives and chemicals are unavoidable so don't get your panties in a twist if you cannot find foods that are one-hundred percent organic with zero added chemicals. There is no need to strive for a "perfect," "clean" diet. Simply by cooking at home more often and focusing on a more plant-based approach to eating, you are supporting your body's natural ability to cleanse your system and keep you and your loved ones healthy. It's good for the planet, too.

Grains (choose whole grains though it is OK to have grains like white pasta once in a while)

Whole grain bread

Whole wheat pasta (many are blends of white and whole wheat flour, which is OK)

Oatmeal, rolled, steel cut, or traditional oats

Brown rice noodles (I've gotten them at Whole Foods)

Brown rice pasta

100% whole-grain ready-to-eat cereals (e.g., shredded wheat)

Whole-grain crackers (e.g., Triscuits, Wasa, Ak-Mak)

Whole-grain tortillas, pita chips

Quinoa

Kasha (buckwheat)

Brown and wild rices

Faro

Barley

Whole wheat couscous

Freekeh

Rice cakes

PROTEIN AND FAT

Soy foods:

Tofu

Edamame

Yuba (it may be hard to find, but
I love this stuff)

Unsweetened soy milk

Soy nuts

Tempeh

Soy sauce

Tamari

Legumes: kidney beans, chickpeas,
black-eyed peas, lentils, split
peas, fava, etc. (hint: rinse
beans out of the can to reduce
the sodium). All beans are
good. Canned, dried, or frozen.

OILS

Extra virgin, unfiltered olive oil

Olive

Canola (expeller pressed, organic)

Sesame

Walnut

Nut butters ("natural," no added
palm oil, sugar, or salt, never
hydrogenated)

Peanut

Almond

Cashew

Soy nut

Sunflower seed

NUTS *(roasted or raw, unsalted)*

Peanuts

Pistachios

Almonds

Cashews

Walnuts

Macadamia

Brazil

Mixed nuts, etc.

Seeds: pumpkin, sunflower, chia,
sesame, ground flax (flax meal)

CONDIMENTS 'N' MORE

Mustard

Relish

Ketchup

Capers

Salsa

Roasted peppers

Bamboo shoots

Artichoke hearts, canned, frozen,
or jarred

Olives, black, green, Kalamata, etc.

Palm hearts

Horseradish

Vinegars: balsamic, cider, wine,
raspberry, et al

Mrs. Dash

Fresh and dried herbs and spices
(all are good)

Tomatoes Canned, no sodium added, chopped, whole or crushed

Tomato sauce

Vegan broths/stocks

Tortilla chips

Popped corn

Chutney

FRUITS AND VEGETABLES

All Fruits

All Vegetables

Dried fruits such as figs, dates, apricots, fresh or frozen (no salt or sauce added)

Edamame (frozen) (shelled for using in recipes, in the shell for snacking)

MILKS *(unsweetened)*

Soy

Almond

Rice

Coconut

Hemp

Oat

The After Cleanse

You did it! You finished the 14-Day *Only Cleanse* Plan. Woohooo! Chances are, by following the plan you are feeling better than you were before the plan. Let's see. Circle the answer that most applies to you right now:

FATIGUE	Very	Somewhat	A little	None	
ACHY JOINTS, MUSCLES	Very	Somewhat	A little	None	
FEELING FOGGY	Very	Somewhat	A little	None	
ENERGY LEVEL	High	Adequate	Low	Running on Fumes	
GASTROIN-TESTINAL SYMPTOMS (crampy, bloating, constipation, diarrhea, dis-comfort, etc.)	Constant	Intermittent	Occasional	Not a problem	
SLEEP QUALITY	Great	Good	Adequate	Poor	What is sleep?
MOOD – IN GENERAL	Great	Good	Neutral	Cranky	Sad/depressed

Compare your answers with your answers on page 125 in chapter 7. Record the other differences you have noticed in your body, mind, and well-being. You may notice changes in energy, sleep, digestive processes, or mood. Perhaps *The Only Cleanse* Plan helped you realized just how much cheese you had been eating, or maybe you were surprised at the amount of highly processed foods you ate during your day. Did you discover where in your body you hold the most tension? Your jaw or shoulders? As you integrated the Space Cleanses and Mindful Moments into your day, you may have realized that certain areas needed work, such as taking a technology break more often or maintaining inner positivity and muting negative self-talk.

Keep track of your body and mind. Recording how you are feeling physically, emotionally, and mentally is important because we tend to forget how we are feeling on any given day. This way you can connect the dots between actions, food, stress, and your mental and physical state of being.

A healthy lifestyle needs to be something you can continue forever. This does not mean you cannot have bananas Foster or champagne once in a while. The plan was created for you to learn that you can incorporate mind and body strategies, healthy eating, and a mostly plant-based diet into your life, all of which support your body's innate ability to be healthy. The plan is your guide to adopting new cleansing, detoxing, healthy behaviors.

Even though you have finished *The Only Cleanse* 14-Day Plan, it is best that you continue to practice the skills you have learned.

- **Keep tracking your fitness and food.**
- **Make regular exercise an integral part of your life.**
- **Commit to two to three meatless days a week.**
- **Practice the Space Cleanses that need attention, such as positive self-talk.**
- **Mindful Moments can be found in many books and spiritual guides.**
- **Maintain a primarily plant-based diet.**
- **Continue the sleep hygiene practices.**
- **Stress Assess and de-stress daily.**

If the plan becomes your lifestyle, you will need to add certain supplements such as vitamin D, vitamin B12, and vegan omega-3 fatty acids. To learn more about what to do, visit with a registered dietitian-nutritionist, who can help guide you.

Expand your horizons by adding vegan foods such as vegetable or bean burgers, vegan mayonnaise, cheeses, or soy or TVP (textured vegetable protein) crumbles. If you choose to reintroduce dairy foods, go organic. If possible, go local. There are vegan and vegetarian frozen foods and dinners for times when you are busy. Please read the tiny print in the ingredient lists so you know what you are putting into your body. Some products are better than others.

After a few months you may find yourself slipping back into old habits, reboot with the 14-Day Plan or the 7-Day Demi-Plan.

Incorporating *The Only Cleanse* philosophy into daily life is very doable. An *Only Cleanse* Plan follower, Michael, was concerned that he had "food-related events" and work dinners coming up and did not want to "cheat" on the plan. Hey, life is life. Enjoy special occasions. You don't always need to eat at every event, by the way. Have a meal before you go. If you are in charge of the event, you can make healthy options for people. There are many great cookbooks on the market and free vegetarian or vegan recipes online. At parties at my house I offer vegan options because some guests cannot eat dairy. I also have people with celiac disease and nut allergies, so I serve gluten- and nut-free dishes. With a bit of forethought, it is quite manageable.

Your Journey to Awesomeness

You may find that not everyone is supportive of the changes you are making. As you traverse the road of life, there will be potholes. Kathi was in the middle of the 14-Day *Only Cleanse* Plan when she went to a brunch with several friends. She told me her companions labeled her a "no-fun, teetotaling vegan." All in good fun, and yet sometimes people feel threatened or annoyed when you are trying to make healthy lifestyle changes and they are not. I am often the focus of food-related "jokes" or comments, and I have learned to smile and let it go. Interestingly the effects of the Mindful Moments or Space Cleanses, such as a positive attitude, acts of kindness, or appreciation of others, are looked upon as good things. When food comes into the mix, attitudes may change. We have complex emotional and psychological relationships with food. It is best to focus on your needs and well-being and to let other people's negative attitudes roll off your back. Do not argue or preach. Enjoy your newfound energy and health. If someone is interested in the plan, refer them to *The Only Cleanse* and let them discover the wonderful benefits of a healthy lifestyle for themselves.

You are worth the effort it takes to be energized and happy. You deserve to be healthy and feel fantastic. You owe it to yourself to be respectful, kind and supportive of yourself. It's a process. Life is an ever-changing motif, and we change with it. The ebb and flow of energy, food, experiences, aging, health, happiness, and sadness are all part of this thing we call life on Earth.

Eat well. Laugh often. Be kind. Embrace compassion. Seek inner peace. Breathe.

REFERENCES

Chapter 1

References The Only Cleanse
Chapter 1
American Cancer Society. "Colorectal Cancer: What Is Colorectal Cancer?" American Cancer Society, http://www.cancer.org/cancer/colon andrectumcancer/detailedguide/colorectal-cancer-key-statistics.

Azpiroz Fernando. "Understanding Intestinal Gas." International Foundation for Functional Gastrointestinal Disorders, http://www.giresearch .org.

Beck DE. "Colonic Physiology." In *The Ascrs Textbook of Colon and Rectal Surgery*. Springer, 2011.

Galvez, Julio, M. Elena Rodriguez-Cabezas, and Antonio Zarzuelo. "Effects of Dietary Fiber on Inflammatory Bowel Disease." *Molecular Nutrition & Food Research* 49, no. 6 (2005): 601–8.

"Gas-Related Complaints." In *The Merck Manual,* edited Merck Sharp & Dohme Corp, 2007. http://www.merckmanuals.com/professional/ gastrointestinal_disorders/approach_to_the_patient_with_lower_gi_ complaints/gas-related_complaints.html?qt=&sc=&alt=.

Henningsson Asa, Bjorck Inger, and Nyman Margareta. "Short-Chainfatty Acid Formation at Fermentation of Indigestible Carbohydrates." *Scandinavian Journal of 'Nutrition* 45 (2001): 165–68.

Hijova E, and Chmelarova A. "Short-Chain Fatty Acids and Colonic Health." *Bratisl Lek Listy* 108, no. 8 (2007): 354—58.

———. "Short-Chain Fatty Acids and Colonic Health." *Bratisl Lek Listy* 108, no. 8 (2007): 354 58.

Johns Hopkins Gastroenterology & Helatology. "The Inside Tract." edited by Johns Hopkins Medicine: The Johns Hopkins University and The Johns Hopkins Health System Corporation, 2012.

Mahan, Kathleen L., and Marian Arlin. *Krause's Food, Nutrition & Diet Therapy.* 8th ed. Philadelphia: W.B. Saunders Company, 1992.

Molodecky, Natalie A., Ing Shian Soon, Doreen M. Rabi, William A. Ghali, Mollie Ferris, Greg Chernoff, Eric I. Benchimol, *et al.* "Increasing Incidence and Prevalence of the Inflammatory Bowel Diseases with Time, Based on Systematic Review." *Gastroenterology* 142, no. 1 (2012): 46–54.e42.

Ng, Siew C, Charles N Bernstein, Morten H Vatn, Peter Laszlo Lakatos, Edward V Loftus, Curt Tysk, Colm O'Morain, *et al.* "Geographical Variability and Environmental Risk Factors in Inflammatory Bowel Disease." *Gut* 62, no. 4 (April 1, 2013 2013): 630–49.

Roy, Claude C., C. Lawrence Kien, Lise Bouthillier, and Emile Levy. "Short-Chain Fatty Acids: Ready for Prime Time?". *Nutrition in Clinical Practice* 21, no. 4 (2006): 351–66.

Said, Hamid M. "Biotin: The Forgotten Vitamin." *The American Journal of Clinical Nutrition* 75, no. 2 (February 1, 2002 2002): 179–80.

Said, Hamid M., Alvaro Ortiz, Veedamali S. Subramanian, Ellis J. Neufeld, Mary Pat Moyer, and Pradeep K. Dudeja. "Mechanism of Thiamine Uptake by Human Colonocytes: Studies with Cultured Colonic Epithelial Cell Line Ncm460." *American Journal of Physiology—Gastrointestinal and Liver Physiology* 281, no. 1 (July 1, 2001 2001): G144-G50.

SANDLE, G I. "Salt and Water Absorption in the Human Colon: A Modern Appraisal." *Gut* 43, no. 2 (August 1, 1998 1998): 294–99.

Chapter 2

Albenberg, L. G., and G. D. Wu. "Diet and the Intestinal Microbiome: Associations, Functions, and Implications for Health and Disease." [In eng]. *Gastroenterology* 146, no. 6 (May 2014): 1564–72.

Alessio Fasano, and Susie Flaherty. *Gluten Freedom: The Nation's Leading Expert Offers the Essential Guide to a Healthy, Gluten-Free Lifestyle.* New York: Wiley, 2014.

Association, American Gastroenterological. "Probiotics: What They Are and What They Can Do for You." American Gastroenterological Association, http://www.gastro.org/patient-center/diet-medications/probiotics.

Boyle, Robert J, Roy M Robins-Browne, and Mimi LK Tang. "Probiotic Use in Clinical Practice: What Are the Risks?". *The American Journal of Clinical Nutrition* 83, no. 6 (June 1, 2006 2006): 1256–64.

Brown Rebecca J, Mary Ann De Banate, Kristina L. Rother. "Artificial Sweeteners: A Systematic Review of Metabolic Effects in Youth." *International Journal of Pediatric Obesity* 5, no. 4 (2010): 305–12.

Carpenter Siri. "That Gut Feeling: With a Sophisticated Neural Network Transmitting Messages from Trillions of Bacteria, the Brain in Your Gut Exerts a Powerful Influence over the One in Your Head, New Research Suggests.". *Monitor on Psycholigy* 43, no. 8 (2012).

Center for Science in the Public Interest. "Chemical Cuisine: Learn About Food Additives." http://www.cspinet.org/reports/chemcuisine.htm.

Centers for Disease Control and Prevention. "Clostridium Difficile Infection." Centers for Disease Control and Prevention,

USA.Gov, http://www.cdc.gov/hai/organisms/cdiff/cdiff_infect.html.

Chen, Jia, Xianzhi He, and Jinhai Huang. "Diet Effects in Gut Microbiome and Obesity." *Journal of Food Science* 79, no. 4 (2014): R442-R51.

Clarke, Siobhan F, Eileen F Murphy, Orla O'Sullivan, Alice J Lucey, Margaret Humphreys, Aileen Hogan, Paula Hayes, *et al.* "Exercise and Associated Dietary Extremes Impact on Gut Microbial Diversity." *Gut* (June 9, 2014 2014).

David Lawrence A, Arne C Materna, Jonathan Friedman, Maria I Campos-Baptista, Matthew C Blackburn, Allison Perotta, Susan E Erdman, and Eric J. Alm. "Host Lifestyle Affects Human Microbiota on Daily Timescales." *Genome Biology* 15, no. R89 (2014).

David, Lawrence A., Corinne F. Maurice, Rachel N. Carmody, David B. Gootenberg, Julie E. Button, Benjamin E. Wolfe, Alisha V. Ling, *et al.* "Diet Rapidly and Reproducibly Alters the Human Gut Microbiome." *Nature* 505, no. 7484 (01/23/print 2014): 559-63.

Devaraj Sridevi, Peera Hemarajata, and James Versalovic. "The Human Gut Microbiome and Body Metabolism: Implications for Obesity and Diabetes." *Clinical Chemistry* 59, no. 4 (2013): 617-28.

Deweerdt, Sarah. "Microbiome: A Complicated Relationship Status." *Nature* 508, no. 7496 (04/17/print 2014): S61-S63.

Du, Huaidong, Daphne L van der A, Hendriek C Boshuizen, Nita G Forouhi, Nicolas J Wareham, Jytte Halkjær, Anne Tjønneland, *et al.* "Dietary Fiber and Subsequent Changes in Body Weight and Waist Circumference in European Men and Women." *The American Journal of Clinical Nutrition* 91, no. 2 (February 1, 2010 2010): 329-36.

EBSCO Complementary and Alternative Medicine (CAM) Review Board. "Beta-glucan." http://www.med.nyu.edu/content?ChunkIID=104429.

EurekAlert! "The Surface Area of the Digestive Tract 'Only' as Large as a Studio Apartment." American Association for the Advancement of Science http://www.eurekalert.org/pub_releases/2014-04/uog-tsa042314.php.

Food and Agriculture Organization of the United Nations, and World Health Organization. "Guidelines for the Evaluation of Probiotics in Food." In *Joint FAO/WHO Working Group Report on Drafting Guidelines for the Evaluation of Probiotics in Food.* London, Ontario, Canada, 2002.

Furness, J. B., W. A. Kunze, and N. Clerc. "Nutrient Tasting and Signaling Mechanisms in the Gut. Ii. The Intestine as a Sensory Organ: Neural, Endocrine, and Immune Responses." [In eng]. *Am J Physiol* 277, no. 5 Pt 1 (Nov 1999): G922-8.

Gaurner Francisco, and Juan R Malagelada. "Gut Flora in Health and Disease." *Lancet* 361 (February 8 2003): 512-19.

Guarner, F., A. G. Khan, J. Garisch, R. Eliakim, A. Gangl, A. Thomson, J. Krabshuis, *et al.* "World Gastroenterology Organisation Global Guidelines:

Probiotics and Prebiotics October 2011." [In eng]. *J Clin Gastroenterol* 46, no. 6 (Jul 2012): 468–81.

Haahtela, T., S. Holgate, R. Pawankar, C. A. Akdis, S. Benjaponpitak, L. Caraballo, J. Demain, J. Portnoy, and L. von Hertzen. "The Biodiversity Hypothesis and Allergic Disease: World Allergy Organization Position Statement." [In eng]. *World Allergy Organ J* 6, no. 1 (2013): 3.

Hanage, W. P. "Microbiology: Microbiome Science Needs a Healthy Dose of Scepticism." *Nature* 512, no. 7514 (2014): 247–8.

Harris, Kristina, Amira Kassis, Genevi Major, #232, ve, and Chieh J. Chou. "Is the Gut Microbiota a New Factor Contributing to Obesity and Its Metabolic Disorders?". *Journal of Obesity* 2012 (2012): 14.

Harvard School of Public Health. "Health Gains from Whole Grains." Harvard School of PUblic Health, http://www.hsph.harvard.edu/nutritionsource/what-should-you-eat/health-gains-from-whole-grains/.

Hemarajata, Peera, and James Versalovic. "Effects of Probiotics on Gut Microbiota: Mechanisms of Intestinal Immunomodulation and Neuromodulation." *Therapeutic Advances in Gastroenterology* 6, no. 1 (2013): 39–51.

Hill, J. M., S. Bhattacharjee, A. I. Pogue, and W. J. Lukiw. "The Gastrointestinal Tract Microbiome and Potential Link to Alzheimer's Disease." [In eng]. *Front Neurol* 5 (2014): 43.

"The Integrative Human Microbiome Project: Dynamic Analysis of Microbiome-Host Omics Profiles During Periods of Human Health and Disease." *Cell Host & Microbe* 16, no. 3 (2014): 276–89.

Kelesidis, Theodoros, and Charalabos Pothoulakis. "Efficacy and Safety of the Probiotic *Saccharomyces Boulardii* for the Prevention and Therapy of Gastrointestinal Disorders." *Therapeutic Advances in Gastroenterology* 5, no. 2 (2012): 111–25.

Kinross James M, Ara W. Darzi, and Jeremy K. Nicholson. "Gut Microbiome-Host Interactions in Health and Disease." *Genome Medicine* 3, no. 14 (2011).

Kligler, B., and A. Cohrssen. "Probiotics." [In eng]. *Am Fam Physician* 78, no. 9 (Nov 1 2008): 1073–8.

Lassenius, Mariann I., Kirsi H. Pietiläinen, Kati Kaartinen, Pirkko J. Pussinen, Jaana Syrjänen, Carol Forsblom, Ilkka Pörsti, *et al.* "Bacterial Endotoxin Activity in Human Serum Is Associated with Dyslipidemia, Insulin Resistance, Obesity, and Chronic Inflammation." *Diabetes Care* 34, no. 8 (August 1, 2011 2011): 1809–15.

Leach Jeff D, and Sobolik Kristin D. "High Dietary Intake of Prebiotic Inulin-Type Fructans from Prehistoric Chihuahuan Desert." *British Journal of Nutrition* 103 (2010): 1558–61.

Ley Ruth E. "Obesity and the Human Microbiome." *Current Opinion in Gastroenterology* 26, no. 1 (2010): 5–11.

Macfarlane, S., G. T. Macfarlane, and J. H. Cummings. "Review Article: Prebiotics in the Gastrointestinal Tract." *Alimentary Pharmacology & Therapeutics* 24, no. 5 (2006): 701–14.

Marshall, Bonnie M., and Stuart B. Levy. "Food Animals and Antimicrobials: Impacts on Human Health." *Clinical Microbiology Reviews* 24, no. 4 (October 1, 2011 2011): 718–33.

Mayo Clinic. "H. Pylori Infection." Mayo Foundation for Medical Education and Research, http://www.mayoclinic.org/diseases-conditions/h-pylori/basics/definition/con-20030903.

———. "Is Our Microbiome a Predictor of Cardiac Risk?": Mayo Foundation for Medical Education and Research, 2014.

Medicine, Physicians Commitee for Responsible. "Meat Consumption and Cancer Risk." The Physicians COmmittee, http://www.pcrm.org/health/cancer-resources/diet-cancer/facts/meat-consumption-and-cancer-risk.

Mendelsohn, A. R., and J. W. Larrick. "Dietary Modification of the Microbiome Affects Risk for Cardiovascular Disease." [In eng]. *Rejuvenation Res* 16, no. 3 (Jun 2013): 241–4.

Natural Resources Defense Council. "The Ecosystem Within." Natural Resources Defense Council, http://www.nrdc.org/thisgreenlife/1208.asp.

Orel, Rok, and Tina Kamhi Trop. "Intestinal Microbiota, Probiotics and Prebiotics in Inflammatory Bowel Disease." *World Journal Of Gastroenterology: WJG* 20, no. 33 (2014): 11505–24.

Ou, Junhai, Franck Carbonero, Erwin G. Zoetendal, James P. DeLany, Mei Wang, Keith Newton, H. Rex Gaskins, and Stephen J.D. O'Keefe. "Diet, Microbiota, and Microbial Metabolites in Colon Cancer Risk in Rural Africans and African Americans." *The American Journal of Clinical Nutrition* 98, no. 1 (July 1, 2013 2013): 111–20.

Palca Joe. "Bacteria on Your Fingertips Could Identify You." NPR, http://www.npr.org/templates/story/story.php?storyId=124709981.

Park Yikyung, Amy F. Subar, Albert Hollenbeck, and Arthur Schatzkin. "Dietary Fiber Intake and Mortality in the Nih-Aarp Diet and Health Study." *Archives of Internal Medicine* (February 14 2011).

Reid Ann, and Shannon Greene. "The Human Microbiome Faq." The American Academy of Microbiology, 2012.

Schnabl, B., and D. A. Brenner. "Interactions between the Intestinal Microbiome and Liver Diseases." *Gastroenterology* 146, no. 6 (1513–24.

Seekatz, Anna M., Johannes Aas, Charles E. Gessert, Timothy A. Rubin, Daniel M. Saman, Johan S. Bakken, and Vincent B. Young. "Recovery of the

Gut Microbiome Following Fecal Microbiota Transplantation." *mBio* 5, no. 3 (July 1, 2014 2014).

Sheh, A., and J. G. Fox. "The Role of the Gastrointestinal Microbiome in Helicobacter Pylori Pathogenesis." *Gut Microbes* 4, no. 6 (2013): 505–31.

Slavin, J. "Fiber and Prebiotics: Mechanisms and Health Benefits." [In eng]. *Nutrients* 5, no. 4 (Apr 2013): 1417–35.

Suez, Jotham, Tal Korem, David Zeevi, Gili Zilberman-Schapira, Christoph A. Thaiss, Ori Maza, David Israeli, *et al.* "Artificial Sweeteners Induce Glucose Intolerance by Altering the Gut Microbiota." *Nature* advance online publication (09/17/online 2014).

Sun, Jun, and Eugene B. Chang. "Exploring Gut Microbes in Human Health and Disease: Pushing the Envelope." *Genes & Diseases*, no. 0 (

Synopsis. "Bile Acids: Toxicology and Bioactivity." edited by Jenkins Gareth J and Hardie Laura. RSC Publishing, 2008.

Thomas Francois, Jan-Hendrik Hehemann, Etienne Rebuffet, Mirjam Czjzek, and Michel Gurvan. "Environmental and Gut Bacteroidetes: The Food Connection." *Frontiers in Microbiology* 2, no. 93 (May 2011).

"What Is a Genome?". US National Library of Medicine, National Institutes of Health, Lister Hill National Center for Biomedical Communications, Department of Health & Human Services, http://ghr.nlm.nih.gov/handbook/hgp/genome.

Yan, Fang, and D. B. Polk. "Probiotics and Immune Health." *Current Opinion in Gastroenterology* 27, no. 6 (2011): 496–501.

Yang, Q. "Gain Weight by "Going Diet?" Artificial Sweeteners and the Neurobiology of Sugar Cravings: Neuroscience 2010." [In eng]. *Yale J Biol Med* 83, no. 2 (Jun 2010): 101–8.

Chapter 3

Acosta, Ruben D., and Brooks D. Cash. "Clinical Effects of Colonic Cleansing for General Health Promotion: A Systematic Review." *American Journal of Gastroenterology* 104, no. 11 (2009): 2830–6; quiz 37.

American Cancer Society. "Gerson Therapy." American Cancer Society, http://www.cancer.org/treatment/treatmentsandsideeffects/complementaryandalternativemedicine/dietandnutrition/gerson-therapy.

Anand Preetha, Ajakumar B. Kunnumakara, Chitra Sundaram, and Harikumar B. Kuzhuvelil. "Cancer Is a Preventable Disease That Requires Major Lifestyle Changes." *Pharmaceutical Research* 25, no. 9 (2008): 2097–116.

Bellany Alastair, and Andrew McRae. "Early Stuart Libels: An Edition of Poetry from Manuscript Sources: H. The Overbury Murder Scandal 1615–1616." In *Early Modern Literary Studies Text Series*: Arts & Humanities Research Council, 2005.

Daily Mail Reporter. "Colonic Irrigation 'Unproven and Dangerous': Diana's Fad Is Actually Bad for You and Can Cause Renal Failure." *The Daily Mail,* 2011.

Dixon Laurina S. "Some Penetrating Insights: The Imagery of Enemas in Art." *Art Journal* 52, no. 3 (Autumn 1993): 28–35.

Doyle D. "Per Rectum: A History of Enemata." *J R Coll Physicians Edinb* 35 (2005): 367–70.

"The Enema—Heir to the Clyster." *South African Medical Journal* 21, no. 8 (April 26 1947).

Ernst, E. "Colonic Irrigation and the Theory of Autointoxication: A Triumph of Ignorance over Science." *Journal of Clinical Gastroenterology* 24, no. 4 (Jun 1997): 196–8.

Gayer, G., R. Zissin, S. Apter, A. Oscadchy, and M. Hertz. "Perforations of the Rectosigmoid Colon Induced by Cleansing Enema: Ct Findings in 14 Patients." *Abdominal Imaging* 27, no. 4 (2002): 453–7.

Gosselink, M. P., M. Darby, D. D. E. Zimmerman, A. A. A. Smits, I. van Kessel, W. C. Hop, J. W. Briel, and W. R. Schouten. "Long-Term Follow-up of Retrograde Colonic Irrigation for Defaecation Disturbances." *Colorectal Disease* 7, no. 1 (2005): 65–9.

Handley, Doug V., Nick A. Rieger, and David J. Rodda. "Rectal Perforation from Colonic Irrigation Administered by Alternative Practitioners." *Medical Journal of Australia* 181, no. 10 (Nov 15 2004): 575–6.

Hijova, E., and A. Chmelarova. "Short-chain Fatty Acids and Colonic Health." [In eng]. *Bratisl Lek Listy* 108, no. 8 (2007): 354–8.

Jessica, L. LaBond, H. Stroeters Nicholas, A. Benvenuto Mark, and S. Roberts-Kirchhoff Elizabeth. "Analysis of Nine Edible Clay Supplements with a Handheld Xrf Analyzer." Chap. 8 In *Chemistry of Food, Food Supplements, and Food Contact Materials: From Production to Plate.* Acs Symposium Series, 99–111: American Chemical Society, 2014.

Jones, Aminah Alleyne, Ranit Mishori, and Aye Otubu. "The Dangers of Colon Cleansing: Patients May Look to Colon Cleansing as a Way to "Enhance Their Well-Being," but in Reality They May Be Doing Themselves Harm." *Journal of Family Practice,* 2011/08// 2011, 454+.

Lawrance Ian Craig. "Novel Topical Therapies for Distal Colitis." *World Journal of Gastrointestinal Pharmacology and Therapeutics* 1, no. 5 (October 6 2010): 87–93.

Love Bryan L, Saima Siddiqui, J. McCallum Brown, and Richard M. Helman. "Severe Chemical Colitis Due to Hydrogen Peroxide Enema." *J Clin Gastroenterol* 46, no. 1 (January 2012 2012).

Markel, H. "John Harvey Kellogg and the Pursuit of Wellness." *JAMA* 305, no. 17 (2011): 1814–15.

Medlins Plus. "Fecal Impaction." US National Library of Medicine, National

Institutes of Health, http://www.nlm.nih.gov/medlineplus/ency/article/000230.htm.

Mishori Ranit, Otubu Aye, and Jones Alleyne Aminah. "The Dangers of Colon Cleansing." *The Journal of Family Practice* 60, no. 8 (2011): 454-57.

Mishori, Ranit M. D. M. H. S., Aye M. D. M. P. H. Otubu, and Aminah Alleyne M. D. M. P. H. Jones. "The Dangers of Colon Cleansing." *Journal of Family Practice* 60, no. 8 (2011): 454-57.

National Cancer Institute. "Fecal Impaction." National Institutes of Health, http://www.cancer.gov/cancertopics/pdq/supportivecare/gastro intestinalcomplications/Patient/page3.

Ori Y, B. Rozen-Zvi, A. Chagnac, M. Herman, B. Zingerman, E. Atar, U. Gafter, and A. Korzets. "Fatalities and Severe Metabolic Disorders Associated with the Use of Sodium Phosphate Enemas: A Single Center's Experience." *Arch Intern Med.* 172, no. 3 (Feb 13 2012): 263-5. doi: 10.1001/archinternmed.2011.694.

Rosenhek Jackie. "The Royal Flush." Doctor's Review: Medicine on the Move, Parkhurst, http://www.doctorsreview.com/history/ju105-history/.

Sinha, Rashmi, Ulrike Peters, Amanda J. Cross, Martin Kulldorff, Joel L. Weissfeld, Paul F. Pinsky, Nathaniel Rothman, Richard B. Hayes, and Lung Colorectal and Ovarian Cancer Project Team Prostate. "Meat, Meat Cooking Methods and Preservation, and Risk for Colorectal Adenoma." *Cancer Res* 65, no. 17 (September 1, 2005 2005): 8034-41.

TCM. "The Poisoners of Other Times." *The Cincinnati Lancet-Clinic* 86 (1901): 303-06.

Welkos Robert W. "New Chapter in the Mystery of Marilyn: Her Own Words?" *Los Angeles Times*, August 5 2005 2005.

Williams, Lynda B., and Shelley E. Haydel. "Evaluation of the Medicinal Use of Clay Minerals as Antibacterial Agents." *International geology review* 52, no. 7/8 (2010): 745-70.

Williams, Lynda B., Shelley E. Haydel, and Ray E. Ferrell. "Bentonite, Bandaids, and Borborygmi." *Elements (Quebec, Quebec)* 5, no. 2 (2009): 99-104.

Chapter 4

Azevedo, Fernanda de, Dimas Ikeoka, and Bruno Caramelli. "Effects of Intermittent Fasting on Metabolism in Men." *Revista da Associação Médica Brasileira* 59, no. 2 (3// 2013): 167-73.

Getting, J. E., J. R. Gregoire, A. Phul, and M. J. Kasten. "Oxalate Nephropathy Due to 'Juicing': Case Report and Review." *American Journal of Medicine* 126, no. 9 (2013): 768-72.

Kerndt, Peter R., James L. Naughton, Charles E. Driscoll, and David A. Loxterkamp. "Fasting: The History, Pathophysiology and Complications." *Western Journal of Medicine* 137, no. 5 (1982): 379–99.

Muraki, Isao, Fumiaki Imamura, JoAnn E Manson, Frank B Hu, Walter C Willett, Rob M van Dam, and Qi Sun. *Fruit Consumption and Risk of Type 2 Diabetes: Results from Three Prospective Longitudinal Cohort Studies.* Vol. 347,2013. Journal Article. doi:10.1136/bmj.f5001.

Nestle, Marion, and Nesheim Malden. *Why Calories Count: From Science to Politics.* Berkely, CA.: University of California Press, 2012.

Chapter 5

US Food and Drug Administration, . "Warning on Hydroxy Cut Products." US Department of Health and Human Services, http://www.fda.gov/ForConsumers/ConsumerUpdates/ucm152152.htm.

American Council on Science and Health. "How Clean Should Your Colon Be?" THE AMERICAN COUNCIL ON SCIENCE AND HEALTH http://acsh.org/2003/02/how-clean-should-your-colon-be/.

Boganen, H., K. van Hee, and H. G. L. M. Grundmeijer. "[Hypertension Due to Liquorice and Liquorice Tea Consumption]." *Nederlands Tijdschrift voor Geneeskunde* 151, no. 51 (2007): 2825–8.

Celik, M. M., A. Karakus, C. Zeren, M. Demir, H. Bayarogullari, M. Duru, and M. Al. "Licorice Induced Hypokalemia, Edema, and Thrombocytopenia." *Human & Experimental Toxicology* 31, no. 12 (2012): 1295–8.

Center for Science in the Public Interest. "DNA Testing Reveals Herbal Supplements Often Missing the Advertised Herb." http://cspinet.org/new/201502023.html.

Dara Lily, Hewett Jennifer, and Lim Joseph Kartaik. "Hydroxycut Hepatotoxicity: A Case Series and Review of Liver Toxicity from Herbal Weight Loss Supplements." *World Journal of Gastroenterology* 14, no. 45 (December 7 2008): 6999–7004.

FDA. "Consumer Advisory: Black Licorice Can Be a Dangerous Treat for Some." edited by US Food and Drug Administration. http://www.fda.gov/food/resourcesforyou/consumers/ucm231078.htm, 2014.

———. "Public Notification: Lingzhi Cleansed Slim Tea Contains Hidden Drug Ingredient." US Food and Drug Administration, http://www.fda.gov/Drugs/ResourcesForYou/Consumers/BuyingUsingMedicineSafely/MedicationHealthFraud/ucm404302.htm.

Food and Drug Administration. *Bad Bug Book, Foodborne Pathogenic Microorganisms and Natural Toxins. Second Edition.* 2012.

Gabardi, Steven, Kristin Munz, and Catherine Ulbricht. "A Review of Dietary Supplement-Induced Renal Dysfunction." *Clinical Journal of the American Society of Nephrology* 2, no. 4 (July 1, 2007 2007): 757–65.

REFERENCES

Joo, J. S., E. D. Ehrenpreis, L. Gonzalez, M. Kaye, S. Breno, S. D. Wexner, D. Zaitman, and K. Secrest. "Alterations in Colonic Anatomy Induced by Chronic Stimulant Laxatives: The Cathartic Colon Revisited." *Journal of Clinical Gastroenterology* 26, no. 4 (1998): 283–6.

Klerk Gerty J de, Marietje G Nieuwenhuis, and Jaap J Beutler. "Hypoka-laemia and Hypertension Associated with Use of Liquorice Flavoured Chewing Gum." *BMJ* 314 (March 8 1997): 731–32.

Lawrence James, and Lin Chong Lina Paul. "The Dangers of Drinking Liquorice Tea." *Endocrine Abstracts* 21, no. p75 (2010).

Lin, Shih-Hua, Sung-Sen Yang, Tom Chau, and Mitchell L. Halperin. "An Unusual Cause of Hypokalemic Paralysis: Chronic Licorice Ingestion." *American Journal of the Medical Sciences* 325, no. 3 (2003): 153–6.

MedlinePlus. "Licorice." In *Natural Medicines Comprehensive Database* US National Library of Medicine, National Institutes of Health, 2014.

NYU Langone Medical Center. "Licorice." EBSCO Publishing, 2013.

O'Connor Anahad. "Spike in Harm to Liver Is Tied to Dietary Aids." *New York Times,* December 21 2013.

Omar, R. Hersham, Irinia Komarova, Mohamed El-Ghonemi, Ahmed Fathy, Rania Rashas, Harry D. Abdelmalak, Muralidnar Reddy Yerramadha, Engy Helal, and Enrico M. Camporesi. "Licorice Abuse: Time to Send a Warning Message." *Endocrinology and Metabolism* 3, no. 4 (2012): 125–38.

US National Library of Medicine. "Drug Record: Cascara (Cascara Sagrada)." US National Library of Medicine, http://livertox.nih.gov/Cascara.htm.

US National Library of Medicine, and National Institute of Diabetes and Digestive and Kidney Diseases. "Drug Record: Green Tea (Camellia Sine-sis)." US National Library of Medicine, http://livertox.nih.gov/GreenTea.htm.

University of Maryland Medical Center. "Licorice." In *Medical Reference Guide: Complementary and Alternative Medicine Guide,* 2014.

———. "Uva Ursi." University of Maryland Medical Center http://umm.edu/health/medical/altmed/herb/uva-ursi—ixzz3lbc38MFo

US Food and Drug Administration. "More Weight Loss Products Added to Consumer Alert." FDA, http://www.fda.gov/ForConsumers/ConsumerUpdates/ucm103184.htm.

Vanderperren Benedicte, Michaela Rizzo, Luc Angenot, Vincent Haufroid, Jadoul Michel, and Hantson Phillippe. "Acute Liver Failure with Renal Impairment Related to the Abuse of Senna Anthraquinone Glycosides." *Ann Pharmacother* 39 (2005): 1353–7.

WebMD, and Natural Medicines Comprehensive Database Consumer Version. "Cascara Overview Information." http://www.webmd.com/

vitamins-supplements/ingredientmono-773-cascara.aspx?activeingred
ientid=773&activeingredientname=cascara.

Chapter 6

References

Bray, George A. "How Bad Is Fructose?". *The American Journal of Clinical Nutrition* 86, no. 4 (October 1, 2007 2007): 895–96.

Guyton Arthur C, and John E. Hall. *Textbook of Medical Physiology.* 9 ed. Philadelphia: W.B. Saunders, 1996.

Harvard Health Publications. "Abundance of Fructose Not Good for the Liver, Heart." Harvard Health Publications, Harvard University, http://www.health.harvard.edu/newsletters/Harvard_Heart_Letter/2011/September/abundance-of-fructose-not-good-for-the-liver-heart.

Harvard Medical School. "The Dubious Practice of Detox." http://www.health.harvard.edu/fhg/updates/The-dubious-practice-of-detox.shtml.

Herrera Jorge L. "Medications and the Liver." http://patients.gi.org/topics/medications-and-the-liver/.

Jenne, Craig N., and Paul Kubes. "Immune Surveillance by the Liver." *Nat Immunol* 14, no. 10 (2013): 996–1006.

Kang, A. Y., L. R. Young, C. Dingfelder, and S. Peterson. "Effects of Furanocoumarins from Apiaceous Vegetables on the Catalytic Activity of Recombinant Human Cytochrome P-450 1a2." [In eng]. *Protein J* 30, no. 7 (Oct 2011): 447–56.

Liu Jiawang, Sridhar Jayalakshmi, and Foroozesh Maryam. "Cytochrome P450 Family 1 Inhibitors and Structure-Activity Relationships." *Molecules* 18 (2013): 14470–95.

Park Sohyun, Liping Pan, Bettylou Sherry, and Heidi M. Blanck. "Consumption of Sugar-Sweetened Beverages among Us Adults in 6 States: Behavioral Risk Factor Surveillance System, 2011." *Centers for Disease Control and Prevention: Preventing Chronic Disease* 11 (April 24 2014).

Peterson, S., J. W. Lampe, T. K. Bammler, K. Gross-Steinmeyer, and D. L. Eaton. "Apiaceous Vegetable Constituents Inhibit Human Cytochrome P-450 1a2 (Hcyp1a2) Activity and Hcyp1a2-Mediated Mutagenicity of Aflatoxin B1." [In eng]. *Food Chem Toxicol* 44, no. 9 (Sep 2006): 1474–84.

Rosqvist, F., D. Iggman, J. Kullberg, J. Cedernaes, H. E. Johansson, A. Larsson, L. Johansson, *et al.* "Overfeeding Polyunsaturated and Saturated Fat Causes Distinct Effects on Liver and Visceral Fat Accumulation in Humans." [In eng]. *Diabetes* 63, no. 7 (Jul 2014): 2356–68.

Roy Heli, Shanna Lundy, Beth Kalicki, Phillip Brantley, and Clause Bouchard. "Health Benefits of Cruciferous Vegetables." Pennington Biomedical Research Center.

Singal, Ashwani K., and S. Anand Bhupinderjit. "Recent Trends in the Epidemiology of Alcoholic Liver Disease." *Clinical Liver Disease* 2, no. 2 (2013): 53–56.

Talalay, Paul, and Jed W. Fahey. "Phytochemicals from Cruciferous Plants Protect against Cancer by Modulating Carcinogen Metabolism." *The Journal of Nutrition* 131, no. 11 (November 1, 2001 2001): 3027S-33S.

US Department of Health & Human Services, National Institutes of Health, and National INstitute on Alcohol Abuse and Alcoholism. "Alcohol Metabolism: An Update." US Department of Health & Human Services, http://pubs.niaaa.nih.gov/publications/AA72/AA72.htm.

Williams, Roger, Richard Aspinall, Mark Bellis, Ginette Camps-Walsh, Matthew Cramp, Anil Dhawan, James Ferguson, *et al.* "Addressing Liver Disease in the Uk: A Blueprint for Attaining Excellence in Health Care and Reducing Premature Mortality from Lifestyle Issues of Excess Consumption of Alcohol, Obesity, and Viral Hepatitis." *The Lancet* (2014).

American Kidney Fund. "Chronic Kidney Disease (Ckd)." American Kidney Fund, Inc, http://www.kidneyfund.org/kidney-disease/chronic-kidney-disease/—VH5Z30tSxuY.

Centers for Disease Control and Prevention. " National Chronic Kidney Disease Fact Sheet 2014." http://www.cdc.gov/diabetes/pubs/pdf/kidney_factsheet.pdf.

Colman Sara. "Top 15 Healthy Foods for People with Kidney Disease." DaVita HealthCare Partners, Inc., http://www.davita.com/kidney-disease/diet-and-nutrition/lifestyle/top-15-healthy-foods-for-people-with-kidney-disease/e/5347.

Garibotto, Giacomo, Antonella Sofia, Stefano Saffioti, Alice Bonanni, Irene Mannucci, and Daniela Verzola. "Amino Acid and Protein Metabolism in the Human Kidney and in Patients with Chronic Kidney Disease." *Clinical Nutrition* 29, no. 4 (2010): 424–33.

International Diabetes Federation. "Idf Diabetes Atlas Sixth Edition Poster Update 2014." International Diabetes Federation, http://www.idf.org/diabetesatlas/update-2014.

Nestle, Marion. *Food Politics.* Berkeley: University of California Press, 2002.

Paddon-Jones, Douglas, Kevin R. Short, Wayne W. Campbell, Elena Volpi, and Robert R. Wolfe. "Role of Dietary Protein in the Sarcopenia of Aging." *Am J Clin Nutr* 87, no. 5 (May 1, 2008 2008): 1562S-66.

Ravera, Maura, Michela Re, Luca Deferrari, Simone Vettoretti, and Giacomo Deferrari. "Importance of Blood Pressure Control in Chronic Kidney Disease." *Journal of the American Society of Nephrology* 17, no. 4 suppl 2 (April 1, 2006 2006): S98-S103.

Schwingshackl, Lukas, and Georg Hoffmann. "Comparison of High Vs. Normal/Low Protein Diets on Renal Function in Subjects without Chronic Kidney Disease: A Systematic Review and Meta-Analysis." *PLoS ONE* 9, no. 5 (2014): e97656.

Tortora Gerard J, and Nicholas P Agnostakos. *Principles of Anatomy and Physiology*. 4th ed.: Harper & Row, 1984.

United States Department of Agriculture, and Agricultural Research Service. "A Plant-Based Diet Is a Healthy Choice." ARS, USDA, http://www.ars.usda.gov/News/docs.htm?docid=9246.

USDA Center for Nutrition Policy and Promotion. "Insight 3: Dietary Guidance on Sodium: Should We Take It with a Grain of Salt?" In *Nutrition Insights*, 1-2: Center for Nutrition Policy and Promotion, 1997.

Eneli, I U, T Skybo, and C A Camargo. "Weight Loss and Asthma: A Systematic Review." *Thorax* 63, no. 8 (August 1, 2008 2008): 671-76.

Environmental Protection Agency. "Mold Remediation in Schools and Commercial Buildings Appendi B—Intorduction to Molds." http://www.epa.gov/mold/append_b.html.

Jensen, M. E., P. G. Gibson, C. E. Collins, J. M. Hilton, and L. G. Wood. "Diet-Induced Weight Loss in Obese Children with Asthma: A Randomized Controlled Trial." *Clinical & Experimental Allergy* 43, no. 7 (2013): 775-84.

Penn Medicine. "Anatomy and Function of the Respiratory System." http://www.pennmedicine.org/health_info/asthma/000141.html

National Institutes of Health, US Department of Health and Human Services, and National Heart Lung and Blood Institute. "How the Lungs Work." National Institutes of Health,

US Department of Health & Human Services, http://www.nhlbi.nih.gov/health/health-topics/topics/ipf/lungworks.

———. "Understanding Lung Problems—Make Each Breath Healthy." National Institutes of Health,

US Department of Health & Human Services, http://www.nia.nih.gov/health/publication/understanding-lung-problems.

Phoades Rodney A. "Respiratory Physiology." In *Medical Physiology, Principles for Clinical Medicine*, edited by Phoades Rodney A and Bell R David. Baltimore: Lippincott Williams & Wilkins, Wolters Kluwer, 2013.

Pramanik, Tapas, Hari Om Sharma, Suchita Mishra, Anurag Mishra, Rajesh Prajapati, and Smriti Singh. "Immediate Effect of Slow Pace Bhastrika Pranayama on Blood Pressure and Heart Rate." *Journal of Alternative & Complementary Medicine* 15, no. 3 (2009): 293-5.

REFERENCES

Prevention, Centers for Disease Control and. "Mold in the Environment." http://www.cdc.gov/mold/faqs.htm.

Richardson Marion. "The Physiology of Mucus and Sputum Production in the Respiratory System." *Nursing Times* 99, no. 23 (June.

Sivakumar, G., K. Prabhu, R. Baliga, M. K. Pai, and S. Manjunatha. "Acute Effects of Deep Breathing for a Short Duration (2–10 Minutes) on Pulmonary Functions in Healthy Young Volunteers." [In eng]. *Indian J Physiol Pharmacol* 55, no. 2 (Apr-Jun 2011): 154–9.

Varraso, Raphaelle, Stephanie E. Chiuve, Teresa T Fung, Barr R Graham, Frank B. Hu, Walter C Willett, and C A Camargo. "Alternate Healthy Eating Index 2010 and Risk of Chronic Obstructive Pulmonary Disease among Us Women and Men: Prospective Study." *BMJ* (2015).

Academy of General Dentistry. "Nutrition." http://www.agd.org.

Asokan, Sharath, Raghuraman Chamundeswari, and Pamela Emmadi. "Effect of Oil Pulling on Plaque Induced Gingivitis: A Randomized, Controlled, Triple-Blind Study." [In English]. *Indian Journal of Dental Research* 20 (2009 January-March

// 2009): 47.

Asokan, Sharath, Pamela Emmadi, R. Kumar, R. Raghuraman, and N. Sivakumar. "Effect of Oil Pulling on Halitosis and Microorganisms Causing Halitosis: A Randomized Controlled Pilot Trial." *Journal of Indian Society of Pedodontics and Preventive Dentistry*, 2011 April-June 2011, 90.

Center, University of Rochester Medical. "The Best and Worst Foods for Your Teeth." University of Rochester Medical Center, http://www.urmc.rochester.edu/encyclopedia/content.aspx?ContentTypeID=1&ContentID=4062.

Dentistry, Academy of General. "Gum. . . . Disease?" http://www.agd.org.

Hirasawa, M., K. Takada, and S. Otake. "Inhibition of Acid Production in Dental Plaque Bacteria by Green Tea Catechins." [In eng]. *Caries Res* 40, no. 3 (2006): 265–70.

Kim, J. Y., J. W. Jung, J. C. Choi, J. W. Shin, I. W. Park, and B. W. Choi. "Recurrent Lipoid Pneumonia Associated with Oil Pulling." [In eng]. *Int J Tuberc Lung Dis* 18, no. 2 (Feb 2014): 251–2.

Novella Steven. "Oil Pulling Your Leg." http://www.sciencebasedmedicine.org/oil-pulling-your-leg/.

Shalala Donna E, and US Department of Health and Human Services. " Oral Health in America: A Report of the Surgeon General: Executive Summary." Rockville, MD Department of Health and Human Services, National Institute of Dental and Craniofacial Research, National Institutes of Health, 2000.

Singh, Abhinav, and Bharathi Purohit. "Tooth Brushing, Oil Pulling and Tissue Regeneration: A Review of Holistic Approaches to Oral Health." *Journal of Ayurveda and Integrative Medicine* 2, no. 2 (Apr-Jun 2011): 64–68.

Venkateswara, Babu, K. Sirisha, and Vijay K. Chava. "Green Tea Extract for Periodontal Health." *Journal of Indian Society of Periodontology* 15, no. 1 (Jan-Mar 2011): 18–22.

National Library of Medicine, and National Institutes of Health. "The Ear: How Can You Keep It Clean and What Helps If Earwax Builds Up?" Institute for Quality and Efficiency in Health Care, http://www.ncbi.nlm.nih.gov/pubmedhealth/PMH0010389/?report=printable.

Rafferty, J., A. Tsikoudas, and B. C. Davis. "Ear Candling: Should General Practitioners Recommend It?". *Canadian Family Physician* 53, no. 12 (2007): 2121–22.

Spankovich, C., and C. G. Le Prell. "Healthy Diets, Healthy Hearing: National Health and Nutrition Examination Survey, 1999–2002." [In eng]. *Int J Audiol* 52, no. 6 (Jun 2013): 369–76.

Section II

Bennett MP, J.M. Zeller, L. Rosenberg, and J. McCann. "The Effect of Mirthful Laughter on Stress and Natural Killer Cell Activity." *Alternative Therapies in Health & Medicine* 9, no. 2 (March-April 2003): 38–45.

Carter Sherrie Bourg. "The Hidden Health Hazards of Toxic Relationships." Sussex Publishers, LLC, http://www.psychologytoday.com/blog/high-octane-women/201108/the-hidden-health-hazards-toxic-relationships.

Centers for Disease Control and Prevention. "Centers for Disease Control and Prevention. National Diabetes Fact Sheet: General Information and National Estimates on Diabetes in the United States, 2003. Rev Ed. Atlanta, Ga:, 2004.", 8: US Department of Health and Human Services, Centers for Disease Control and Prevention, 2004.

———. "Insufficient Sleep Is a Public Health Epidemic." National Center for Chronic Disease and Prevention and Health Promotion, Division of Adult and Community Health, http://www.cdc.gov/features/dssleep/.

Seventh Day Adventist Church,. "Living a Healthful Life." Seventh Day Adventist World Chruch, http://www.adventist.org/vitality/health/.

Cohen Gene D. "Research on Creativity and Aging: The Positive Impact of the Arts on Health and Illness." *Generations* 30, no. 1 (2006): 7.

Cohen Geoffrey L, and Sherman David K. "The Psychology of Change: Self-Affirmation and Social Psychological Intervention." *Annual Review of Psychology* 65 (2014): 333–71.

De Vogli, R., T. Chandola, and M. Marmot. "Negative Aspects of Close Relationships and Heart Disease." *Archives of Internal Medicine* 167, no. 18 (2007): 1951–57.

Doghramji Karl. "The Effects of Alcohol on Sleep." *Medscapre Family Medicine* 7, no. 1 (2005): http://www.medscape.org/viewarticle/497982.

Emmons, R. A., and M. E. McCullough. "Counting Blessings Versus Burdens: An Experimental Investigation of Gratitude and Subjective Well-Being in Daily Life." [In eng]. *J Pers Soc Psychol* 84, no. 2 (Feb 2003): 377–89.

Esposito, Katherine, and Dario Giugliano. "Diet and Inflammation: A Link to Metabolic and Cardiovascular Diseases." *Eur Heart J %R 10.1093/ eurheartj/ehi605* 27, no. 1 (January 1, 2006 2006): 15–20.

EurekAlert! "Lack of Exercise Responsible for Twice as Many Deaths as Obesity." American Association for the Advancement of Science http:// www.eurekalert.org/pub_releases/2015–01/uoc-loe011315.php.

HAWKINS, MARQUIS S., MARY ANN SEVICK, CAROLINE R. RICHARDSON, LINDA F. FRIED, VINCENT C. ARENA, and ANDREA M. KRISKA. "Association between Physical Activity and Kidney Function: National Health and Nutrition Examination Survey." *Medicine & Science in Sports & Exercise* 43, no. 8 (2011): 1457–64 10.249/MSS.0b013e31820c0130.

Hays, N. P., R. D. Starling, X. Liu, D. H. Sullivan, T. A. Trappe, J. D. Fluckey, and W. J. Evans. "Effects of an Ad Libitum Low-Fat, High-Carbohydrate Diet on Body Weight, Body Composition, and Fat Distribution in Older Men and Women: A Randomized Controlled Trial.[See Comment]." *Archives of Internal Medicine* 164, no. 2 (Jan 26 2004): 210–7.

Hu, Frank B. "Plant-Based Foods and Prevention of Cardiovascular Disease: An Overview." *Am J Clin Nutr* 78, no. 3 (September 1, 2003 2003): 544S–51.

Jerath, R., J. W. Edry, V. A. Barnes, and V. Jerath. "Physiology of Long Pranayamic Breathing: Neural Respiratory Elements May Provide a Mechanism That Explains How Slow Deep Breathing Shifts the Autonomic Nervous System." [In eng]. *Med Hypotheses* 67, no. 3 (2006): 566–71.

Jerath, Ravinder, John W. Edry, Vernon A. Barnes, and Vandna Jerath. "Physiology of Long Pranayamic Breathing: Neural Respiratory Elements May Provide a Mechanism That Explains How Slow Deep Breathing Shifts the Autonomic Nervous System." *Medical Hypotheses* 67, no. 3 (2006): 566–71.

Jie Ji, Su-qing Wang, Yu-jian Liu, and Qi-qiang He. "Physical Activity and Lung Function Growth in a Cohort of Chinese School Children: A Prospective Study." *PLoS ONE [Electronic Resource]* 8, no. 6 (2013).

Jonnalagadda, Satya S., Lisa Harnack, Rui Hai Liu, Nicola McKeown, Chris Seal, Simin Liu, and George C. Fahey. "Putting the Whole Grain Puzzle Together: Health Benefits Associated with Whole Grains—Summary of

American Society for Nutrition 2010 Satellite Symposium." *Journal of Nutrition* 141, no. 5 (2011): 1011S-22S.

Keogh, J. B., J. A. Grieger, M. Noakes, and P. M. Clifton. "Flow-Mediated Dilatation Is Impaired by a High-Saturated Fat Diet but Not by a High-Carbohydrate Diet." *Arteriosclerosis, Thrombosis & Vascular Biology* 25, no. 6 (Jun 2005): 1274–9.

Kim, Sang Hwan, Suzanne M. Schneider, Len Kravitz, Christine Mermier, and Mark R. Burge. "Mind-Body Practices for Posttraumatic Stress Disorder." *Journal of Investigative Medicine* 61, no. 5 (2013): 827–34.

Kurzweil, Raymond. "Live Forever." *Psychology Today* 33, no. 1 (2000): 66.

Linus Pauling Institute. "Essential Fatty Acids." http://lpi.oregonstate.edu/infocenter/othernuts/omega3fa/.

Lyubomirsky Sonja, and Layous Kristin. "How Do Simple Positive Activities Increase Well-Being?". *Current Directions in Psychological Science* 22, no. 1 (2013): 57–62.

Merchant, Anwar T., Linda E. Kelemen, Lawrence de Koning, Eva Lonn, Vlad Vuksan, Ruby Jacobs, Bonnie Davis, *et al.* "Interrelation of Saturated Fat, Trans Fat, Alcohol Intake, and Subclinical Atherosclerosis." *Am J Clin Nutr* 87, no. 1 (January 1, 2008 2008): 168–74.

Mori, Hisao, Hareaki Yamamoto, Masaomi Kuwashima, Saburo Saito, Hiroshi Ukai, Kouichi Hirao, Mikio Yamauchi, and Satoshi Umemura. "How Does Deep Breathing Affect Office Blood Pressure and Pulse Rate?". *Hypertension Research—Clinical & Experimental* 28, no. 6 (2005): 499–504.

Moss MIchael. *Salt Sugar Fat: How the Food Giants Hooked Us.* New York: Random House, 2013.

Mustad, V. A., T. D. Etherton, A. D. Cooper, A. M. Mastro, T. A. Pearson, S. S. Jonnalagadda, and P. M. Kris-Etherton. "Reducing Saturated Fat Intake Is Associated with Increased Levels of Ldl Receptors on Mononuclear Cells in Healthy Men and Women." *Journal of Lipid Research* 38, no. 3 (Mar 1997): 459–68.

National Center for Complementary and Alternative Medicine (NCCAM). "Massage Therapy for Health Purposes: What You Need to Know,

Nccam Pub No.: D327." US Department of Health & Human Services, National Institutes of Health, http://nccam.nih.gov/health/massage/massageintroduction.htm.

Newby PK. "Plant Based Diet May Help Control Weight." *Agricultural Research Magazine, United States Department of Agriculture* 54, no. 3 (March 2006).

Non-GMO Project. "Gmos and Your Family." Non-GMO Project, http://www.nongmoproject.org/learn-more/gmos-and-your-family/

Norris Jack. "Omega-3 Fatty Acid Recommendations for Vegetarians."

VeganHealthorg, Vegan Outreach, http://www.veganhealth.org/articles/omega3.

Office of Dietary Supplements, and National Institutes of Health. "Omega-3 Fatty Acids and Health." http://dietary-supplements.info.nih.gov/FactSheets/Omega3FattyAcidsandHealth.asp.

Orlich MJ, Singh P, Sabaté J,. "Vegetarian Dietary Patterns and Mortality in Adventist Health Study 2." *JAMA Intern Med.* 173, no. 13 (2013): 1230-38.

Pan, An, Qi Sun, Adam M. Bernstein, Matthias B. Schulze, JoAnn E. Manson, Meir J. Stampfer, Walter C. Willett, and Frank B. Hu. "Red Meat Consumption and Mortality: Results from 2 Prospective Cohort Studies." *Arch Intern Med* (March 12, 2012 2012): archinternmed.2011.287.

Pirro Matteo, GiuseppeSchillaci , Gianluca Savarese, Fabio Gemelli, Massimo R. Mannarino, Donatella Siepi, Francesco Bagaglia, and Elmo Mannarino. "Attenutation of Inflammation with Short-Term Dietary Intervention Is Associated with a Reduction of Arterial Stiffness in Subjects with Hypercholesterolaemia." *European Journal of Cardiovascular Prevention and Rehabilitation* 11 (2004): 497-502.

Schaefer, Ernst J. "Lipoproteins, Nutrition, and Heart Disease." *Am J Clin Nutr* 75, no. 2 (February 1, 2002 2002): 191-212.

Schnall, Simone, Jean Roper, and Daniel M.T. Fessler. "Elevation Leads to Altruistic Behavior." *Psychological Science* 21, no. 3 (March 1, 2010 2010): 315-20.

Seligman Martin EP, Tracy A. Steen, Nansook Park, and Christopher Peterson. "Positive Psychology Progress-Empirical Validation of Interventions." *American Psychologist* 60, no. 5 (Juy-August 2005 2005): 410-21.

Sinha, Rashmi, Amanda J. Cross, Barry I. Graubard, Michael F. Leitzmann, and Arthur Schatzkin. "Meat Intake and Mortality: A Prospective Study of over Half a Million People." *Arch Intern Med* 169, no. 6 (March 23, 2009 2009): 562-71.

Small, Gary W., Daniel H. S. Silverman, Prabha Siddarth, Linda M. Ercoli, Karen J. Miller, Helen Lavretsky, Benjamin C. Wright, *et al.* "Effects of a 14-Day Healthy Longevity Lifestyle Program on Cognition and Brain Function." *American Journal of Geriatric Psychiatry* 14, no. 6 (Jun 2006): 538-45.

Southern Cherokee Nation of Kentucky, Inc. "Smudging." Southern Cherokee Nation of Kentucky, Inc. , http://www.southerncherokeenationky.com/cultur/smudging/.

Stuckey, Heather L., and Jeremy Nobel. "The Connection between Art, Healing, and Public Health: A Review of Current Literature." *American Journal of Public Health* 100, no. 2 (2010): 254-63.

Sung Jidong, Jamie R. DeRegis, Anita C. Bacher, Katherine L. Turner, Paul S. Turner, Mark D. Keleman, Pamela Ouyang, and Kerry J. Stewart. "Lower

Dietary Polyunsaturated to Saturated Fat Ratio Is Associated with Increased Visceral Adiposity." Paper presented at the American College of Cardiology Annual Meeting. Lipids—Clinical and Prevention, Chicago. Absrtact, March 30 2003.

Tunajeck Sandra K. "A Place for Stuff: Clutter Can Be Hazardous to Your Health." American Association of Nurse Anesthesists, http://www.aana.com/resources2/health-wellness/Documents/nb_milestone_0809.pdf.

United States Department of Agriculture, and Agricultural Research Service. "A Plant-Based Diet Is a Healthy Choice." ARS, USDA, http://www.ars.usda.gov/News/docs.htm?docid=9246.

Vallim T, and A.M. Salte. "Regulation of Hepatic Gene Expression by Saturated Fatty Acids." *Prostaglandins Leukot Essent Fatty Acids* 82, no. 4–6 (2010): 211–18.

Wang, Lu, Aaron R. Folsom, Zhi-Jie Zheng, James S. Pankow, and John H. Eckfeldt. "Plasma Fatty Acid Composition and Incidence of Diabetes in Middle-Aged Adults: The Atherosclerosis Risk in Communities (Aric) Study." *Am J Clin Nutr* 78, no. 1 (July 1, 2003 2003): 91–98.

Wu, H., A. J. Flint, Q. Qi, R. M. van Dam, L. A. Sampson, E. B. Rimm, M. D. Holmes, *et al.* "Association between Dietary Whole Grain Intake and Risk of Mortality: Two Large Prospective Studies in Us Men and Women." [In Eng]. *JAMA Intern Med* (Jan 5 2015).

Xie, Lulu, Hongyi Kang, Qiwu Xu, Michael J. Chen, Yonghong Liao, Meenakshisundaram Thiyagarajan, John O'Donnell, *et al.* "Sleep Drives Metabolite Clearance from the Adult Brain." *Science* 342, no. 6156 (373-7.

INDEX